The Southampton Press

Trail Guide

to

the South Fork

THE SOUTHAMPTON PRESS

TRAIL GUIDE

TO

THE SOUTH FORK

WITH A NATURAL HISTORY

MIKE BOTTINI

GROUP FOR THE SOUTH FORK

NEW YORK   SAG HARBOR

HARBOR ELECTRONIC PUBLISHING

2003

WWW.HEPdigital.COM

To the many people who worked for and supported open space
and greenbelt trails preservation on Long Island's South Fork

© 2003 by Michael Bottini
Library of Congress Control Number: 2003103698
ISBN 0-9707039-8-8 (paper)
ISBN 0-9707039-9-6 (eBook)

Printed in the United States of America

First printing: May 2003

This print version of the book does not include an index. Readers who need an
index are directed to the eBook version, which is fully word-searchable.

CREDITS

Editors: Anne Sanow, Charles Monaco

Cover design: Dimitri Drjuchin

A NOTE ON THE TYPE

This book is set in Adobe Garamond. Based on the design of sixteenth-
century typsetter Claude Garamond, the many Garamond faces have proved
among the most durable and popular typefaces of the last 400 years. Adobe
designer Robert Slimbach went to the Plantin-Moretus museum in Antwerp,
Belgium, to study the original Garamond typefaces. These served as the basis
for the design of the Adobe Garamond romans; the italics are based on types
by Robert Granjon, a contemporary of Garamond's. This elegant, versatile
design, especially suited to both screen and print, was the first Adobe Origi-
nals typeface, released in 1989. The display type is Goudy.

CONTENTS

Foreword: Mike's Hikes 7
Introduction 10

SHINNECOCK HILLS/NORTH SEA
Shinnecock Hills Preserve 17
Tuckahoe Hill Preserve 23
Marguerite Crabbe Greef Preserve 28
Wolf Swamp Preserve 33
Elliston Park 36
Big Fresh Pond Nature Trail 39

SOUTHAMPTON VILLAGE/NOYAC
Richard L. Fowler Preserve 47
Munn Point Preserve 52
Laurel Valley Preserve 57
Morton National Wildlife Refuge 62
Clam Island Preserve 68
Trout Pond Preserve 73

BRIDGEHAMPTON/SAG HARBOR/SAGAPONACK
Brick Hill Preserve 83
Long Pond Greenbelt: North Loop 86
Long Pond Greenbelt: South Loop 90
Poxabogue Preserve 94
Sagg Swamp Preserve 99

EAST HAMPTON VILLAGE/WAINSCOTT
East Hampton Village Nature Preserve 105
▲ Paumanok Path: Wainscott Section 110
Miller's Ground Preserve 114
Buckskill Preserve 118

NORTHWEST
Barcelona Neck Preserve 125
▲ Paumanok Path: Northwest Section I 130

Grace Estate Preserve 136
Cedar Point County Park 141
▲ Paumanok Path: Northwest Section II 146
Sammy's Beach Preserve 151

SPRINGS/AMAGANSETT
▲ Paumanok Path: Stony Hill Section 159
Springs Woodblock Preserve 164
Accabonac Preserve 168

NAPEAGUE/MONTAUK
▲ Paumanok Path: Napeague Section 175
Walking Dunes 180
▲ Paumanok Path: Hither Woods Section 189
Hither Hills Preserve: Fresh Pond Loop 196
Hither Woods Preserve: Ram Level Loop 203
Montauk Mountain Preserve 207
▲ Paumanok Path: Montauk Village Section 212
Shadmoor Preserve 217
Big Reed Pond Nature Trails 222
▲ Paumanok Path: Montauk Point Section 240
Seal Haulout Trail 247
Money Pond Trail 253
Point Woods Trail 257
Camp Hero State Park 262

Map and Key 267

▲ Paumanok Path Sections

Foreword: Mike's Hikes

Robert S. DeLuca, President, Group for the South Fork

In his last manuscript, *The Dispersion of Seeds*, Henry Thoreau aptly wrote, "though I do not believe that a plant will spring up where no seed has been, I have great faith in a seed. Convince me you have a seed there, and I am prepared to expect wonders."

And so it has been with eastern Long Island's long-rooted and now blooming trail preservation movement and the contents of this book.

Although the original cutting, maintenance, and protective interest in trails can be traced to Long Island's first aboriginal inhabitants (whose early paths still define some of today's existing roads like Canoe Place and Noyac Path), colonial settlers also placed significant value on local trails as a resource of unprecedented importance to the public.

Whether for access to timber, open water, game, or salt hay, the public's common interest in having access to the bounty of the local South Fork landscape was a staple of the cultural philosophy of the time and reinforced in the text of early patents passed down from the Crown to the region's fledgling colonial leadership.

In the 130 years that followed, growing passions for ownership, private property, and limited governmental authority over land in part stoked the flames of revolution that led to the creation of this country.

On eastern Long Island, however, a century and a half of entrenched colonial settlement, governance, and custom established a culture and political philosophy that would not easily disappear—though surely it would be challenged.

Although it is hard to imagine today, eastern Long Island was relatively slow to change from its rural and agrarian past. As a result, active use of the region's trails made significant sense for much of the resident population well into the early part of the last century. Most people farmed, fished, hunted, took others hunting, and utilized timber from local stocks made accessible by common trails. The existence of these trails truly facilitated daily routine in much the same way that our system of paved roads does today.

Outside of the region's historic village centers, the subdivision of open land was a smoldered concern that eventually developed into the firestorm of development we experience today. By the early 1970s, major improvements in Long Island's roadways opened access to and widened investment interest in the South Fork and began a forty-year assault on the local landscape that has not yet subsided.

As open land was carved up into an ever-expanding number of individual development lots, the region's trail system was an early casualty. Private property rights confronted centuries of historic tradition and across the region trails began to disappear under the blade of the bulldozer. Without adequate legislative and public reinforcement of the trails tradition, a resource that had served the common interests of residents from every socio-economic group for centuries was on track to disappear in the span of single human lifetime.

But like many things on the South Fork, the future of the South Fork trail system was not predetermined.

Perhaps because of its smaller size, or simply because of the personal commitment of a few passionate individuals the Town of East Hampton was first to take up the issue of trails preservation and soon became the epicenter of the South Fork trails movement.

By the late 1970s the East Hampton Trails Preservation Society had formed as a volunteer organization dedicated the protection and preservation of the town's trails. Within ten years, Southampton would also have its own Trails Preservation Society and the development of a regional constituency for trail mapping, protection, preservation, and maintenance was substantially in place.

Nonetheless, in the face of escalating land conversion and unprecedented real estate values, the process of assuring continuous political and legislative support for trails protection has been—and remains—a daily challenge. Dedicated volunteers and centuries of tradition have been pitted against highly motivated developers, high-priced lawyers, and some less than stellar public officials, in a legal and ideological battle between private land and public good.

From the earliest days of the South Fork's trail preservation movement the Group for the South Fork has served as the region's principal professional support system, tactical strategist, and organizing advocate in support of the trails movement. The Group has committed its staff and financial resources to empowering and adding value to the individual and collective efforts of the region's now numerous trails volunteers. From grant-writing and litigation to trail clearing and mapping, the Group and its generous members have honored a commitment to trails preservation with the specific goal of creating a new generation of trail advocates and enthusiasts who will speak up knowledgeably and passionately for the protection of our public trails.

Over the course of the last two decades staff professionals, including the author of this book, have sought new ways to broaden public awareness, and deepen an appreciation for the region's trails. And so it was that in the spring of 1998, our Environmental Planner, Mike Bottini, working with the *The Southampton Press*, researched and produced the very first trail article for publication—a "seed" that would subsequently give rise to every wondrous hike that is covered in the pages of this book!

Over the past five years, working in partnership with the *The Southampton Press*, the Group was able to commit a substantial portion of Mike's professional time to the development of some 150 specific nature hikes, canoe paddles, and other outings that have now appeared in print.

The exceptional quality and detail of these articles recently earned Mike's now regular "South Fork Outdoors" column the New York Press Association's first place award for Best Outdoor Column.

The excellence of Mike's work will inspire others to speak up for the protection of the natural world. We have selected an array of outings that will give every reader an opportunity to experience the beauty, diversity, exhilaration, and inner peace that comes from a deepening experience of nature.

In return, we ask only that you help us in our efforts preserve and maintain our local environment and historic trail systems by becoming an active member of the organizations that have dedicated themselves to the preservation of the South Fork's trails. Your support allows the public voice for trails protection to grow stronger and more effective as the challenges grow larger and more significant.

We think Thoreau had it right. We have seen the seed for trails preservation planted, we have watched it grow, and we are certain that with your help we can protect our precious trails forever.

Introduction

The South Fork of Long Island, spanning the townships of East Hampton and Southampton, is more widely known as "the Hamptons," a playground of the rich and famous. Among its best known natural resources are its beautiful ocean beaches. Less well known are its many and diverse nature preserves and greenbelt trails scattered along a narrow, forty-mile-long peninsula.

The number of preserves on the South Fork and the linear miles of its greenbelt trails may surprise many who have witnessed firsthand the intense development pressure the area has been subject to over the past twenty years. While development brought dramatic changes to our once rural landscape, several key environmental initiatives have enabled the acreage of preserved lands on the South Fork, and its public trail system, to greatly expand as well.

This did not happen by chance. These initiatives—a mandatory cluster law, the land transfer tax, and trail preservation ordinances to name a few—were the fruits of hard work by a number of dedicated organizations, individuals, and public officials. And the work is not over yet. For example, much remains to be done to complete the portion of the Paumanok Path from the Shinnecock Canal to Town Line Road in eastern Southampton; there is still a lot of vacant land that needs to be protected from development on the moraine; and nearly all these trails are maintained by volunteers.

And that is the reason for this book. My hope is that it may prompt people to visit a preserve, perhaps learn something new about this unique area, and inspire them to get involved in some way.

This book describes approximately one hundred miles of trails crossing through fifty different preserves and greenbelts. These hikes can be done at any time of the year: different seasons, and even different times of the day, offer a uniqueness that makes a hike worthwhile. And don't forget to plan a few full moon hikes over the coming year.

A few words of caution before heading out into the field. Bow hunting for deer takes place in our larger preserves from October 1 to December 31 (including weekends). The limited range of accuracy for bow hunting makes it unlikely that a hunter will mistake you for a deer, so I'm comfortable using the trails then. Shotgun season (weekdays for three weeks in January) is another matter; for those fifteen days, stay out of the areas where deer hunting is allowed.

Deer ticks are a problem in that many of them carry the bacteria that can give you Lyme disease. I've had this twice since moving here in 1988, but went on antibiotics early enough to knock it out both times. I should point out that I often pick up ticks while doing off-trail field work, never on a well-maintained trail. Ticks can be active anytime of the year, including a warm winter day. But they are usually found in grassy or brushy areas. If you are hiking an overgrown trail, wear light-colored, long pants and tuck them into your boot tops or white socks and check yourself periodically during the hike and later at home. It takes at least twenty-four hours after the tick has started feeding for the bacteria to be transferred to your bloodstream. Some people insist ticks can be removed by simply showering; don't believe them. A steady pull on carefully positioned tweezers will do the trick.

A chigger is the larva of a parasitic mite that causes severe itching. They are not uncommon in the grasslands of Montauk, but I've been fortunate enough never to have experienced them firsthand. Poison ivy is not uncommon here, so it is a good idea to learn to recognize this plant by its leaves, berries, and hair-like aerial roots. As with ticks, chiggers and poison ivy are not problems on well-maintained trails. There are no poisonous snakes here. In the event you encounter a snake, consider yourself lucky to be able to observe one.

ACKNOWLEDGEMENTS

In my work over the past fourteen years as an environmental planner with the Group for the South Fork, I have had the great fortune of spending time in the field with many of the most knowledgeable naturalists and ecologists on Long Island, all of whom contributed in some way to this book. These include: Eric Lamont of the Long Island Botanical Society; John Turner, Dr. Stuart Lowry, and Dr. Marilyn Jordan of the Nature Conservancy; Marty Shea and Larry Penny of the Natural Resources Departments from Southampton and East Hampton respectively; Andy Sabin, Jean Held, and Jim Ash of the South Fork Natural History Society; Rob Villani and Don Reipe of the American Littoral Society; Dr. Howard Reisman, Sam Sadove, and Dr. Paul Forestell of Southampton College; and Bob DeLuca and Steve Biasetti of the Group for the South Fork. Tom Wessels, one of my field ecology professors at Antioch New England graduate school many years ago, continues to help me out with answers to ecological questions.

Richard G. Hendrickson, Nancy Kane, William Mulvihill, Russell Drum, and Amund "Swede" Edwards contributed much to the historical information found in the book. Thanks also to Diana Dayton, the reference librarian at the incredibly well-organized Long Island Room of the East Hampton library, truly a community gem. Special thanks to Rick Whalen who, in addition to providing a wealth of historical information, first introduced me to the trails of East Hampton. Kurt Billing enthusiastically shared his knowledge of the trails in the North Sea area, and the potential for future greenbelts, some of which have come to fruition. Tom MacNiven, leading the way on morning runs, showed me many of the trail connections in East Hampton.

The daunting task of checking the hundred miles of trails mapped in this book was greatly expedited by Group for the South Fork staff (Steve Biasetti, Jodi Grinrod, Anita Wright, Adrian Drake, Elise Jacobs, and Madeleine Meek) and volunteers from the East Hampton Trails Preservation Society (Richard Lupoletti, Ed Porco, Ken Beiger, Ken Kindler, Bill Good, Nancy Kane, and Bill Nichols). In addition to correcting maps, many provided useful comments that were incorporated in the text.

This book would not have been possible without the support of the Group for the South Fork and the *The Southampton Press*. Many thanks to Bob DeLuca, president of the Group for the South Fork, for allowing me the luxury of writing a weekly column over the past five years, and Joe Shaw, editor of the *The Southampton Press Eastern Edition*, for publishing them and showing incredible patience with my inability to meet deadlines. Joe Louchheim, publisher of the *The Southampton Press*, was instrumental in the creation of this book: he first proposed the idea of having me write the South Fork Outdoors column, and the idea of publishing a book based on those articles. Thanks, too, to John Zack and Kerri Cunningham for their work on earlier versions of the maps.

My friend and writing mentor Greg Donaldson coached me through my first articles and provided much needed encouragement over the months I was trying to convert a weekly column into a book. A special note of thanks is due my publisher, James Monaco of Harbor Electronic Publishing, for steering me around the pitfalls that keep so many manuscripts from making it to the printers.

Mike Bottini
Springs
April 2003

TO GET INVOLVED OR JOIN A HIKE
    Group for the South Fork (631 537 1400)
    East Hampton Trails Preservation Society (631 329 4227)
    Southampton Trails Preservation Society (631 537 5202)
    Friends of the Long Pond Greenbelt (631 537 0660)
    Long Island Greenbelt Trails Conference (631 360 0753)
    Visit www.hike-LI.com and Peconic.org

ABOUT THE MAPS
    Please see the Main Key at the back of the book for a general guide. Keys for individual maps include only additional information. These maps were accurate as of Spring 2003 but please remember that trails often change.

SHINNECOCK HILLS

NORTH SEA

SHINNECOCK HILLS PRESERVE

A narrow wedge of open space just north of the Southampton College campus, the 26-acre Shinnecock Hills Preserve is nestled between the LIRR, County Road 39, and St. Andrews Road. Once part of the Shinnecock Golf Club (located directly across C.R. 39 from the Preserve), it was purchased in 1994 by The Nature Conservancy as an excellent example of the rare ecological community known as a "maritime grassland."

As defined in the New York State Department of Environmental Conservation publication *Ecological Communities of New York State*, this grassland community occurs on the glaciated portion of the Atlantic coastal plain near the ocean and within the influence of offshore winds and salt spray. Little bluestem (*Schizachyrium scoparium*), common hairgrass (*Deschampsia flexuosa*), and poverty-grass (*Danthonia spicata*) are the dominant grasses. As is the case at the Shinnecock Hills Preserve, this community often intergrades, or occurs together in a mosaic pattern, with the "maritime heathland" community, dominated by shrubs such as bearberry, beach heather, lowbush blueberry, huckleberry, bayberry, and beach plum.

Once covering extensive areas of the Shinnecock Hills, Montauk, Block Island, Cape Cod, and the offshore islands in Massachusetts, this plant community is now among the most threatened natural communities in the East. Today, New York's remnant maritime grasslands total less than 150 acres and are being lost even on "preserved" lands. Time, and a process called "ecological succession," have greatly altered the grassland landscape both here and in Montauk, to one of woody shrubs and trees. Pitch pine, red cedar, oak, and black cherry are forming ever-widening groves at the Shinnecock Hills Preserve, and seem to indicate that something other than wind and salt spray are necessary for the long-term survival and competitive edge of the grassland community.

In the September–October 1996 issue of the Long Island Botanical Society Newsletter, Ann F. Johnson attempts to document this process of ecological succession in the Shinnecock Hills in her article "The Shinnecock Hills: From Drifting Dunes To Pine Forest in 160 Years." By examining historical accounts dating back to the early 1800s, coastal and geodetic survey maps, and aerial photographs, Ms. Johnson pieces together the changes in the landscape and concludes that succession proceeded from bare sand to grassy heath between 1822 and 1897, and from grassy heath to pitch pine forest between 1897 and 1983. She ends with the question: "Will the Hills remain in pine forest, or will this in turn be superseded by oaks?" Something to ponder as you amble through the Preserve.

From the Preserve entrance, follow the yellow and green trail markers onto a narrow footpath which climbs steeply through an area of woody shrubs and scattered mature eastern red cedar, oaks and pitch pine. Approximately halfway up the hill (1), the trail passes through a very large and dense patch of trailing arbutus. Most hikers associate this prostrate evergreen with the edges of old woodland roads and trails, clinging to the thin boundary between the unvegetated, compacted soils of the path and the undisturbed adjacent forest. In such places, it forms narrow ribbons of green unlike the broad expanses found here. This fact was noted by botanist Willard N. Clute in his 1899 article "Spring in the Shinnecock Hills": "most interesting was the Arbutus (*Epigea*), which here almost covered some of the open places, in full sun. The Wintergreen (*Gaultheria*), was also plentiful with the Arbutus, and both seemed decidedly out of place, since they usually occur in woods or at least thickets."

Further along the trail passes through a waist-high, stout-twigged thicket of beach plum shrubs (*Prunus maritima*) (2). The trail soon veers left, levels off and contours along the side of the hill, skirting a large swath of catbriar on the downhill side (3) before emerging from the scattered trees and thickets and offering the first view over the grasslands. Here the trail forks: follow the arrow directing you to the right, up onto a ridge just below the high point of the preserve. From this vantage point you can view the mosaic of grasses, shrubs, and trees which comprise the preserve today. In order to maintain the grass portions, Nature Conservancy staff have been cutting down pitch pine, eastern red cedar, and black cherry trees as evidenced by the remaining stumps at 4.

Dropping down off the ridge, the trail cuts through an unnatural rectangular-shaped pit (5) largely vegetated with a reindeer lichen (*Cladonia* spp.). This appears to be one of the sand traps associated with the golf fairways constructed here many years ago. According to Elliot Vose, president of the Shinnecock Hills Golf Club, most of the Club's original fairways were located south of what is now Route 27 (C.R. 39). The golf course was rearranged in the 1930s with the construction of the highway, and all fairways were relocated on the north side of the new road, where the original clubhouse was situated.

Once abandoned, the bare, sterile sand found in the trap was the perfect habitat for *Cladonia* to colonize. Based on Willard Clute's observations from 1899, *Cladonia* may have been much more prevalent in this area than it is today. He reported that "in spite of all these adverse conditions, a considerable number of plants manage to exist in the sterile soil. Foremost among them must be placed the reindeer moss (*Cladonia*). When the sun shines, its existence seems to stand still. It crunches under the foot like crusted snow. But a day of moist air revives it, and it becomes soft, pliant and full of life."

Clute also reported that prickly pear (*Opuntia*) could often be found growing in amongst the *Cladonia*. Although I may have missed a few specimens, I was not able to locate any of the former, our native cactus, anywhere along the trail. It appears that this species is another victim of time, change, and ecological succession.

At 6, the trail winds through a small grove of evergreens: red cedar, pitch pine, and a non-native pine with two needles per fascicle and numerous cones quite a bit smaller than those of the nearby pitch pine. My guess is Scotch pine (*Pinus sylvestris*). As I stood examining the buds and unopened yearling cones on a warm sunny afternoon, I could actually hear the snap and crackle of the cones beginning to open to shed their seeds.

Just before reaching a small wooden footbridge, the trail passes close by two more old sand traps, one on the left and the other on the right. Beach heather (*Hudsonia tomentosa*) can be found in both. The footbridge spans a steep-sided ditch which runs straight through the entire preserve. I was not able to find any information on the purpose or origin of the ditch. After the bridge, the trail begins to swing north for the return loop. At 7, you will find a variety of woody shrubs, including both species of *Lyonia* (staggerbush, *L. mariana* and male-berry, *L. ligustrina*) and many good examples of the maritime heathland community such as bayberry, winged sumac, huckleberry, lowbush blueberry, and beach plum. Two key members of this community seem to have greatly diminished in numbers in the area: bearberry (I did find some on the dirt road just below the preserve's high point) and beach heather (*Hudsonia tomentosa*). Both of these were reported as quite abundant in earlier (1800s) botanical accounts of the Shinnecock Hills.

The trail next descends into a depression (8) that marks the lowest elevation in the preserve (44 feet above mean sea level, or AMSL). Here I was finally able to locate several shadbush (*Amelanchier*) specimens: three distinct clumps reaching approximately ten feet in height. I'm not sure if these are the rare Nantucket shads, or our more common *Amelanchier canadensis*.

According to Southampton Town Chief Environmental Analyst Marty Shea, the Nantucket shadbush is much smaller in size.

With regard to the issue of whether the dwarf form is actually a separate species from the ubiquitous *A. canadensis,* or that it is merely an expression of environmental conditions, there is much debate. Veteran landscaper and nurseryman Charlie Whitmore was skeptical with regards to the separate species idea, being of the opinion that size reflected a particular site's growing conditions. George W. D. Symonds, author of *The Shrub Identification Book,* has this to say about *Amelanchier:* "This is a large and confusing genus; there is considerable difference of opinion regarding the various species." I'll give the final word to noted botanist Robert Zaremba of The Nature Conservancy, who writes: "A part of the taxonomic confusion of the Rose family, Nantucket Shadbush has not been listed as endangered because it may be a distinctive hybrid."

Before climbing back out of this protected swale, look for the young hickory growing near the bottom, the only hickory specimen I noticed along the trail.

Just beyond a point where the trail crests a knoll, it passes through a clearing dotted with half-inch stumps (9). This area was cleared of sumac in 1999 to allow for the expansion of the maritime grassland community: a form of reverse succession to provide a stage for the early successional grasses to thrive.

The trail next enters a pine and cedar grove (10) and skirts a depression on the left. Here again you will find Scotch pine in the mix. Further along (11), some older, large pitch pines show signs of past fire on their blackened trunks. The unmarked fork in the trail there is confusing; the main trail to the right leads out to St. Andrews Road. Look to the left and head uphill towards the trail signpost. At the intersection near the ditch, backtrack to the parking area. Consider continuing straight ahead onto the high point (101 feet AMSL) where a view of Peconic Bay can be had to the northwest. Note the flat-topped, level pitch of the knoll and the rich soil—this may have been one of the old golf course greens. An old roadway leads off the knoll and back to the trailhead area, traversing through a large patch of bearberry enroute.

While offering a pleasant walk at any time of the year, the best time to visit the Shinnecock Hills preserve is in late spring (May and early June) when the shrubs (shadbush and beach plum) and the wildflowers (bird's-foot violet, lupine and bushy rockrose (*Helianthemum dumosum*)) are in bloom. The latter is described by Robert Zaremba of The Nature Conservancy as "perhaps the signature species for the maritime grassland community." Before planning a visit, consider contacting the South Fork Chapter of The Nature Conservancy (631-329-7689) to see if they are scheduling a guided tour of this interesting preserve.

Directions: The entrance to this Nature Conservancy preserve is located on St. Andrews Road, which intersects C.R. 39 (Rte. 27) just west of the Southampton College exit (the traffic light at Tuckahoe Road). Please be aware that this section of Rte. 27 is extremely dangerous, with traffic often moving very fast through the curves on either side of St. Andrews. Once safely on St. Andrews, look for the parking area and trailhead on the left, approximately 0.3 mile from C.R. 39.

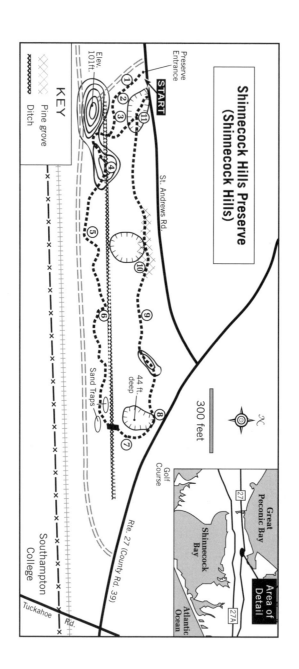

Shinnecock Hills Preserve
(Shinnecock Hills)

START

Preserve
Entrance

Elev.
101ft.

① ② ③ ⑪ ④ ⑤ ⑩ ⑥ ⑨ ⑦ ⑧

St. Andrews Rd.

Sand Traps

44 ft.
deep

300 feet

N

KEY

⋈⋈⋈ Pine grove
∞∞∞∞ Ditch

Golf
Course

Rte. 27 (County Rd. 39)

Southampton
College

Tuckahoe Rd.

Great
Peconic Bay

Shinnecock
Bay

Atlantic
Ocean

Area of
Detail

27

27A

22

Tuckahoe Hill Preserve

Despite its close proximity to the highly congested, strip-mall style development of County Road 39, Tuckahoe Hill offers the hiker a wonderful escape into a diverse and interesting forest. In the late 1980s, with the help of local resident Kurt Billings, Group for the South Fork led an effort to interest the town and county in preserving the 200-acre woodland that covers the hill. Our arguments for preservation included protecting one of the Suffolk County Water Authority well fields that supplied public water to Southampton Village; preserving wildlife habitat, including that of several rare species; and providing a corridor for the Paumanok Path that included one of the most magnificent views on the South Fork. As of early 2003, 140 acres have been preserved.

In addition to the ubiquitous oak–hickory forest, Tuckahoe Hill has stands of red maple, tupelo, pitch pine, and American beech, and quite a few survivors of the chestnut blight which continue to resprout from roots systems that are over one hundred years old. The many perched freshwater wetlands found in the area add to the forest's diversity, enabling it to support a wide variety of amphibians such as spotted salamanders, spring peepers, spadefoot and Fowlers toads, and gray tree frogs and wood frogs, in addition to the usual woodland inhabitants: red fox, white-tail deer, box turtles, milk snakes, red-tailed hawks, and great-horned owls.

The 127-foot-high section of glacial deposits known as Tuckahoe Hill is somewhat isolated from the rest of the east–west trending Ronkonkoma moraine. Topographic maps of the area reveal low-lying lands on its east and west flanks which are part of several distinct north–south troughs. One connects North Sea Harbor, Little Fresh Pond, and Agawam Lake, the other connects North Sea Harbor, Big Fresh Pond, and Heady Creek, at the east end of Shinnecock Bay. According to the 1957 U.S. Geological Survey for this area, these north–south trending channels developed as a result of rivers of glacial meltwater carving through the morainal deposits between the slowly receding glacier to the north and the Atlantic Ocean to the south.

The trail entrance is on Sebonac Road, directly across from Tuckahoe School, and adjacent to the stop sign at the North Magee Street intersection (1). The narrow, recently cut footpath winds through a mature oak and hickory forest, skirting a large swamp off to the right. Many of the understory shrubs are sweet pepperbush and swamp azalea, head high woody plants often found in or adjacent to wetlands.

Within a few hundred feet the footpath joins a fairly wide, unpaved road (2) whose sandy roadbed is a good place to look for animal tracks. Deer, fox, and raccoon imprints are often discernible, even to the novice tracker. After a short distance, you may notice a few wetland plants growing along both sides of the road: tupelo and red maple trees, and sweet pepperbush and highbush blueberry shrubs (3). In the winter months, with most of the leaves gone, the low areas of both wetlands are fairly visible. Clumps of Tussock sedge can be seen in the bottom of the wetland off to the left, while the one on the right is dominated by old tires.

Termed "vernal" wetlands, these low-lying areas usually have standing water in them early in the year from winter and spring precipitation, but are often dry in the summer months. The temporary nature and small size of these wetlands has been a huge liability for them: many people, including generally conservation-minded sportsmen, do not see the value of wetlands that support neither gamefish or waterfowl. Fortunately, the South Fork has local ordinances that do, as both these wetlands are the haunts of a variety of unusual amphibians, including some of our beautiful and rare mole salamanders.

As the road gradually steepens and comes within sight of a large wood and brush pile, look for a foot trail on the left (4). Although it is a well-worn and quite visible path, it is easily missed.

According to William Wallace Tooker's book on Indian names, Tuckahoe has several possible meanings. His best guess is that it is the Shinnecock name for *Arisaema triphyllum*, commonly called jack-in-the-pulpit or Indian turnip and quite abundant in the damp soils of the Tuckahoe and North Sea area. While the name "Indian turnip" suggests it is a wild edible, this may be a case of a misleading common name. It and a close relative, skunk cabbage, are riddled with calcium oxalate crystals which cause a severe burning sensation in the mouth. The crystals may be a built-in defense against browsing. In any case, the turnip needs to be repeatedly boiled and strained in order to purge the crystal, a process that uses more energy in preparation than is gained in eating.

At the first trail intersection (5), note the abundant swamp azaleas (*Rhododendron viscosum*) growing along both sides of the trail. Although normally found in wet soils at the edge of swamps, marshes, and freshwater ponds, here it is thriving in dry sandy soil quite a distance uphill from the kettlehole wetland off to the left (west).

Continue straight (north) and look for several American chestnut trees close to the trail at and before the next intersection (6). American chestnut (*Castanea dentata*) was once one of the most common forest trees throughout much of its range, accounting for a third to half of the canopy species. Not only was it common, but it grew fast and lived long, the latter a reflection of its status as the most rot-resistant of our native trees. All that changed quite quickly and dramatically beginning in 1890 when nursery stock from China infected with the Asian fungus *Cryphonectria parasitica* was brought into New York City. Spreading at a rate of up to fifty miles per year, 99.9% of all chestnut canopy trees in North America were dead by 1950.

For some reason, the mature canopy trees initially infected by the fungus were not able to regenerate by root sprouts. However, their offspring, trees grown from nuts produced before the magnificent canopy specimens succumbed to the blight, could stump-sprout after attack by the fungus. The vast majority of today's multiple-trunked understory chestnuts arise from root systems established by nuts which germinated at the onset of the blight.

While this allows the American chestnut to survive as a member of the forest community here, the fungus kills the above-ground portion of the tree before it reaches an age where it can produce fertile nuts. This fact severely reduces the American chestnut's stature and role in today's forest community.

We are waiting for a few more public acquisitions in the Tuckahoe Hill area before designing a better trail loop; for the time being you will have to backtrack to (5). Turn left there and follow alongside some snow fencing into a slight depression, then up to the top of Tuckahoe Hill, owned by Southampton Village. As you climb you may notice that the size—both height and girth—of the oak trees along the trail diminishes dramatically. This phenomenon is very common all along the South Fork moraine, particularly on the northern slopes. The strong northerly winds and porous, dry soils near the morainal ridge combine to stunt the growth of the typical assortment of oaks and hickories which, further downhill, grow much larger. This process mimics, in some ways, the better-known "krummholz" phenomenon in the mountains of New England.

Someone recently cleared many of the oaks growing on the north side of the summit, probably to enhance the panoramic view: one of the best on the South Fork. Slivers of water on either side of Cow Neck mark Little and Great Peconic Bays; the sandy bluffs of Robins Island and the North Fork are also clearly visible. The only obvious structure in the 180-degree view is the barn and silo on Cow Neck.

As an alternative to cutting down trees, perhaps a small observation tower, five or six feet high, would suffice; it could be constructed over the concrete foundation of the old World War II lookout station, which was located at the hill's highest point.

To return to the trailhead, simply follow the roadway on the south side of the hill: a direct and quick route back, passing the Village police pistol range, a storage area for dead street trees (some nice firewood there), and an abandoned dog kennel.

Directions: Situated north of Route 27 (a.k.a. County Road 39) between Southampton College and Southampton Village, Tuckahoe Hill is bounded on the west by North Magee Street, on the east by Sandy Hollow Road, on the north by West Neck Road, and on the south by Sebonac Road. The trailhead is located in the northeast corner of the intersection of Sebonac Road and North Magee Street, directly across from Tuckahoe School.

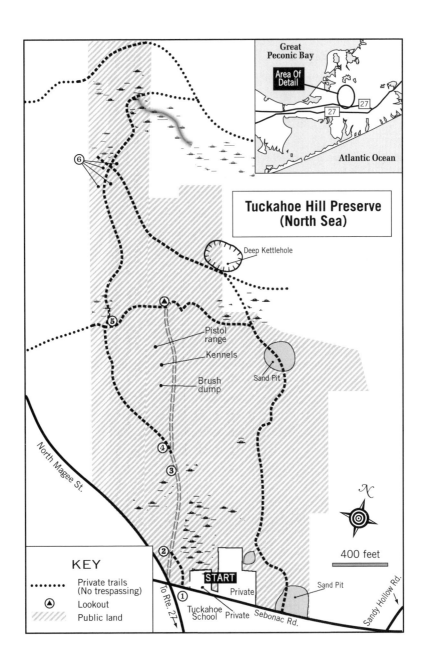

Great
Peconic Bay

Area Of
Detail

27

27

Atlantic Ocean

6

Tuckahoe Hill Preserve
(North Sea)

Deep Kettlehole

5

Pistol
range

Kennels

Brush
dump

Sand Pit

North Magee St.

4

3

𝒩

400 feet

KEY

.... Private trails
(No trespassing)

Ⓐ Lookout

//////// Public land

To Rte. 27

2

1

START

Private

Tuckahoe
School

Private

Sebonac Rd.

Sand Pit

Sandy Hollow Rd.

Marguerite Crabbe Greef Preserve

The Big Woods Preserve, a 90-acre tract of mature forest, freshwater wetlands, and salt marsh, is situated adjacent to and south of one of the oldest preserves in the township: Elliston Park. Forming the western border of the preserve is one of the most beautiful estuaries on the South Fork: Sebonac Creek. Big Woods, formerly part of the extensive Salm estate that once included nearby Cow Neck, was preserved through a joint acquisition utilizing private funding secured by The Nature Conservancy from the Greeff family and public funds available through the town's environmental bond. The town took title to the northern half of the property, that which was adjacent to its Elliston Park preserve, while The Nature Conservancy will be managing the southern forty-five acres.

The following is a description of the one-mile-long loop trail (marked with yellow-on-green blazes) through The Nature Conservancy's portion of the Big Woods, which has been named the Marguerite Crabbe Greeff Wildlife Sanctuary in honor of a woman whose family made TNC's purchase possible. Visitors to this beautiful and diverse wildlife sanctuary will traverse an upland forest with several large stands of American beech and smaller groves of stately white pines, and a wetland forest of tupelo and red maple underlain with a wide variety of wetland shrubs, ferns, and sedges, and will be treated to views over the Sebonac Creek tidal marshlands.

The trail begins in a mixed hardwood forest containing some large American beech trees and, within 75 yards, intersects with the main "loop" trail (1). Here, a large eastern white pine is found growing close to the trail. Several small stands of white pines are scattered throughout the preserve, and they contain the tallest trees in the Big Woods area. Although white pines are long-lived trees, reaching old age at 250 years, their size in this case reflects their ability to grow fast rather than their longevity. A rough approximation of a white pine's age can be made by carefully counting the number of whorled lateral branches along the main trunk; each whorl represents one year's growth. The distance between each whorl, which may vary from several inches to several feet, represents the growth rate for a particular year and, therefore, can provide some indication of growing conditions (temperature,

28

rainfall, etc.) for that season. In the case of the pine specimen at (1), it is a youngster at approximately sixty years of age.

Turning left at the intersection, note the change in both the forest canopy (oak, pine, and beech to red maple and tupelo) and the shrub layer (lowbush blueberry and huckleberry to sweet pepperbush and swamp azalea) along the trail between (1) and (2). An almost imperceptible descent of ten feet in elevation is enough to alter the soil conditions from dry to moist, giving wetland-tolerant species a competitive edge.

Off to the left, out of sight, is a tiny freshwater creek which drains into the tidal waters of Sebonac Creek. According to Hank Billing, a long-time resident of the area who is now deceased, this "dreen" once continued under Millstone Brook Road, through a swale, under Big Fresh Pond Road, and into the pond itself, providing a second outlet for Big Fresh Pond: one to the Sebonac Creek estuary and one to the North Sea Harbor estuary. The latter still exists today.

At (3) is the first of two short sections of boardwalk where the trail surface periodically intersects the water table. Alongside the walkways, hikers can get a close view of a wide variety of wetland plants including trees, shrubs, ferns, and sedges. Most times of the year the trees and shrubs, such as winterberry holly, chokeberry, swamp azalea, sweet pepperbush, and highbush blueberry, can be identified using any one of a number of field guides that describe bark, twig, and bud characteristics. One of my favorites is the non-technical, two-book series called *The Tree Identification Book* and *The Shrub Identification Book* by George Symonds. Identification of the herbaceous plants is best done in the warm months when in flower.

Back in the upland forest at (4), there is an excellent example of how the American beech reproduces by developing new shoots directly out of its root system. This asexual reproduction results in clones with all the physical characteristics of the mother plant, and directly connected to one another via the shared root system.

A short spur trail to the left at (5) provides the best access to the Sebonac Creek tidal marsh, where an ecological phenomenon known as plant zonation can be observed. In this case, the distinct bands or zones of vegetation correlate to position in the overall intertidal zone, with subtle changes in elevation above mean sea level on the order of centimeters determining the number of hours per day and frequency per month during which any particular area is covered with salt water. The sequence of zones, from least frequently inundated to most, is defined by the predominance of the following plants: groundsel bush, phragmites, salt hay (*Spartina patens*), and cordgrass

(*Spartina alterniflora*). A close examination of the salt hay zone will reveal several other grass-like plants: black rush (*Juncus Gerardi*) and spikegrass (*Distichlis spicata*), the dominance by one or the other further subdividing the salt hay zone by inundation time. Also within this particular zone are found a group of unusual succulent plants (*Salicornia* spp.) commonly called glasswort, and the salt marsh aster and sea lavender, which both have colorful flowers to add to the late summer salt marsh landscape.

The northernmost section of the trail loop, between (5) and (7) on the accompanying map, skirts the edge of the Sebonac Creek salt marsh but is tucked just inside the adjacent freshwater swamp so as to preclude any views over the marsh. Several sections of boardwalk in this area enable passage in all but the worst flood conditions.

At the edge of one of the larger stands of white pines, growing on a large oak tree in the vicinity of (7), is a huge clump of bracket fungi clearly visible from the trail. Mushrooms, which are the reproductive (fruiting) structures of fungi, are most numerous and visible in the late summer and fall. Most are soft, fleshy appendages that do not persist for very long. Because of their woody character, bracket fungi last longer and are apparent throughout the year. As with all fungi, these organisms lack chlorophyll and cannot photosynthesize; food is obtained via a network of tiny strands called hyphae, which lumped together are known as the mycelium of the fungus. This network penetrates dead leaves, branches, tree trunks, animal carcasses, and, in some cases, living root systems and even hikers (the dreaded athlete's foot fungus). By way of secreting digestive enzymes which dissolve complex compounds, a process called decomposition, the hyphae are able to absorb simple food molecules for their own growth and reproduction. Much of the dissolved material not used by the fungi is available to the roots of nearby plants which, in turn, convert these simple minerals and nutrients back into complex compounds via the process called photosynthesis. Thus a cycle is created, one in which the fungi play a critical role as the ultimate recyclers.

Just beyond the bracket fungi (7) is a major trail intersection. The Nature Conservancy loop is well-marked, while the well-defined but unmarked trail leading off to the left connects to the town portion of the Big Woods and Elliston Park. The latter is proposed to be designated part of the Paumanok Path. Stay on The Nature Conservancy trail which ascends a small knoll (8) to a height of 32 feet above mean sea level: the highest elevation on the preserve. The knoll is covered with American beech, whose smooth gray bark is a striking in the leafless months of winter and early spring. As far as I know, American beech is the only tree in the northeast with smooth, unbroken bark, even on the oldest specimens. I've often wondered about this odd feature and its ecological advantage. In his book *Reading the Forested Landscape: A Natural History of New England*, Tom Wessels offers an explanation: American beech is a member of a family of trees that evolved in the tropics, where the growth of epiphytes can actually break branches and topple entire trees. Smooth bark is an adaptation which inhibits the growth of epiphytes by reducing potential rootholds: an adaptation which the species didn't lose over time and climate changes. A fascinating answer and a good example of why I love the subject of field ecology!

Directions: From County Road 39, turn north onto North Magee Street (one traffic light east of Southampton College). Proceed past Tuckahoe School, straight through the intersection with Sebonac Road, to a five-way intersection, at which you turn right onto Millstone Brook Road (don't make the extreme sharp right onto West Neck Road). The entrance to the Big Woods Preserve is marked with a wooden sign on the left directly opposite from the intersection of Big Fresh Pond Road.

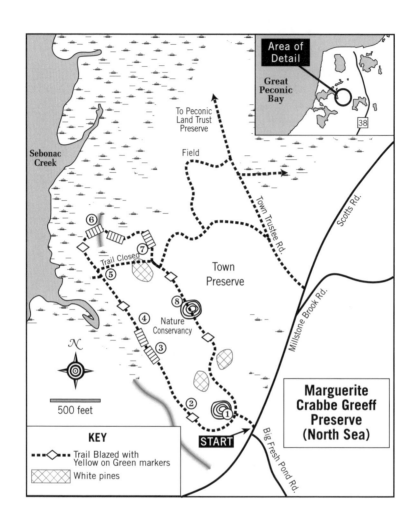

Area of
Detail

Great
Peconic
Bay

38

To Peconic
Land Trust
Preserve

Sebonac
Creek

Field

Town
Trustee Rd.

Scotts Rd.

⑥

Trail Closed

⑦

⑤

Town
Preserve

Millstone Brook Rd.

⑧

④

Nature
Conservancy

③

𝒩

②

①

500 feet

Marguerite
Crabbe Greeff
Preserve
(North Sea)

START

Big Fresh Pond Rd.

KEY

Trail Blazed with
Yellow on Green markers

White pines

WOLF SWAMP PRESERVE

The 20-acre Wolf Swamp Preserve was donated to The Nature Conservancy in 1957 by Elizabeth Morton Tilton who, three years earlier, had donated Jessups Neck to the U.S. Fish and Wildlife Service to become the Morton National Wildlife Refuge. Wolf Swamp is one of the first preserves established by The Nature Conservancy in this area; at that time TNC owned only ten preserves on all of Long Island.

The Wolf Swamp Preserve is situated on the northwest corner of Big Fresh Pond. The swamp itself is about five acres in size, or 25% of the preserve, with the remaining 15 acres composed of typical upland (or "xeric") forest: white, scarlet, black, post, and northern red oaks; mockernut and pignut hickories; some American beech, American holly, white pine, and pitch pine. A 0.75-mile-long loop trail marked with yellow-on-green blazes traverses both the swamp and upland forest. Visitors to the preserve in the spring will be serenaded by an assortment of birds establishing nesting territories and amphibians seeking mates: go early in the day to best hear the former, and around dusk for the latter. One animal you won't see or hear is the wolf, for which the swamp is named. The gray wolf was exterminated from all of Long Island well before 1800 as a result of a bounty system instituted by the first Dutch and English settlers in the 1600s and early 1700s.

Entering through the preserve's wooden gate (1), turn right where the trail forks and head south towards a stand of mountain laurel growing on the side of a hill which the trail ascends (2). A careful look at this stand will reveal an interesting growth pattern: the mountain laurel have sprouted along a low, man-made berm, possibly the spoils of a boundary ditch used to mark property lines much as rock walls were used in New England. The elevated and sloped berm, with its exposed mineral soil, provides a suitable substrate for mosses to develop which, in turn, have a symbiotic relationship with mountain laurel. According to Neil Jorgensen's excellent book *A Sierra Club Naturalist's Guide to Southern New England*, the tiny seeds of this laurel usually require a bed of moss to germinate. Further along the trail, at (3), is a toppled beech whose uplifted root system has also created a mound of exposed mineral soil which has been colonized by moss. Some day it too might provide a germination site for mountain laurel.

As the trail begins to descend the hill, a winter view of Big Fresh Pond, formerly known as Lake Missapogue, can be had through the leafless forest. Contouring along the edge of the pond, with representatives of the upland forest (beech, white pine, oaks, hickories) on the left and an assortment of wetland shrubs and trees (swamp azalea, sweet pepperbush, highbush blueberry, chokeberry, tupelo, and red maple) growing thickly on the right, the trail soon reaches an old road and wooden terracing at (4). Prior to its becoming a wildlife sanctuary in 1957, this was a favorite swimming spot among some locals who referred to it fondly as "B. A. Beach."

The cleared areas at the end of the old roadway, with their sandy soils and southern exposure, are ideally suited for white pine seedlings, which are abundant here. Take some time to scan the pond for waterfowl and osprey before continuing to the boardwalk at (5).

The boardwalk crosses a man-made vector control ditch which accelerates drainage of Wolf Swamp into the pond. This low-lying area is dominated by two species of tree which are particularly well-adapted to growing in wet, poorly aerated soils. One species, tupelo (*Nyssa sylvatica*) is rarely found outside these freshwater swamps. The other, red maple (*Acer rubrum*) is well-adapted to a wide range of soil types and is not uncommon in the upland forest. Note the thicket of catbriar (*Smilax rotundifolia*) in the swamp to the left of the trail. This bright green-stemmed and thorny vine is often an indicator of some type of disturbance which enabled it to gain a foothold; once established, it seems to persist long after all other signs of the initial disturbance have disappeared. This aggressive plant can be found in all South Fork plant communities and soil types with the exception of the salt marsh.

Exiting the swamp, the trail passes by a large pitch pine (6) and reenters the upland forest. Stay left at the next intersection; to the right is a trail that links to Elliston Park and the Paumanok Path. Of interest along the trail between (6) and the head of the swamp and boardwalk (7) is the contrast between the forest canopy and shrub layer. The latter reflects a wetland environment with scattered swamp azaleas and highbush blueberry plants, while the canopy is composed of oaks indicative of xeric (dry) soils.

The final stop, the boardwalks at (7), offer an opportunity to view one of the first plants to flower each spring: skunk cabbage. The oddly shaped, reddish-purple and green spathe which surrounds the tiny, inconspicuous flowers protrudes from the marsh soil (and snow) as early as February. Ready to be pollinated in March, this intriguing plant gets its name from the putrid odor it emits, mimicking rotten flesh, which helps it attract the few flies available at this early date. Another hundred yards down the trail will complete the loop at the preserve entrance.

Over the years, land acquisitions and donations involving the town, The Nature Conservancy, Peconic Land Trust and conservation-minded individuals in the immediate vicinity of Wolf Swamp have created a swath of several hundred acres of preserved land extending from the salt marshes and tidal creeks of the Sebonac estuary eastward to North Sea Road and including the entire northern shoreline of Big Fresh.

Directions: From County Road 39 (Rte. 27), turn north onto North Sea Road, travel two miles and turn left onto Millstone Brook Road. Continue to the next intersection (Scott's Road) and park. The well-marked entrance to the preserve is near this intersection, on the east side of Millstone Brook Road.

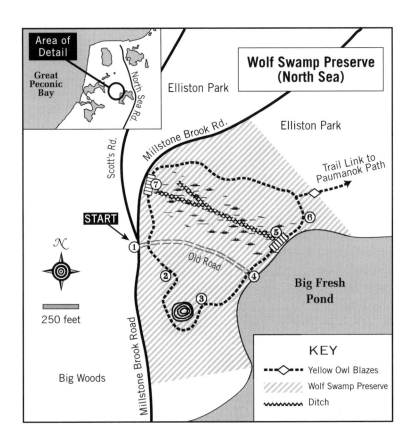

ELLISTON PARK

Most town residents familiar with Elliston Park, avid hunters and fishermen excluded, think of this beautiful preserve as the area in and around the Big Fresh Pond swimming beach. Unbeknownst to many, this 133-acre park extends westward from the pond, across Millstone Brook and Scott's Road, to the expansive tidal mashes of Island and West Neck Creeks. This section describes a route which traverses the entire park. Be sure to bring your binoculars, as there are several excellent vantage points to scan over both fresh and salt water bodies for herons, egrets, and waterfowl.

Heading toward the pond from the park's main entrance, go past the rest rooms to the fenced, terraced area (1). The trail, a narrow footpath, is on the right within sight of the pond and marked with the white rectangular blazes of the Paumanok Path. Within fifty yards, the trail swings through an open area vegetated with a variety of mosses and lichens (2). There are also many young, white (five-needled) pines in the vicinity. A rough estimate of the age of these fast-growing trees can be made by counting the number of whorls, or sections of lateral branches, along the main trunk; be sure to include the stubs of long-gone lower branches on this sun-loving, self-pruning conifer.

After passing through an upland forest of oak, hickory, and American beech, the trail follows along the edge of a typical freshwater swamp of red (or swamp) maple and tupelo or pepperidge (3) before intersecting with an old road which provides fishing access to the pond. Before turning right to continue out to Millstone Brook Road, take a short detour to the pond's edge, passing by several big pitch (three-needled) pines (4), for a view of one of the pond's coves not visible from the main swimming beach.

Crossing Millstone Brook Road, the trail enters a section of the Elliston Park grant not known to many, and rarely visited. Just before ascending a small knoll, keep an eye out for the unusual Siamese oak on the left (5). This mixed hardwood forest also has some fairly large American chestnut trees: look for the silhouettes of their big, burred seed husks in the forest canopy.

After descending partway into a large kettlehole (6), the trail crosses Scott's Road and enters yet another section of the Elliston Park forest. Here, the trail passes by one of the largest American chestnut trees I have seen on the South Fork (7). Once one of the dominant trees east of the Mississippi, it was decimated by the introduction of an Asian fungus in the early 1900s. Today, surviving specimens are limited to 20–30-foot-tall trunks sprouting from the old root system. Once they reach that size and age, the fungus kills the above-ground portion of the tree again. Although some specimens live long enough to bear fruit (chestnuts, of course), research has found that most of the seeds are not viable, or capable of germinating.

This beautiful section of trail, eventually connecting with an old Trustee road, was laid out by Kurt Billing, a nearby resident who served on the boards of several local environmental organizations including the Group for the South Fork, and who spearheaded land preservation efforts in this area. This trail section provides a spectacular view (8) across the marshes of Island Creek towards Cow Neck, and traverses some delightful groves of beech and shadbush.

At the intersection with the main access road, turn right and look for the first left fork, not far ahead (9). At this point, the access road passes close by a salt marsh (with an upland fringe of phragmites) to the east, a farm field to the west, and hardwood forest to the north and south. In ecological terms, this small area is called an ecotone: the boundary between two or more (in this case three) plant communities. In the general vicinity of an ecotone, one would expect to find representative wildlife species from each of the different ecological communities; hence, ecotones are generally areas of high species diversity. During a short visit there, I was not surprised to record a flock of chickadees and tufted titmice, a white-breasted nuthatch, a rufous-sided towhee, and a red-bellied woodpecker working the forested area, robins and crows in the farm field and catbriars, and a great blue heron, a pair of red-tailed hawks, and a flock of Canada geese in and over the salt marsh.

The main access road continues straight onto land managed by the Peconic Land Trust, for which permission is required to visit. Taking the left turn at (9), follow the southern edge of a farm field that is also part of the Elliston Park complex. It and another field on the eastern edge of Elliston Park (visible from North Sea Road) have long been leased to a local farmer for growing crops. The adjacent Big Woods property was leased by the North Sea Gun Club for many years as a hunting area.

Look for a trail heading back into the beech forest at the southwest corner of the field (10). This somewhat overgrown trail soon intersects a wider, well-worn trail (11); turn left to return to the Trustee road via the town's Big Woods Preserve. For future reference, a right turn at (11) eventually leads to The Nature Conservancy's Marguerite Crabbe Greeff Wildlife Sanctuary. Both the Greeff Wildlife Sanctuary and the Big Woods Preserve, totaling

100 acres, were once part of the Salm estate centered at Cow Neck, and, fortunately, both were preserved in the mid-1990s.

Back at the Trustee road, turn right and follow the road a short distance to Scott Road. Consider returning via the Wolf Swamp Preserve, described in the previous section.

Directions: From County Road 39 near Southampton Village, turn north onto North Sea Road. Travel 2 miles and look for a wooden sign which reads "Elliston Park" and marks the left turn onto Millstone Brook Road. The park entrance is 1/4 mile on the left.

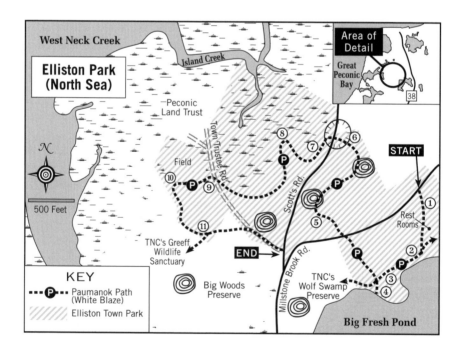

BIG FRESH POND NATURE TRAIL

Elliston Park is named in honor of Emma Rose Elliston (1856–1933). The daughter of Captain Jetur Rose, Emma was born aboard her father's whaling ship off the island of Honolulu and spent much of her early life at sea with her parents. The park was established in 1952 by her husband Joshua Edward Elliston in what is believed to be the first land grant to the town of Southampton for conservation purposes. Its 133 acres lie between Island Creek on the west and North Sea Road on the east and include tidal wetlands, freshwater swamps, upland forest, the northern shoreline of Big Fresh Pond and the upper reaches of an unnamed brook known locally as the alewife dreen. The nature trail is a one-mile loop through a small section of the park, but includes a wide variety of plant communities and wildlife habitats such as oak-hickory forest, red maple and tupelo swamps, small groves of American beech, Norway spruce and pitch pine; it crosses the alewife dreen in two places and provides several views of the pond. The quiet observer can glimpse a variety of interesting wildlife at various times of the year including spawning alewives and their predators (egrets, herons, osprey), great horned owls, nesting turtles, and an assortment of waterfowl.

As you walk from the parking area off Millstone Brook Road towards Big Fresh Pond, look for the trail (marked with yellow blazes) on your left before the restrooms. The trail begins in a classic oak–hickory forest, the dominant forest type on the South Fork (1). There are several species of hickory and many of oak common to this area; all produce nuts (called "mast") which are an important source of food for white-tail deer in the autumn, enabling them to fatten up for the rigors of the rut and winter. Other species which depend on mast and can be found here are gray squirrels, chipmunks, blue jays, and crows.

The trail gradually descends toward a red maple and tupelo swamp (2), and makes a sharp left turn. On the right side of the trail the lower elevation intercepts the water table and standing water is often visible, as are typical wetland plants: skunk cabbage, ostrich and royal ferns, red maple and tupelo trees. Despite the fact that these pools of freshwater may completely dry up in mid-summer, they are important breeding areas for salamanders, frogs, and toads. Such temporary waterbodies are called "vernal wetlands."

The upland area on the left side of the trail is predominately black cherry and black locust, two "pioneer" or early successional tree species. These species indicate that this area was cleared many years ago and is beginning to revert back to forest. An aerial photograph dated 1942 shows this area under cultivation.

Further along is a large downed red maple that has been sawn through to accommodate the trail. Note its shallow network of roots and lack of a large tap root, an adaptation to growing in wet soils devoid of oxygen. A disadvantage of having no tap root to anchor the tree is its susceptibility to being blown down. This is compensated for by the red maple's ability to lose most of its root system, send out new stems from the horizontal trunk, and continue to grow.

The next area (3) is an assortment of shrubs and vines, including wild grape, honeysuckle, and bittersweet, indicative of an early successional stage between abandoned farmland and forest. Note the small black cherries already established here but not yet large enough to shade out the shrubs.

Beyond the shrub patch, you will enter a grove of Norway spruce. This is one of several such groves planted in the park by the town in the late 1950s. The year-round shade created by this evergreen severely limits the amount of ground cover underneath it. As the spruces grow, they not only shade out the understory vegetation but each other, causing the lower branches (and, in the case of slow growing specimens, whole trees) to lose their needles. In this and the other two spruce groves along the trail, many specimens that appear to be dead still have healthy foliage in their upper crown.

Between this and the next, larger spruce grove the trail skirts a red maple swamp (4). The name "red" maple is derived from its small but striking red flowers (visible in late April and early May), conspicuous red seeds, and fall foliage. Although this tree is tolerant of a wide range of soil types, its ability to thrive in wet soils is the source of its other common name: "swamp" maple.

The second and third sections of spruce grove are favorite daytime haunts of great horned owls. For some unknown reason, crows have a habit of harassing owls should they discover one in their territory. Taking turns buzzing the roosting owl until it takes flight, the whole flock flies off in pursuit with a din of cawing until the owl perches again, usually not far from the previous perching spot. I've been able to glimpse a great horned owl on several visits here by following the noisy crows. A sharp eye in these groves might also turn up an owl "pellet": bones (sometimes including a whole skull), teeth, feathers, fur, and other indigestible material compressed into a tight cylinder and coughed up by the owl from the seclusion of its roosting spot.

Another stand of red maples and a thick section of sweet pepperbush are traversed before reaching the first footbridge (5). Look for an unusual herbaceous plant called jack-in-the-pulpit in the red maple stand. It is easily recognized in spring and summer by its distinctive flower: an outer hood or "pulpit" surrounding and covering an inner spike or "jack," and in the fall by its distinctive cluster of large red berries. Inside the pulpit, the base of the jack is surrounded by tiny flowers; if the flowers are berry-like the plant is female, if the flowers are thread-like it is male. The sex of individual plants is determined by the amount of energy stored in its corm (part of the root system) the previous growing season: large corms produce females, small corms produce males, and the smallest corms will not produce any flower, just one compound leaf. Therefore, one plant can change its sex from year to year depending on the growing conditions.

On either end of the footbridge are this area's dominant wetland trees: red maple (*Acer rubrum*) on the west side and tupelo (*Nyssa sylvatica*) on the east. Both are easily recognized from a distance, even in the winter, by their distinctive branching patterns: the maple's paired twigs and buds and gently curving pattern and the tupelo's sharply angled zig-zag pattern. The footbridge spans the alewife dreen, which connects Big Fresh Pond (upstream) with the tidal waters of North Sea Harbor (downstream). During the alewife spawning run (April through June) look for herons and egrets perched in the trees nearby and the silvery carcasses of partially eaten alewives along the banks.

On the far side of the bridge, enter the third and last section of Norway spruce. On the far end of this grove, reenter the oak–hickory forest and note the abundance of young spruce seedlings interspersed under the canopy of hardwoods (6). The presence of so many healthy spruce seedlings in the forest understory indicates that, over time, spruces may replace the oaks and hickories in this section of the park. This is the approximate halfway point on the nature trail.

After passing under a large pitch pine, which contained a red-tailed hawk nest in 1996, note the intersection with the Paumanok Path on your left. From this point to (11), the nature trail overlaps with the regional path. Ahead is a small stand of American beech with its conspicuous smooth, light-gray bark and shrub-free understory (7). Beech nuts, small triangular seeds in a spiny husk, were a favorite food of the black bear as it fattened up each fall in preparation for its long winter's sleep. This agile tree climber is no longer listed among Long Island's fauna, having been one of the first large mammals extirpated by the island's European settlers.

The trail turns right along a high, sandy embankment covered with tall pitch pines (8). There are views of Big Fresh Pond, a classic kettlehole pond formed during the last ice age, and opportunities to scan the area with binoculars for waterfowl and fishing osprey. Between here and the next footbridge the sharp-eyed naturalist might notice a fairly large American chestnut. Once one of the dominant trees east of the Mississippi, it was decimated by the introduction of an Asian fungus in the early 1900s. Today, surviving specimens are limited to 20–30 foot tall sprouts from old roots. Once they reach that size, the fungus kills it back again to the roots. Also look for roosting herons, egrets, cormorants, and osprey, which congregate in this area of the park during the alewife spawning run. All of these piscivores have various adaptations for catching fish: the long-legged herons and egrets stalk their prey by walking in the pond's shallows, spearing fish with their lance-like beaks; osprey hunt on the wing over open water catching fish near the surface with their sharp talons and rough, scaly toes; and cormorants, excellent divers and underwater swimmers, pursue their prey into the deepest waters by propelling their streamlined bodies with webbed feet.

The footbridge (9) is a good vantage point to observe the alewife run. Station yourself there just before sunset during the months of April, May, and June. The alewife is a type of herring, 12–15 inches in length, found from Newfoundland to South Carolina. They are anadromous, that is, they live most of their lives in salt water but migrate to freshwater to spawn. Each spring (approximately mid-March here) the adults congregate at the mouth of the brook in North Sea Harbor (not coincidentally, this date also marks the arrival of osprey from their overwintering areas further south). Although the adult alewives can detect their natal pond waters, studies have shown that they will utilize different spawning sites and there is much mixing of populations. Schools of alewives make the trip upstream mostly at night, and most spawning activity takes place after dark. This event is triggered when the water temperature reaches 50F, and after a period of about five days in the brook or pond the adults head back to sea. At least 50% of the adults will not survive the rigors of spawning and the gauntlet of predators patrolling the shallow brook, and only 0.02% of the eggs laid will produce 3–4 inch long juveniles that make it to sea the following fall. However, each female lays 45,000 to 350,000 eggs, so the 0.02% survival rate still yields a not insignificant 9–70 juveniles per female. This fascinating creature is an important ecological link in the food chain between its prey (zooplankton) and this area's top piscivores, such as the birds discussed previously.

After crossing the bridge, proceed along a berm through another red maple–tupelo swamp with some particularly large tupelos. The trail ascends steeply back into the oak–hickory forest, passing several American chestnuts. The understory of the oak–hickory forest is a thick shrubby mix of huckleberry and lowbush blueberry which flowers in May and produces edible berries in mid-summer.

The trail emerges from the forest and crosses an open area near the bathing beach (10). During the month of June, snapping and painted turtles from the pond and box turtles from the forest seek out nesting sites in this sandy, sunny area. You may be fortunate enough to observe them excavating a hole to deposit their leathery eggs; please do not interrupt this reproductive process that has remained unchanged since the age of the dinosaurs.

The wooden terraces near the bathing beach (11) complete the loop. This access to the pond was once known as the "sheep pens"; perhaps sheep grazed in the nearby area and were watered and sheared here. Before leaving, reflect on the foresight of the park's donor, Joshua Edward Elliston, and the words etched on his tombstone: "Sympathy with Nature is a part of the good man's religion."

Directions: From County Road 39 near Southampton Village, turn north onto North Sea Road. Travel 2 miles and turn left onto Millstone Brook Road. Park entrance is 1/4 mile on left. NOTE: This park is open to town residents only.

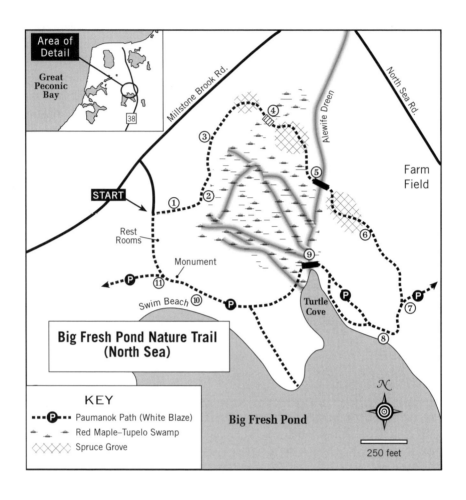

Area of Detail

Great Peconic Bay

38

Millstone Brook Rd.

North Sea Rd.

Alewife Dreen

④

③

START

①

②

⑤

Farm Field

⑥

Rest Rooms

Monument

⑨

Ⓟ

⑪

Swim Beach

⑩

Ⓟ

Turtle Cove

Ⓟ

Ⓟ

⑦

⑧

Big Fresh Pond Nature Trail (North Sea)

𝒩

KEY

- ▪▪Ⓟ▪▪ Paumanok Path (White Blaze)
- Red Maple–Tupelo Swamp
- ⟨⟨⟨⟨⟨ Spruce Grove

Big Fresh Pond

250 feet

SOUTHAMPTON

VILLAGE

NOYAC

Richard L. Fowler Preserve

Nestled in a narrow greenbelt amidst some of the oldest working farms in New York State, this short (0.3 mile) little-known Southampton Village trail is named for a well-known Village resident with a long history of public service. As stated on the bronze plaque which marks the beginning of the trail, it was dedicated in 1986 "In memory of, and gratitude for, the years of dedicated service to the residents of the Village of Southampton: 1968–1985." Mr. Fowler, a farmer whose family farm is located just to the east on Wickapogue Road, served as a Village Trustee for fourteen consecutive years beginning in 1972, until his death in 1985.

The nature walk is essentially an interesting out-and-back traverse through a typical South Fork hedgerow: a study in exotic "pioneer" vegetation which is well-adapted to re-vegetating disturbed sites. These species tend to be quite aggressive and fast growing, with the result being an impenetrable thicket of trees, shrubs, and vines; a perfect haven for deer, fox, raccoon, cottontail rabbit, box turtles, garter snakes, pheasant, bobwhite quail, and an assortment of resident and migratory songbirds.

What makes this "hedgerow walk" somewhat unique is its location alongside a shallow gully which eventually leads to the northern end of Wickapogue Pond, an 11.6-acre coastal freshwater pond. So, in addition to the hedgerow's inhabitants, a visitor to the preserve might glimpse one or more of the wetland species that reside or hunt in the pond: muskrat, painted turtles, green frogs, osprey, egrets, and herons.

From the road, the trail drops down into a large, shallow swale forested with a mix of maples and black cherries. My botanical knowledge, limited as it is, encounters a huge vacuum when it comes to ornamental plants. Knowing I'd come across a lot of non-native shrubs, vines and herbaceous plants on this trail, I took along my Newcomb's Guide to key a few things out. I'm fairly confident identifying trees and so I didn't bother bringing my tree guide but could have used it to key out the maples growing here. I assumed they were Norway maples (*Acer platanoides*), our most common "non-native maples," but something about the leaf edge didn't look quite right. Back at home with the keys out (but no leaf in hand), the Sycamore maple (*Acer pseudoplatanus*) looks like a better guess. Both are hardy immigrants from Europe.

Within one hundred feet, the first of three wooden footbridges, short spans over the usually dry drainage gully, is crossed. Continue along this shaded, wooded section; most of the trailside vegetation here yields a variety of fruits that is a source of food for wildlife: black cherry, bittersweet, arrow-wood, honeysuckle, and wild grape to name a few.

Just before reaching the second footbridge, the dirt trail emerges from the woods and becomes a grass path. On the left is a wild tangle of vegetation including a vine, "deadly nightshade," with a small but striking flower with purple lobes and a bright yellow center (anther). Its bright red fruits, resembling miniature tomatoes to which they are related, are "somewhat" poisonous. Another common plant here, pokeweed, also has poisonous berries, although the small purple fruits (still green as of last week) are much sought after by robins, catbirds, mourning doves, mockingbirds, and cedar waxwings. This species is one of a group of pioneer plants that specialize in growing on "disturbed" sites by having extremely long-lived seeds that can wait many years in the soil until conditions are just right for germination. Once the seeds sprout, this stout plant can grow ten feet in a single season, becoming one of the largest non-woody plants in our area.

At the footbridge is a large shrub, either an autumn olive or a Russian olive (*Elaeagnus* spp.), that needs to be pruned back. Both of these fast-growing, non-native species are considered nuisance plants in many Long Island nature preserves, and are the target of eradication programs. Growing in among its branches is a blackberry bush, with the large tasty fruits dotting the wooden bridge.

Just beyond the bridge, to the left of the trail, is a twelve-foot-high wall of bittersweet vines completely engulfing an unidentifiable shrub. Note that the bittersweet berries are still green as of August 1. They, along with many other fruit-bearing trees, shrubs, and vines, will have ripened berries in time to fuel the big southward migration of birds.

The next stretch of the trail is notable for the honeysuckle, whose ripe berries are a striking red color. At a fork in the trail, go right towards the last of the wooden bridges. On the left side of the bridge is a tree-of-heaven (*Ailanthus altissima*), a species originally from Asia, and a nice patch of jewelweed, a wetland plant limited to the moist soil in the very lowest part of the swale. As described in Harlow's *Trees of the Eastern and Central U.S. and Canada*, tree-of-heaven "will withstand perhaps a greater handicap in the way of poor, hard, trampled, or sunbaked earth than any native tree. When cut, this tree sprouts with great vigor, sometimes to a height of 12 feet the first season, and it is practically impossible to get rid of it unless the entire root system is grubbed out."

On the bridge itself was a densely-packed cylinder of blackberry seeds, the work of a raccoon who, as a general rule, has a habit of leaving its scat on elevated, prominent places such as tree stumps, boulders, and, in this case, the bridge. From here the trail passes through a wide grassy sunlit area with a variety of goldenrods and asters. During the summer months, a riot of purple is provided courtesy of the purple loosestrife, another obnoxious, non-native on the "aggressive alien" hit list. Unfortunately, this beautiful wetland plant is out-competing many of our important native wetland plants, disrupting the ecological balance of wetland systems.

As the trail ducks back into the black cherry forest, look for the token shadbush on the right and a couple of eastern red cedars before entering another open area of wetland vegetation: loosestrife and sensitive ferns. In the background is a row of some type of spruce, probably planted as screening for a nearby home.

Next you will pass under two arches created by arrowwood (*Viburnum dentatum*), a native wetland shrub very common in Montauk's clay soils whose clusters of berries ripen to a dark purple. Off to the left is another of the wetland "bullies," phragmites, extending all the way down to Wickapogue Pond and along most of its shoreline. Interspersed with this reed is another vine: grape (*Vitis* spp.). At the next fork (go left) the grape has blanketed a black cherry tree.

A vine is a growth form that uses other plants or objects for supporting their leaves. By doing this, they are able to save the energy normally required to develop woody (support) tissue and, as a result, they can put that energy into growing outward and upward. This enables them to quickly exploit new openings in the forest or along edges. They use several strategies for climbing: nightshade drapes itself over other plants; grapes climb using curling stems called "tendrils"; honeysuckle, bittersweet, and hedge bindweed climb by entwining themselves around other plants or objects. The latter, bindweed, is easily identified along the trail by its large pink-with-white-stripes and funnel-shaped flowers.

Reaching the edge of Wickapogue Pond, I managed to glimpse a muskrat swimming among the lilies and a kingbird "hawking" insects over the water from a narrow slot in the phragmites. Stepping out further for a better vantage point, I watched four fisherman intent in their pursuit of prey. A father and two sons cast into the pond's deeper waters in hopes of hooking a big one, while a great egret worked the near-shore shallows for something it could swallow in one quick gulp. After some minutes with none having any success, I turned to retrace my steps.

As a final note, the accompanying map shows a Village greenbelt, albeit a very narrow one, connecting this nature trail with the Village property at Old Town Pond. Perhaps this trail system could be extended some day to include this connection and, hopefully, a view over some protected farmland from it north to Wickapogue Road.

Directions: The entrance to the preserve is on the south side of Wickapogue Road, approximately 0.4 mile east of Old Town Road. The trail starts in a hedgerow just east of the intersection of Wickapogue Road and Narrow Lane; look for a large rock tucked in a gully just off the south side of the road.

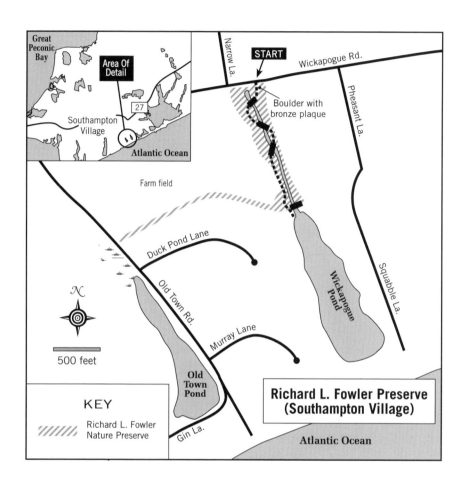

Richard L. Fowler Preserve
(Southampton Village)

Munn Point Preserve

Standing on the edge of Shinnecock Bay, enjoying one of the ever diminishing unspoiled views of the bay's shoreline, I reflected on the destruction of Meadow Lane's natural beauty over the past thirteen years, an onslaught still very much in progress. As if to reinforce the message of poor planning and our failure to manage our natural resources, a least tern and pair of piping plovers lands fifty feet to my right. Both officially listed as endangered species, their habit of choosing prime beach front for nesting puts them in direct conflict with *Homo sapiens*, a conflict they are losing. Reaching for a borrowed camera, fully automated but with countless features and overrides, I locate the two species in the viewfinder and steady the camera for an unusual and lucky shot. Apparently hitting the zoom button instead of the shutter, the camera makes some noises but no click, and while I fumble with it my subjects take leave.

The lost photo op was more than made up for by the sights and sounds enjoyed on my visit to the seven-acre Orson D. Munn Point Preserve in Southampton Village. A 200-yard-long boardwalk connects the parking area on Meadow Lane to the bayfront beach and, enroute, visitors are treated to a close-up view of the salt marsh and its resident and migratory wildlife. Depending on the season and time of day, a visit to the preserve could turn up some interesting sightings: diamondback terrapins come ashore to lay eggs; foxes have used a den nearby; snowy owls, northern harriers, and short-eared owls hunt over the marsh grasses; and a wide assortment of shorebirds and waterfowl congregate during the spring and fall migrations.

Some may question the wisdom of constructing a boardwalk through the marsh as the antithesis of what a "preserve" is all about, and rightly so. There are always impacts and tradeoffs to be weighed and considered, and hopefully a balance struck between providing access and an educational opportunity for people and quiet solitude for wildlife.

On the edge of the parking area, standing like sentries guarding the entrance to the wooden boardwalk, are a small number of Japanese black pine trees of assorted ages and sizes (1). Similar in habitat preferences but faster growing and having longer, more lush-looking needles than our native pitch pine, this Asian import was once the pine of choice among landscapers and was planted all along Long Island's parkways and beach fronts. At a certain age, it is subject to a fatal disease and today its use in landscaping is much diminished. Surrounding the pines are knee- to waist-high thickets of roses. Other plants found growing in this zone of dry sandy soil above the reach of the tide are American beach grass, seaside goldenrod, and the incredibly tenacious and adaptable poison ivy.

To the left of the boardwalk is a granite boulder with a bronze plaque (2) which reads:

> Munn Point
> Dedicated to Orson D. Munn
> Southampton Village Trustee from 1967–1985

Mr. Munn's eighteen-year tenure as Village trustee was quite a long one, and included some quite controversial times as development pressure in the Village, particularly along Meadow Lane, mounted.

At (3) the relatively thick-bladed beachgrass gives way to a thin and wiry-stemmed grass called salt hay (*Spartina patens*). This grass marks a seemingly imperceptible change in gradient which allows the incoming full and new moon (spring) tide to completely inundate the soil there with salt-water, while the nearby beachgrass area remains dry. Look for the serpentine line of flotsam and jetsam that weaves through this plant zone and delineates the most recent high tide mark. The composition of the "wrack line" changes over time and reflects some of the estuarine life cycles; at times it is mostly pieces of phragmites or reed grass, at other times it may be eel grass, or a line of empty crab shells. In the latter case, what appears at first glance to be evidence of a massive shellfish die-off is actually a sign of life, growth and synchronicity in nature: the cast-off exoskeletons of crabs following a molt.

Growing quite close to the boardwalk are two shrubs which mark the furthest advance of any woody plants into the salt marsh: groundsel (*Baccharis halimifolia*) and marsh-elder (*Iva frutescens*). Their overall shape and leaves are quite similar, but a careful examination of their branching pattern and leaf arrangement easily distinguishes one from the other. Groundsel's leaves are lined up along its twigs in an alternating pattern, while marsh-elder's are arranged in pairs, one opposite another, along the twigs. Once you get an eye for telling them apart, you will notice that marsh-elder generally ventures further out into the intertidal zone, its roots having a better tolerance for regular immersion in salt water.

At (4), salt hay is replaced by another broad-bladed grass which superficially resembles American beachgrass: cordgrass (*Spartina alterniflora*). This is the dominant plant of the Munn Point preserve and the most abundant plant found in the lower salt marsh zone, an area which is inundated twice daily by even the lowest (neap) high tide. It is also the "pioneer" plant of the salt marsh, colonizing sand and mud flats and, if protected from waves, eventually forming new areas of marshland. A recently established section of marsh can be observed at (9). As a result of extreme fluctuations in salinity and ambient temperature over short periods of time (consider the salinity change over the course of a few hours between high and low tide during a hard rain, or the temperature shift as 35-degree water recedes and exposes the marsh to a winter air temperature of below zero), plant diversity is low here. The most conspicuous plant visible among the cordgrass is *Salicornia* or glasswort, a succulent resembling a tiny cactus.

In terms of fauna, of the two most visible and numerous inhabitants, the ribbed mussel and the fiddler crab, each has a unique and opposite strategy for coping with the twice-daily change between marine and terrestrial environments. The mussels, of course, are active during high tide; while exposed to air this bivalve shuts down tight and waits it out. The air-breathing fiddler crab, on the other hand, is actively feeding when the tide is out; it retreats into its tunnel in the peat as the tide comes in and, by positioning a peat "plug" near the tunnel entrance, it creates an air chamber which can last through several hours of tidal inundation.

Near its mid-point, the boardwalk takes a jog around a small salt pond (5) which seldom dries out even at low tide. Here, a variety of small fish can take refuge during low tide without having to retreat to the deeper waters of the nearby bay. Without a net, it is difficult to identify the numerous finfish swimming about, but on a visit one June several brightly colored individuals stood out quite well. Their brilliant blue backs and contrasting orange sides were the unmistakable markings of male sheepshead minnows (*Cyprinodon variegatus*) ready for breeding. This common killifish can live in waters with salinities ranging from fresh to 142 ppt (salinity is measured in parts per thousand, with ocean salinity averaging 35 ppt), qualifying it for the special designation euryhaline species.

Watching the water rush through the tidal creek (6) on an outgoing tide, I noticed hundreds of small dark inch-worm-like organisms drifting by: these were mosquito larva. The linear, grid-like network of ditches in this and most salt marshes on the eastern seaboard was created as part of the Depression-era WPA program: a poorly researched make-work project with the goal of eliminating mosquito breeding habitats. Its failure was no surprise to biologists familiar with this pesky insect, and half a century later our salt marshes still suffer the ecological consequences of ditch "maintenance." Moving slowly over the muddy creek bottom are an assortment of snail and whelk shells now inhabited by hermit crabs. In places completely covering the bottom are mud snails (*Illyanassa obsoletus*). These small dark-colored gastropods feed on microscopic plant plankton, particularly diatoms, which cover the surfaces of the peat, mud, sand, and decaying plants in the marsh and bay. Although largely herbivorous, they will also scavenge on the decaying remains of other animals.

The boardwalk terminates at a narrow band of dune sand (7) which protects the marsh from the erosive forces of wind-driven waves on the bay. The bay beach's high tide mark was pockmarked with twelve inch diameter depressions, evidence of recent egg-laying by horseshoe crabs. Masses of the tasty blue mussel, attached to small rocks and pebbles by dozens of thin filaments called byssal threads, lay strewn about closer to the low tide mark (8). Off to the west, an adult osprey perched on the edge of its nest. This pole was erected in 1999 and is the only occupied osprey nest in the Village of Southampton. Obviously a suitable site from the bird's point of view, we may have to move it further back off the beach next year to better avoid conflicts with people walking through the area.

Looking north across the narrows separating the broad expanse of Shinnecock Bay from Heady Creek is a landscape in striking contrast to the scene behind me on the ocean dunes, one uncluttered with monuments to personal wealth and consumption. Realizing that this is one of the longest stretches of undeveloped shoreline on the entire bay, I was struck by the irony of the situation. The nightmarish scene behind me is subject to strict zoning regulations and wetland laws, and has received the attention of two land trusts and state, county, and village funding for open space acquisitions. The tranquil scene before me has benefitted from none of that. I was looking at the Shinnecock Indian Reservation.

Today, whether you call it Dune Road, Beach Lane, or Meadow Lane, the landscape on either side of this road has been transformed dramatically with the importation and installation of topsoil, irrigation systems, rocks, sod, and an assortment of landscaping material that resembles anything but a dune or meadow. Do these homeowners really think their hundreds of thousands of dollars of landscaping look better than the natural vegetation they replaced? Perhaps, feeling guilty for building on a dune or marsh, these homeowners decided to re-create the landscape so as not to be reminded of where they are.

If you think the onslaught is over, think again. Of the twenty acres of marsh and dune land between the Munn Point boardwalk west to where the bay nearly touches the road, fifteen are privately owned, comprising five separate lots. Attorneys and environmental consultants will spend hours before the Village Zoning Board trying to justify building on a sliver of overwash deposited on the marsh during a storm that breached the ocean dunes. The fact that this is a flood zone will be "mitigated" by constructing the house on pilings eight feet above the road!

Directions: The Munn Point Preserve is located on the north (bay) side of Meadow Lane (a.k.a. Beach Lane or Dune Road) in the Village of Southampton approximately one half-mile west of Halsey Neck Lane. A permit, which can be obtained at Southampton Village Hall, is needed to access the preserve.

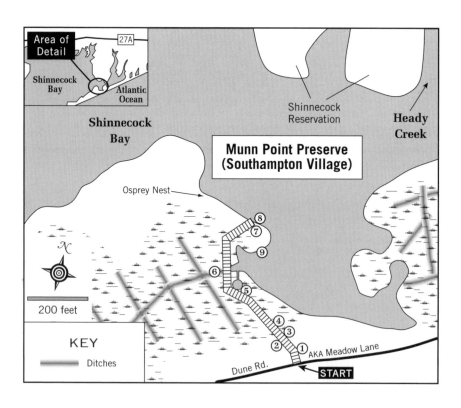

LAUREL VALLEY PRESERVE

The sun had already dipped below the western horizon and dusk had settled in as I approached the edge of a large clearing (10). It was February 21, and I had obviously not left myself enough daylight to complete my fieldwork. I still had a half-mile walk to Deerfield Road and my car, and was moving quickly so as to get there before total darkness descended, when an unusual sound caught my ear and caused me to stop and listen.

The series of loud bubbly chirps sounded nearby, yet I couldn't pin down the exact location or direction of the bird calls. Nor did I see any of what I assumed was a small flock of birds making the noise. Something else was odd here; songbirds are generally quiet at this time of the day.

I was finishing a hike along the loop trails in Laurel Valley County Park, Noyac. The 150-acre county park was purchased in 1990 with funds from the county's 0.25% sales tax program. This open space program targeted important groundwater recharge areas for preservation, and the Laurel Valley area lies over some of the deepest and thickest freshwater deposits on the South Fork. The only area on the South Fork with larger freshwater deposits is found at the Golf at the Bridge property just to the east. Ironically, the Noyac Golf and Country Club, adjacent and to the north of the park, has contaminated its groundwater with chemicals used in turfgrass management.

I had started my late afternoon walk at the Deerfield Road–Deerwood Path trailhead, where the County Parks Department has erected an informational display (1) including a map of the park's trail system. Heading east, I followed the white rectangular blazes that mark the Paumanok Path. A short distance in is a trail intersection and sign (2) pointing out the two hiking options: left for the loop trail that traverses the northern and eastern portions of the park; and right for the Paumanok Path which traverses the park's southern area.

I opted to make a counterclockwise loop of the park by following the white rectangular paint blazes of the Paumanok Path to the kettlehole at (6), and then returning via the loop trail marked with blue-on-white blazes. Turning right, I followed the Paumanok Path up and out of the shallow ravine, onto a prominent hilltop and down into a steep-sided and deep ravine.

A short portion of the ravine here (3) is part of a town reserve area, totaling thirty acres, created by the town planning board through the subdivision approval process. "Cluster" or open-space subdivision laws enable the board to protect natural, recreational, and cultural resources without reducing the developers yield (the total number of lots allowed under zoning) or requiring public acquisition funds. This is accomplished by reducing lot size and locating lots away from the resource being protected. More often than not, as is illustrated with the Fourteen Hills and Goose Down subdivisions on the south side of the park, the designs are not very creative. House sites are located on the hilltops, clearing and paving for roads is maximized, wildlife habitat is needlessly fragmented, and the thin, ribbon-like greenbelts that are created provide poor trail experiences and have little, if any, wildlife value.

Laurel Valley County Park is named for the abundance of mountain laurel and the half-dozen small valleys or ravines found there. The ravines, some quite steep-sided and nearly all northwest–southeast oriented, were most likely carved by meltwater flowing towards Peconic Bay from large blocks of ice left behind by the receding glacier. At or near their upper end one can usually find a large kettlehole where the block of ice broke off the melting glacier.

Mountain laurel and valleys are linked together in more ways than just this park's name. As you hike through this area, note the general correlation between topography (ravines, kettleholes, hilltops, and ridges) and the densest stands of mountain laurel.

Most of the park is an oak-hickory forest with an understory of huckleberry and lowbush blueberry or mountain laurel. One of several exceptions to this rule is found at (3) where the trail crosses through a small grove of American beech. Beech forests are striking for their smooth, light-gray bark and lack of any understory layer. The latter makes for easy walking, with or without a trail. The absence of understory shrubs is due to the beech tree itself: its branches and leaves are layered from the upper canopy right down almost to the forest floor itself, casting a deep shade over anything beneath it, and part of its root system is found right on the surface of the forest floor, effectively out-competing any plants for soil nutrients and moisture.

From the beech grove, the Paumanok Path hugs the bottom of the ravine, weaving through or around the mountain laurel thickets. At (4) is a trail sign that marks the intersection with the shorter of the two loop trails. This loop trail segment crosses over several hilltops and ravines and is worth exploring. It is marked with black-on-white trail markers and connects the Paumanok Path with the larger blue-on-white loop trail at (9).

After passing a lone, tall pitch pine (5), the Paumanok Path intersects with another trail (6). Leave the white blazes, which turn right (south) and climb up out of the ravine to connect with Middle Line Highway, and continue straight ahead into a large, open kettlehole, following the blue-on-white trail markers. The ice block that formed the large kettlehole here was also the source of meltwater that carved out the ravine you just hiked through.

The trail turns north and climbs out of the kettlehole. En route back to Deerfield Road, the trail traverses a series of hilltops, kettleholes, and ravines. By the time you've reached the spur to Wildwood Road (7), you should have figured out the relationship between dense mountain laurel thickets and topography.

Mountain laurel is most prolific on the steep sides of the hills and kettleholes and along the bottom of the ravines. It is nearly absent on the hilltops, where huckleberry and lowbush blueberry dominate the understory shrub layer. It is also more prominent on the north-facing, shadier sides of hills, kettleholes, and ravines, although there are many exceptions to this.

Interestingly, it is generally not found growing in the very bottom of kettleholes, so shade is not the only factor here. Its tiny seeds do not germinate well on leaf litter; steep slopes can be swept clear of leaves by wind, and a hard rain can clear a ravine, but both rain and wind will often deposit leaves in the bottom of a kettle.

At (8), the trail offers a view north across the Noyac Golf course with Peconic Bay and the North Fork visible in the distance. I had lingered there a bit too long talking with a neighbor out walking her dog. She mentioned that she often hears great-horned owls in the park at this hour, but none this evening. And so I found myself standing in the old field (10) at dusk, trying to get a glimpse of the mystery bird when I heard a loud, buzzy "PEENT!" This was repeated loud and clear a half dozen times, enabling even an amateur birder like myself to confirm it as the courtship call of the American Woodcock (*Scolopax minor*).

Courtship takes place in the twilight hours following sunset and preceding sunrise (on bright moonlit nights, courtship may occur on and off throughout the night). It begins with the male quietly flying in wide circles to a height of about fifty feet, after which he continues to ascend in diminishing circles making a loud, twittering sound caused by air rushing over the outer three primary feathers of its wings. At a height of several hundred feet, the wing twitter is replaced by a warbling, musical chirp (also caused by air rushing over the specialized feathers) as the male begins a zig-zag descent back to terra firma. Reaching the ground, he gives a vocalization best described as a buzzy "PEENT!"

A few stars were visible in the darkening sky but there was enough light to follow a male through most of his erratic flight. I always lose sight of the birds as they approach the ground on the descent. The purpose of the aerial display is to attract mates. If impressed, the female will wander over to the male's mating territory, put a brief end to his aerial antics, then head off to a nearby forest or thicket to make a modest nest in the leaf litter. There is no lasting bond between mates; the male resumes his display flights in hopes of attracting other females and has no role in nesting or caring for the young.

The show, which continues into June, takes place in fields and brushy meadows adjacent to wetlands and forested areas. As I continued along the Laurel Valley Loop Trail, I realized that all three clearings in the park (10, 11, and 13 on the accompanying map) were staging areas for this unusual event. Biologists have documented a slow but significant decline in the eastern population of American Woodcock over the twenty-year period 1968-1988. Please be mindful of this when visiting courtship territories and be careful not to disturb the breeding ritual.

Note some of the large tree specimens along the last quarter mile of the loop: very large hickories, oaks and red maples (12). A huge sycamore is growing among black cherries and black locusts near 13. Black locust seems to be particularly susceptible to windthrow; many of the trees here have toppled, making for challenging work for the volunteer trail maintenance crew.

Directions: There are three trail access points for this area: Middle Line Highway, Wildwood Road, and Deerfield Road. The latter is the official trailhead for the park, located on Deerfield Road approximately halfway between Noyac Road and Little Noyac Path at the intersection of Deerwood Path. Travelling south on Deerfield from Noyac Road: Deerwood Path is the first paved road on the right. There is not much of a shoulder on Deerfield Road, so park on Deerwood Path. The trail is blazed and begins in the forest directly across Deerfield Road from Deerwood Path.

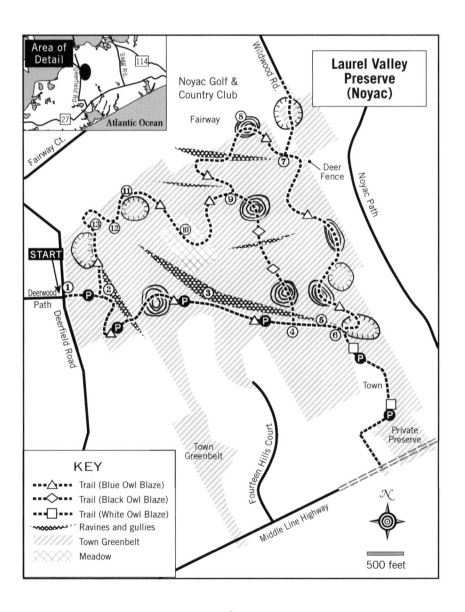

Area of Detail

Sagg Rd.
Deerfield Rd.
114
27
Atlantic Ocean

Laurel Valley
Preserve
(Noyac)

Fairway Ct.

Noyac Golf &
Country Club

Fairway

Wildwood Rd.

8

7

Deer
Fence

Noyac Path

11

9

10

13

12

START

Deerwood
Path

Deerfield Road

1

P

2

P

3

4

5

6

P

Town

P

Private
Preserve

Town
Greenbelt

Fourteen Hills Court

Middle Line Highway

N

KEY

- - -△- - - Trail (Blue Owl Blaze)
- - -◇- - - Trail (Black Owl Blaze)
- - -□- - - Trail (White Owl Blaze)
~~~~~~ Ravines and gullies
///// Town Greenbelt
XXXXX Meadow

500 feet

Morton National Wildlife Refuge

Donated to the U.S. Fish and Wildlife Service in 1954 by its owner, Elizabeth Morton, the refuge's unusual mix of ornamental, non-native plants and brushy second growth reflect a long and interesting history of agriculture on its grounds dating back to the 1600s. Originally named Farrington Point for John Farrington, one of the original founders of the South Hampton Colony, the peninsula took its current name from another member of the newcomers from Lynn, Massachusetts: John Jessup. Jessup was deeded the area in 1679 and, through the ensuing 275 years, ownership was transferred to only two other families.

In 1800, Isaac Osborn acquired the land and began experimenting with a variety of crops and livestock, including mulberry trees for raising silkworms and introducing the first shorthorn cattle and merino sheep to Long Island. During this time, the entire area was cleared and either under cultivation or used as pastureland. Even the salt marsh was periodically mowed and these grasses, collectively called salt hay, were used as winter fodder for cattle and sheep.

It should be noted that, were it not for the generosity of people like Elizabeth Morton, Long Island's National Wildlife Refuge Complex might not even exist. Of the eight refuges on all of Long Island, totalling a paltry 6,100 acres, most have been donated to the U.S. Fish and Wildlife Service. These facts reflect one of the most disappointing failures of Long Island's environmental community: attracting federal funding to create an island-wide system of wildlife refuges that reflect Long Island's ecological diversity and location on the Atlantic flyway.

A vast majority of the 187 acres which comprise the refuge are located on a narrow, nearly two mile-long peninsula, or neck, which juts northward toward the North Fork, in the process forming the boundary between Peconic and Noyac Bays. The three hills that occupy Jessup Neck, rising 20 to 60 feet above the bay, are kames. In his excellent book *Long Island: A Natural History*, Rob Villani describes a kame as "a dome-shaped mound, formed when pebbles and sand accumulate in an opening in a motionless piece of glacial ice. Eventually the ice melts and the kame appears."

These kames are connected, quite tenuously, to the rest of the refuge in the form of a low-lying and narrow section of beach, called a tombolo, in places a mere four feet above mean sea level. It is not unusual, even during a moderate storm, for the neck to be temporarily transformed into an island. The source of the beach material is the bayfront bluffs, including the east and west edges of the eroding kames, and the mechanism of transport is littoral drift. The southern end of Jessup Neck has a double tombolo, with a beautiful salt pond and marsh nestled between the two. Periodic dredging of Noyac Creek prevents the eastern tombolo from connecting to Clam Island.

The refuge's 1.5-mile-long trail system, limited to its mainland section, is easily followed. From the kiosk, which provides interesting information about the National Wildlife Refuge system in general and some specific information about Morton Wildlife Refuge, take the first right off the main trail to the beach (1). This section of trail crosses through an area that was once cleared for farming and is now re-vegetated with a variety of early successional old field vegetation, including black locust trees and honeysuckle and sumac shrubs, all of which are interlaced with vines of catbriar, wild grape, and bittersweet. A large red maple growing here is, according to a refuge trail guide, the oldest measured on Long Island at 130 years of age. In June, you may see a painted, snapping, or box turtle on the trail. At this time of year females of the former two species emerge from the nearby pond, and females of the latter from the nearby woods, seeking open, sunny sites to excavate a shallow depression in the earth into which their soft, leathery eggs are deposited. After covering the nest with soil, the females leave the two to four month job of incubating to the sun and earth.

Shortly after entering the woods, the trail crosses a long section of boardwalk (2) which cuts through a red maple swamp near the south end of a freshwater pond, barely visible off to the left. On either side of the boardwalk are plants well-adapted to growing in the shady, wet soils found underneath the large maples. One species that is hard to miss is skunk cabbage (*Symplocarpus foetidus*), a member of the Arum family whose huge, plate-sized leaves seem to be designed to maximize capture of what little sunlight penetrates the maple canopy. While the plant does have an odor, it is certainly not in the same category as its namesake. Personally, I would describe it a not too unpleasant, earthy-garlic bouquet.

Another member of the Arum family growing nearby is jack-in-the-pulpit, whose one or two compound leaves of three small leaflets are much less conspicuous than its relative, but still easy to spot. Its distinctive and unusual "flower" is worth noting: a green, white and purple striped spathe, or hood (the pulpit) surrounding a spadix, or column (jack). The actual flowers are inside the spathe, at the base of the spadix, and not visible unless you carefully lift the top flap of the spathe and peer inside. Of course, this is all ingeniously engineered and designed to ensure successful pollination by attracting insects. Come back in late summer to look for the large, brilliant red berries.

Despite their succulent leaves and flowers, neither plant is browsed by deer (so say the books!). Given the number of white-tails found in the refuge, it would be interesting to keep an eye on that. Both plants are laced with an anti-browsing agent called calcium oxalate which, in humans, causes a severe burning sensation when chewed.

Several of the taller woody plants growing alongside the boardwalk, near its midpoint, appear to be sapling cottonwoods. A small grove of the adults is growing at the edge of the pond. I've heard mention of a stand of swamp cottonwood (*Populus heterophylla*) in the refuge, but these four-to-eight-foot-tall specimens seem to be some non-native, imported species not found in my tree guides.

En route to the next section of boardwalk over a stream (3), look for a wooden gate on the right; just beyond the gate, on the left side of the trail, are several sweet cherry trees (*Prunus avium*), with a distinctive smooth shiny bark marked with horizontal bands called lenticels. This is another exotic tree, native to parts of Europe and Asia. Nearby is a tuliptree, once part of the hardwood forest found inhabiting the richer soils of the South Fork. These majestic forests were converted to farmland hundreds of years ago; not even a small remnant can be found on the South Fork today. Tuliptrees were the tallest of the eastern hardwoods, growing one hundred feet high and six feet in diameter. In the forest, the trunk grew straight and clear to a height of sixty feet or more before the first branch was reached. Also known as the canoe tree, it was the Native American's tree of choice for building dugouts. In his book *Trees of the Eastern and Central United States and Canada*, noted dendrologist Dr. William Harlow writes that the tuliptree is "unsurpassed in grandeur by any other eastern broadleaved tree."

The boardwalk at 3 spans the outlet of the pond; a small stream whose banks are lined by skunk cabbage and red maple. I can't think of any other plant in this area with a leaf as massive as that of skunk cabbage. According to some field guides, the root system of this herbaceous perennial can live for hundreds of years. Its longevity, some claim, is usually limited by the natural, gradual process of ecological succession which inevitably alters its habitat from wetland to upland, thereby creating an environment in which it can no longer successfully compete with other species.

The trail swings within sight of the pond and a bench which overlooks it (4). The pond was created in a natural depression that was most likely a swamp or marsh before it was excavated. Walk down to the shoreline and watch quietly. Within even a short span of time you are likely to be rewarded with several wildlife sightings: perhaps a muskrat feeding on some aquatic vegetation, a turtle swimming slowly near the surface, or a heron stalking the shallows for fish or green frogs. The latter are lined up along the shoreline roughly every foot or so, a careful eye can pick many of them out despite their excellent camouflage.

The next section of boardwalk (5) spans another small stream which empties into the tidal waters of Noyac Creek, just visible off to the right. From there the trail crosses a large meadow with an osprey pole (6), which should probably be moved closer to Noyac Creek. In the spring of 1999 I received a distressing call from a nearby resident: an osprey had constructed a nest on the roof of a powerboat moored in the creek. The skipper eventually returned and didn't take too kindly to his new shipmates, wasting no time in tossing their nest overboard. Hopefully no eggs had been laid yet.

Back at the intersection with the main trail, turn right to reach the beach, passing through wooded thickets of black cherry and eastern red cedar. Black-capped chickadees, accustomed to handouts, show little of their usual wariness at your approach, and may "buzz" you looking for food. Where the trail opens up at the beach (7), enjoy the beautiful panorama overlooking Peconic and Noyac Bays. To the southwest, the sandy bluff marking Homes Hill and the entrance to North Sea Harbor is clearly visible. Scanning clockwise from that point, you can pick out Cow Neck's long stretch of undeveloped shoreline, Robins Island, the North Fork, the west beach and bluff of Jessup Neck stretching for 1.75 miles to the north, a row of waterfront homes on Shelter Island, the bold sandy bluffs of North Haven, Long Beach, and, just across Noyac Creek, Clam Island County Park. Sound impressive? It certainly is!

Access further north onto Jessup Neck is prohibited from April to August to protect important nesting areas from disturbance. But one need not go any further, as the scenery doesn't get much better than here anyway.

Directions: The well-marked entrance to the refuge is located on Noyac Road (C.R. 38) between Deerfield Road and Millstone Road, directly across from the Noyac Golf and Country Club. From west of the canal, head east on Rte. 27, turn left (north) onto Sandy Hollow Road (C.R. 52) which runs into North Sea Road. Continue north on North Sea Road (C.R. 38) and bear right onto Noyac Road (still C.R. 38) for another 5 miles to the refuge entrance (on the left). There is a $4 visitation fee per vehicle; $2 for pedestrians and bicyclists.

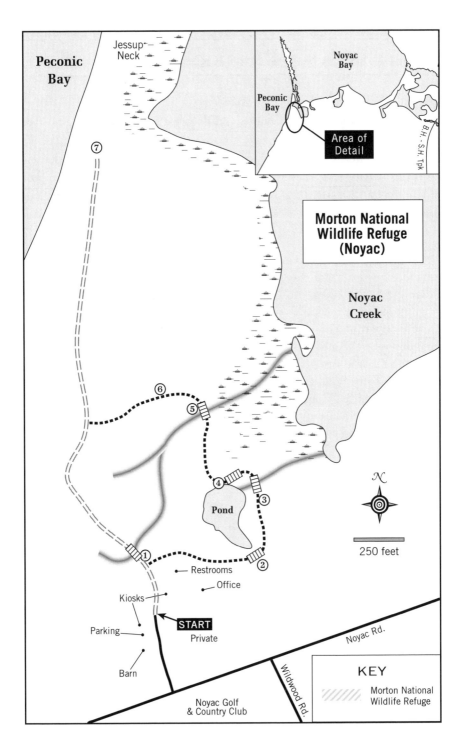

Peconic
Bay

Jessup
Neck

Noyac
Bay

Peconic
Bay

B.H. - S.H. Tpk

Area of
Detail

Morton National
Wildlife Refuge
(Noyac)

Noyac
Creek

⑦

⑥

⑤

⑧

④

③

Pond

①

②

𝒩

250 feet

Restrooms

Office

Kiosks

Parking

START
Private

Barn

Noyac Rd.

Wildwood Rd.

Noyac Golf
& Country Club

KEY

Morton National
Wildlife Refuge

CLAM ISLAND PRESERVE

Despite the name, a visit to Clam Island does not have to involve a boat or swim: a quarter mile-long *tombolo*, a term used by geologists to describe a sand beach connecting an island with the mainland or another island, connects this twenty acre "island" to the mainland of Noyac. The tombolo provides easy foot access to the island's upland forest, salt marsh, beach, and dredge spoil area. A word of caution: be prepared to get at least your feet wet if setting out on a spring high tide.

This small gem was purchased by Suffolk County in 1988 after years of lobbying by Group for the South Fork, the Noyac Civic Council, and the Property Owners Association of Noyac Harbor. The effort involved a campaign, targeted at the U. S. Army Corps of Engineers and the NYS Department of Environmental Conservation, to oppose a development plan which included a bridge and raised roadbed for auto access, and a two hundred foot-long catwalk into Noyac Bay. First proposed for preservation by County Legislator Tony Bullock, the acquisition plan was finally pulled together under Fred Thiele's County tenure, surviving some bickering at the County Legislature in which the island's purchase was temporarily held hostage. In this case, the good guys prevailed.

From the end of Noyac Bay Avenue, head westward along the beach, stopping from time to time to look up and enjoy the panorama over Noyac Bay with views of North Haven, Shelter Island, Southold, and Jessup Neck. The beach here changes from day to day, depending on the presence and size of waves which, in turn, are determined by the strength and duration of wind. If its been blowing hard out of the northwest all day, or your visit is not long after a good Nor'easter, the small but persistent bay surf will have stripped the beach of sand, sweeping it into deeper waters just offshore, and leaving behind a collection of plum-sized, smooth rocks of assorted colors.

Before reaching the tombolo, you pass two big, box-like houses on the left. Set on pilings, they loom above the reedgrass completely out of proportion to the landscape. The entire area on which they sit was once salt marsh; fill was deposited here sometime after 1947 and before the state enacted its Tidal Wetland Regulations. Estimates have put the loss of tidal wetlands on Long Island at approximately 40% of the original acreage, and the South

Fork was not immune to that destruction. Possibly as a token of retribution, one of the big box occupants has erected an osprey nesting pole.

Moving on, look for a slight point protruding into the bay (2) which is vegetated with salt marsh cordgrass (*Spartina alterniflora*), normally found in a more protected location such as found on the creek side of the beach. An examination of the grasses at low tide will reveal a significant deposit of peat upon which the vegetation is growing; such a deposit could only accumulate in a very protected area. This is evidence that the tombolo is acting similar to a barrier beach system in that it is slowly "rolling over" itself and moving landward (south in this case), engulfing the edge of the Noyac Creek salt marsh on its south side and, as seen here on its northern side, uncovering the peat portion of an old marsh that once flourished when the tombolo was situated several hundred feet further north.

At (3), the tombolo is quite low and narrow and, at high tide, barely separates the waters of the creek and the bay. It is not unusual for the tide to overtop the tombolo here; at times the tidal action may scour out a small, temporary channel which, through the same process that created the tombolo, gradually fills in with sand. That process, called littoral drift, involves a source of sand material, such as an eroding shoreline or bluff or sediments, carried downstream and deposited by a river, and a method of transport, generally a complex interaction among tidal and wind driven currents and waves. What's most intriguing to me is trying to figure out the direction of "net" littoral drift and which of the many complex currents dominant over time. This is easily understood on the ocean beaches of the South Fork, but along the extremely uneven coastline of the Peconic–Gardiner's Bay estuary, things are not quite that simple. First of all, the ebb and flood tides race through narrows and fan out over large embayments, creating countercurrents or eddies which complicate matters. And, in some areas having distinctive headlands delineating two embayments: the overriding net effect seems to be for the headlands to erode and the sand to be carried toward each of the embayments; in effect a net littoral drift in opposite directions depending on which side of the headland you look at.

In this case, the overall pattern of sand movement in the bay seems to be southward from the eastern bluffs of Jessup Neck towards Clam Island, and eastward from the island towards Mill Creek. If that is accurate, the source of the tombolo's sand could be a combination of Jessup Neck and Clam Island material.

Continuing to the island itself, evidence of the island's contribution to the littoral drift can be seen at (4). The eroding shoreline has exposed the roots of several eastern red cedar and oak trees, now susceptible to saltwater damage at high tide and dessication at low tide. Several oaks are barely surviving the stress of this bayfront location oriented to the harsh northwesterly winds; their twisted and contorted branches are largely bare of leaves, while specimens growing further inland, protected from the wind and salt spray, are still sporting luxuriant foliage. During low tide, several cedar stumps are visible quite a distance from the edge of today's forest: these forest relics are evidence of long-term erosion and change.

Continuing along the beach to the island's western end (5), enjoy the view across Noyac Creek to Morton Wildlife Refuge, before examining the shrubby clumps of beach plum (*Prunus maritima*) found here. Standing no more than six feet in height, these specimens have put more energy and biomass in lateral growth than vertical, and for good reason. The leaves and buds on the shrubs' windward side, in this case facing northwest, are subject to damaging salt spray which, over time, has retarded branching in that direction. In the lee of these damaged branches, afforded some protection from the wind and salt, other branches have fared better as long as they don't poke their buds and leaves up too high. The result is a very compact, sculpted shrub orienting its growth in a southeasterly direction.

Leaving the beach, head over to the southern side of the island, crossing a large dredge spoil area en route (6). The spoils are from Noyac Creek, which the Town Trustees dredge to maintain a channel for recreational boating and to maintain tidal circulation and salinity levels in the creek. In 1998 an incredible amount of material was dredged and deposited here, leaving quite an unsightly landscape. However, many of these spoil sites make excellent nesting areas for terns and plovers, both species in decline who need all the help they can get.

Following a line of red cedars, note their variation in both form (columnar versus spreading) and color (various shades of yellow-green and blue-green). Unlike the beach plums, the cedars show no signs of salt damage or wind pruning.

My last visit to the island was a late September day. The southern side of the island, overlooking Noyac Creek and in the lee of a stiff northwesterly, was warm and calm. The groundsel-bush was covered with pussy willow-like flowers, while a marsh edge companion and look-alike, marsh elder, had already gone to seed. Brilliant yellow flowers of the seaside goldenrod were everywhere and, in the nearby marsh, glasswort (*Salicornia* spp.) had turned a bright crimson-red, a harbinger of autumn along with the similar-colored Virginia creeper on the edge of the forest. Here, I finally figured out how to work our fully-automated, idiot-proof office camera, and snapped some photos of this beautiful scene before making the return trip.

On the way back, consider taking a new trail (7) through the center of the island's maritime forest, a mix of post oak (*Quercus stellata*), eastern red cedar, and sassafras. Poison ivy is quite abundant here, growing as woody shrubs and climbing vines. It's a good idea to know how to identify this plant after it has dropped its leaves; its berries and aerial roots are good characteristics to recognize. You might also consider exploring the unmarked trail just east of (2) that winds through a town greenbelt.

Directions: The entrance to this small County Park is not marked, but not difficult to find. From Noyac Road, turn north onto Mill Road, which is situated between Trout Pond and Millstone Road (almost directly across Noyac Road from the entrance to the Trout Pond parking area). Go to the end of Mill Road, turn left onto Noyac Bay Avenue, and follow it a short distance around a sharp right turn where it dead ends on Noyac Bay. Park on the side of the road and, facing the bay, walk left (west) along the beach to Clam Island.

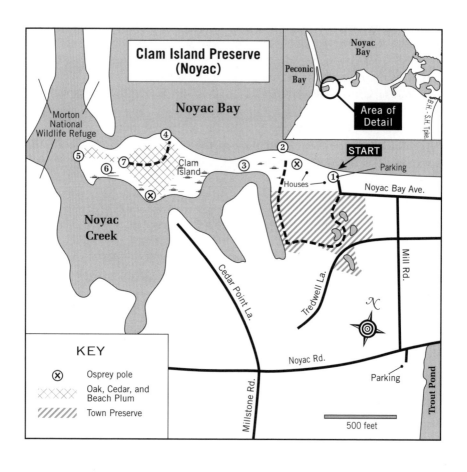

Clam Island Preserve (Noyac)

Noyac Bay

Noyac Bay

Peconic Bay

Area of Detail

B.H.-S.H. Tpke.

Morton National Wildlife Refuge

Clam Island

START

Parking

Houses

Noyac Bay Ave.

Noyac Creek

Cedar Point La.

Tredwell La.

Mill Rd.

Noyac Rd.

Parking

Millstone Rd.

Trout Pond

KEY

⊗ Osprey pole

✕✕✕✕✕ Oak, Cedar, and Beach Plum

▨▨▨ Town Preserve

500 feet

Trout Pond Preserve

The forty acres of woods and freshwater wetlands that comprise Trout Pond Town Park are nestled between the estuarine waters of Mill Creek and Noyac Bay to the north and a ridge of glacial deposits, known as the Ronkonkoma moraine, to the south. Trout Pond is fed by two small brooks that appear, somewhat magically, out of the ground just north of Ruggs Path. Meandering through a diverse forest, the brooks lose 15 feet of altitude before reaching the pond where, at the north end, a spillway over the dam drops another ten feet en route to the tidal waters of Mill Creek. Long a favorite swimming hole for nearby neighbors, in the 1970s town officials began exploring sources of funding to acquire the pond. In 1983, following a town-wide referendum on the matter, the pond and thirty three adjacent acres were purchased to create Trout Pond Town Park.

From the parking lot, follow an asphalt path which cuts through a wooded area heavily laden with vines: a impenetrable mass of cat briar, wild grape, bittersweet, and honeysuckle (1). Vines are commonly associated with "disturbed areas" such as abandoned fields or forest edges. Because very little energy is expended in developing a strong support system (woody tissue), vines have the ability to grow very quickly. They rely on other plants or objects to support their growth, and climb towards the sunlight by a variety of means: hair-like aerial roots (poison ivy), aerial roots with adhesive pads (Virginia creeper), tendrils (tiny curling stems which are actually modified leaves as found on cat brier), entwining (bittersweet), or simply draping themselves over the host plant (wild grape).

The species composition of the forest here is another clue that it was once cleared. Eastern red cedar, tree of heaven, sassafras, black locust and black cherry are all "early successional" or "pioneer" species which prefer open, sunlit areas and can quickly colonize abandoned fields or other clearings, beginning the gradual process of reforestation. Vines often slow the reforestation process by shading out tree seedlings and, in some cases, actually strangling them by entwining tightly around their narrow trunks and damaging their xylem and phloem structures just beneath the outer bark. Some species, such as poison ivy, also inhibit other seedlings by secreting a toxin into the soil.

After exiting the woods, head for the wooden boardwalk and dam (2). This is a good place to scan the water with binoculars for waterfowl and basking turtles. Perhaps the distinctive cries of the kingfisher or osprey, two piscivores which frequent the pond, can be heard on a quiet day.

This area is also a good place to reflect on this site's long and interesting history. Before colonial times, an unimpeded creek known as Noyac River flowed through this narrow, steep-sided valley and into Noyac Bay. "Noyac" is the Native American term for "point or corner of land" which, according to William D. Halsey, author of *Sketches from Local History*, refers to nearby Jessups Neck, one of the most prominent natural features in the area. The close proximity of abundant shellfish, in addition to the excellent supply of freshwater, made Noyac River an ideal summer encampment for a small band of Native Americans who were most likely part of the Shinnecock tribe. In fact, present-day Noyac Road closely follows the pre-colonial Indian route between here and the main Shinnecock settlement in Southampton Village. According to William D. Halsey, evidence of the Native American encampment was clearly visible as recently as the 1960s.

Town historian Robert Keene put the date of the first earth and stone dam sometime in the early 1700s, creating what was then called Mill Pond to power a grist mill. Prior to that (1686), a fulling mill was operated on "the stream at Noyack"; apparently this type of mill could be operated without a dam. The grist mill was owned by Charles Rugg, for which nearby Ruggs Path was named. At one time a windmill was constructed to pump water back uphill and into the pond. Various mills were operated until 1881, when heavy rains overtopped the dam and caused considerable damage. The dam and stone bridge over which Noyac Road crossed were repaired, but not the mill. A rare sedge (*Carex mitchelliana*) inhabits that general area today.

The property was then acquired by George Thompson who stocked the pond with trout, changed its name to Oak Grove Trout Pond, and ran a resort out of a house built near the pond's south end. In 1905, F. E. Mellinger bought the pond and surrounding lands to raise ducks and pigeons (squabs). At one time there were 5,000 pigeons here before a forest fire swept through the area. At least one of the pigeon coops was salvaged and transported to the Hendrickson farm on Lumber Lane in Bridgehampton, where it served many years as a chicken coop. The concrete foundation of the coops can still be seen just south of Ruggs Path (10).

At the eastern end of the boardwalk, near Ruggs Path, is a small patch of cattail (3). Cattails have a distinctive flower structure visible most months of the year: in summer as a dark-brown, sausage-shaped or "cat's tail" flower, and in winter as a buff-colored, fluffy seed head. The minute seeds are attached to downy hairs for efficient wind dispersal; thousands are packed into one head. While the seeds are considered poor wildlife food, the rootstocks and young shoots are highly nutritional and much sought after by muskrat and geese. Perhaps more important than its food value is its habitat value: the dense thicket it creates provides excellent cover for small fish, frogs, a variety of nesting birds, and the insects they all prey on. As you approach the pond's edge here, you are sure to roust a couple of green frogs (*Rana clamitans*) and send them scurrying for deeper water with an "eek!" and a splash.

Continuing south on the east side of the pond, take some time to examine the variety of trees and shrubs growing between the trail and the water's edge. Many of these are wetland species specifically adapted to the moist, occasionally saturated soils found here. The dominant pondshore trees are swamp maple (*Acer rubrum*) and tupelo or sourgum (*Nyssa sylvatica*). Both have a striking scarlet fall foliage, with sourgum turning color quite early (sometimes in late August). "Tupelo" is from the Creek Indian words for "swamp tree." Unlike the swamp or red maple which is commonly found on dry hillsides and ridges in addition to wetlands, tupelo seems much more dependent on water-saturated soils. Part of its scientific name, *nyssa*, is derived from one of the ancient Greek water goddesses of lakes and rivers.

Gray birch (*Betula populifolia*), shadbush (*Amelanchier canadensis*), and smooth alder (*Alnus rugosa*) are small trees (or large shrubs) also found growing along the shoreline. The latter is easily identified throughout the year by its cone-like fruiting structures. Among the common pondshore shrubs are winterberry holly (*Ilex verticillata*), whose bright red berries are visible through most of the winter; highbush blueberry (*Vaccinium corymbosum*), with its delicious berries; swamp azalea (*Rhododendron viscosum*), recognizable by its typical azalea flower (white); and sweet pepperbush (*Clethra alnifolia*), with its fragrant white flowers and persistent seed capsules resembling peppercorns.

Forming a mat-like mass of groundcover along the opposite (upland) side of the trail (4) is the low-growing evergreen *Vinca minor*, commonly called periwinkle or myrtle. Its attractive blue-violet flowers appear in late April, adding a dash of color to an otherwise colorless landscape at that time of year. Because of this, it is a popular cultivar. Its presence in a woodland setting is often evidence of an old cellar hole or foundation nearby, and in fact what appears to be part of an old septic system is visible from the trail.

Another spring-blooming, non-native flower found all along the trail system is Garlic Mustard (*Alliaria officinalis*). Look for clusters of small white flowers and coarsely toothed leaves which, when crushed, smell of garlic. Many of the larger trees along the trail are chestnut oaks (*Quercus prinus*), easily identified by their coarsely-toothed leaves and deeply furrowed bark. A member of the white oak group, which has rounded lobes or teeth and acorns that mature in one year; its bark was considered the best source of white oak tannin.

Halfway down the pond, the eastern hillside steepens and is covered by mountain laurel (5), an attractive native plant that adds greenery to the winter landscape and clusters of showy pink-white flowers in June. A member of the heath family (*Ericaceae*), mountain laurel requires very acidic soils with a pH range of 4–4.5 and does not respond well to liming. In spite of its relatively large and showy flower, the seeds of the laurel are very tiny and have very specific germination requirements: a bed of moss. The moss, in turn, requires patches of leaf-free, bare soil to become established. These areas are most commonly found on the steep sides of kettleholes and hillsides.

Take the first right turn and cross a small wooden footbridge over one of the two inlets which feed the pond (6). Surrounding the footbridge is the typical assortment of wetland shrubs and trees. Growing along the edges of the stream are a variety of ferns and a large plant with striking crimson-orange, irregularly-shaped flowers visible over most of the summer. The latter is *Impatiens capensis*, commonly known as jewelweed (because the leaves trap tiny air bubbles when submerged, giving it a silvery appearance) or touch-me-not (derived from the fact that its seed capsules snap open when touched, projecting the seeds several feet through the air). Sap from its stems relieves itching from poison ivy and insect stings.

At the next intersection, turn left; the trail climbs slightly and enters an oak-hickory woodland (7). Two forest understory shrubs associated with stream banks and moist woods are common here: spicebush (*Lindera benzoin*) and witch hazel (*Hamamelis virginiana*). Spicebush, named for its strongly aromatic leaves (when crushed), is one of the earliest shrubs to flower in the spring, gracing the forest with clusters of small yellow petals. Witch hazel flowers at the other extreme end of the growing season, producing small, stringy yellow petals in November. Because there are few plants in bloom at those times of the year, these plants have little competition in attracting for insect pollinators. On the other hand, there are far fewer insects active at those times of the year.

Several paths lead off to the left and into the red maple swamp surrounding the pond's eastern inlet. This is an excellent place for birding during the spring migration: many insects are attracted to the flowering maples and these, in turn, attract many species of aerial insectivores, such as warblers. A water-filled concrete structure there (8) may have been a tank for raising trout fry before they were released into the pond, an unsuccessful project initiated by George Thompson in the 1890s. The trout, apparently brook trout, died by the hundreds. Since the early 1990s the Southampton Town Trustees have been stocking the pond with rainbow and brown trout.

Veer right (9) onto a footpath that skirts the edge of the western inlet to its source near a nice grove of American beech (11). American beech is easy to identify: smooth, gray bark; long, pointed, cigar-shaped buds; and copper-colored leaves (autumn). In fall, look for its small triangular beech nuts sheathed in a prickly husk. These are a favorite food among many birds and mammals. Since beech can reproduce by sending new shoots up from its roots, it often forms pure stands of clones. Very tolerant of shade, beeches are considered a climax species whose presence is associated with a mature forest. The area beneath beech trees is generally devoid of plants; the growth of understory plants is limited by its shallow root system, combined with the dense shade it casts on the forest floor.

Turn right here and head north, mostly staying within sight of the brook. Nearing the south end of the pond (12), the banks of the brook are lined with skunk cabbage (*Symplocarpus foetidus*), revealing its strong preference for permanently wet soils. Named for the odor emanating from all parts of the plant (a strong garlic-like smell not nearly as bad as an aroused skunk) this interesting perennial is visible at all times of the year. From spring through summer, its plate-sized leaves are hard to miss. Despite their size and succulence, few wildlife seek them out as food. An anti-browsing agent in the form of calcium oxalate keeps all but the resident slugs at bay, including the ubiquitous white-tailed deer. From autumn through winter, next year's flower and leaf buds are visible: the former a mottled purple-yellow and the latter a light green. Both are pointed and up to six inches tall. In late winter, often poking up through the snow and ice, the flower bud begins to enlarge. Despite air temperatures that may hover around freezing, internal heat generated through the process of respiration is trapped beneath the bud's spongy, well-insulated covering (called the spathe), creating an internal temperature of seventy degrees. This unusual phenomenon enables the male and female flowers (a knob-like structure called the spadix) to mature quite early in the year, and can result in a situation where the flower buds are actually melting the surrounding snow; a striking image found in the portfolios of many nature photographers. When in bloom (early spring before the leaves emerge) one side of the spathe opens and the tiny flowers are visible. There are few insects available to pollinate the flowers at that time of the year, but the warmth of the flower and odor of the plant help attract any that are. The pollinated flowers develop into dark, marble-sized seeds in late summer, a source of food for wildlife such as wood ducks and pheasant.

Leading off to the left is a new trail created by the Southampton Trails Preservation Society in 2001 (13). It winds through a mix of vines and second growth forest, much like that seen at (1), to complete a loop back to the parking area. Or you can return by continuing straight ahead on the main trail, enjoying views over the pond from its west side.

Directions: Trout Pond is located on Noyac Road, one mile west of Long Beach and 0.5 mile east of Millstone Road. The parking area is on the south side of Noyac Road, across from Mill Road, just west of the pond.

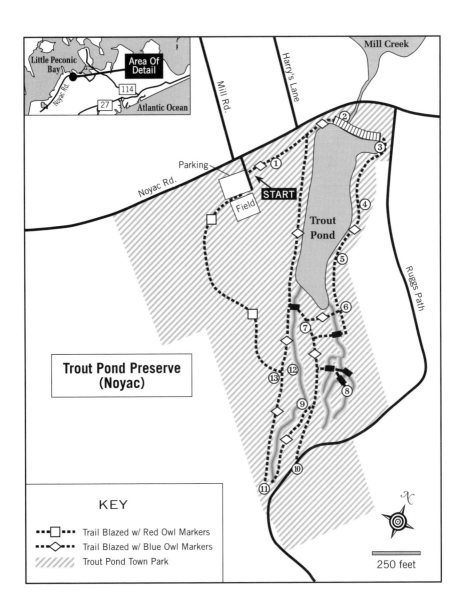

Trout Pond Preserve (Noyac)

Little Peconic Bay

Area Of Detail

Atlantic Ocean

Noyac Rd.

114

27

Mill Creek

Mill Rd.

Harry's Lane

Parking

Noyac Rd.

START

Field

Trout Pond

Ruggs Path

① ② ③ ④ ⑤ ⑥ ⑦ ⑧ ⑨ ⑩ ⑪ ⑫ ⑬

KEY

Trail Blazed w/ Red Owl Markers
Trail Blazed w/ Blue Owl Markers
Trout Pond Town Park

N

250 feet

BRIDGEHAMPTON

SAG HARBOR

SAGAPONACK

BRICK HILL PRESERVE

The view is magnificent. Facing south atop a small knoll on the edge of the Ronkonkoma moraine, Bridgehampton's outwash plain lay at my feet, sloping imperceptibly away to meet the Atlantic, quite visible in the distance. Despite the recent building boom, the landscape is still dominated by large blocks of agricultural land, today a mix of horse pastures, nursery stock, and a vineyard in addition to the fields of potato, corn, and winter rye.

The view is also quite panoramic. A combination of the knoll's location at the edge of the Scuttlehole farm fields, and its elevation at 219 feet above mean sea level, enables one to scan the horizon for several miles through the southern half of the compass circle. In addition to the church steeples, which mark the location of several hamlets, the South Fork's largest coastal lagoon or salt pond, Mecox Bay, is easily discernible. Even after a thick coastal fog has settled in, limiting the view here to the immediate surroundings, the knoll-top setting itself is lovely enough to justify the one-mile-long round-trip hike, so don't let the weather or visibility deter your visit.

Starting at the Bridge Hill Lane cul-de-sac, cross the split rail fence and walk southwesterly along the wide, grass walkway which bisects the forest. This fifty-foot-wide walkway extends for a quarter mile to another cul-de-sac which can be accessed from Lopers Path. The walkway was originally destined to become a paved roadway, part of the network of roads in the controversial Whiskey Hill subdivision, a proposed development that laid out roads and house lots with little regard to slopes, wildlife resources, trails and adjacent open space. Although the oddly-shaped 86-acre parcel had many constraints, making it a challenging area to develop, the proposed subdivision design was one of the worst I've ever reviewed. Even Group for the South Fork staff were surprised when, in the late 1980s, it was deemed satisfactory by the Southampton Planning Board and received final approval.

Fortunately, soon after the woods were cleared for roads and curbing and road drainage structures installed, the owner-developer ran into some trouble and left town. Town approvals expired and the new owner-developer and Planning Board worked out a plan with less roadway and more open space, including the provision for a public trail to the incredible overlook.

There are now signs marking the intersections of the trails with the grass road; continue past the first trail sign to the second (1). Follow the yellow blazes along a narrow footpath to where it meets a wider, more established trail (actually an old woods road). As you diagonal up the slope, look off to the right through the oak-laurel woods for a large, spire-shaped glacial erratic.

As the trail levels off near the top of the knoll, look for a right turn onto a newly created footpath (3), which leads south to another old woods road (4). The blazes here lead across the road and down into a small kettle vegetated with black locust and black cherry trees and bittersweet and catbriar vines. Climbing out of the kettle, the footpath rejoins the old woods road, this new trail section being cut to maintain some distance from a new house constructed off to the right. Continue on the old woods road to another narrow footpath (5). This left turn leads uphill through pitch pines to the scenic overlook.

Enjoy the view and look for one of two (at least that's how many I know of) U.S. Geodesic Survey markers in the ground nearby. One is imprinted "Hildreth 1932" and the other "No. 4 1945." Also, be aware that the top of the knoll hugs the preserve boundary; please don't wander onto adjacent private property.

The names Whiskey Hill and Brick Hill refer to a large, illegal still operation and a small-scale brick-making operation, respectively. It's not clear to me which of the several hills in the vicinity bears each name, but the whiskey operation was one of the largest in the country before it was shut down by federal agents. One of the hills was also the site of a windmill.

On the return trip, take a right at (3), and a quick left (follow the yellow blazes) over the top of a 225-foot-high knoll and down into a small swale with a scattering of red maples among the oaks and mountain laurels. A switchback (7) allows you a moderate descent around a small garden of glacial erratics before reaching the grass road.

Directions: From Scuttlehole Road, turn north onto Brick Kiln Road, traveling for 0.4 mile to the first left turn, which is Bridge Hill Lane. Bridge Hill Lane is a 0.3 mile-long cul-de-sac; park at the far end. Beyond the cul-de-sac is a split rail fence and wide grass path; follow the grass path to the intersection of the town trail approximately 150 yards on the left.

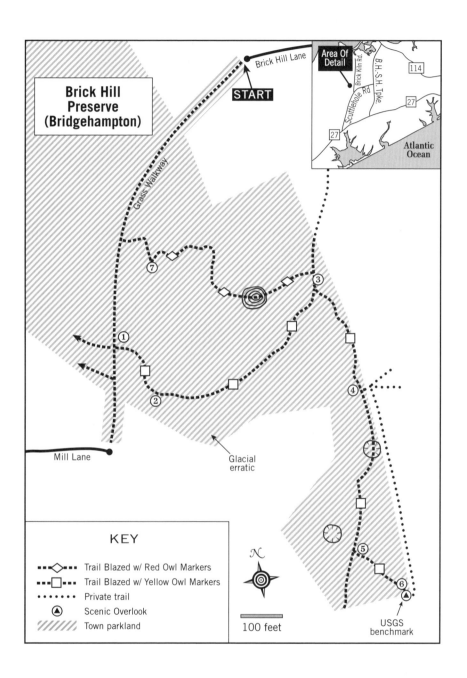

Brick Hill Preserve (Bridgehampton)

Area Of Detail

Brick Hill Lane

START

Grass Walkway

Mill Lane

Glacial erratic

USGS benchmark

KEY

Trail Blazed w/ Red Owl Markers
Trail Blazed w/ Yellow Owl Markers
Private trail
Scenic Overlook
Town parkland

100 feet

Long Pond Greenbelt:

North Loop

The Long Pond Greenbelt is a linear system of ponds, streams, swamps, and adjacent woodlands stretching across the South Fork from Sag Harbor to Sagaponack. The greenbelt includes a coastal salt pond (Sagg Pond), which periodically opens to the Atlantic Ocean, the tidal waters of Otter Pond, and lower reaches of Ligonee Brook which connect directly to the Peconic Estuary, and thirty freshwater ponds, marshes, and swamps of assorted shapes and sizes. The wide variety and number of wetland types is largely responsible for the greenbelt's record number of rare flora and fauna: this relatively small area of approximately 1,000 acres contains more rare species than any other area in New York State.

The north loop is a three-mile hike through the northern section of the greenbelt and includes views of Ligonee Brook, Long Pond, and Little Long Pond. From the Turnpike parking area adjacent to Mashashimuet Park to the greenbelt forest, a distance of only 200 yards, the route (actually an old abandoned railway corridor) is a bit tricky to follow. From the parking area, walk south along the turnpike for twenty yards, passing a private driveway and following alongside a split rail fence. At the opening in the fence, turn left onto a dirt track. A recently constructed wooden kiosk here may have maps and additional information about the greenbelt. Continue straight ahead to a five-foot-high mound of dirt. Cross over the mound: the trail now enters the forest and is very easy to follow.

You are actually on an old, abandoned railway spur that connected the Bridgehampton Station with Long Wharf, Sag Harbor. Completed in 1870, the five miles of track were abandoned in 1939, and the steel rails were removed and recycled during World War II. Not far down the railway trail is a small dreen called Ligonee Brook (1) that flows under the railbed. Depending on the tide in Sag Harbor Cove at one end of the brook, and the height of Long Pond at the other end, the brook may be running in either direction here. This watercourse has been dug out and possibly straightened in the past but still provides a conduit for spawning alewives heading upstream and mature eels heading downstream, the latter to begin their incredible oceanic journey to their spawning area in the Sargasso Sea, one thousand miles away.

Continue straight through the intersection of the Old Railway Trail and Round Pond Trail. Round Pond Trail was once another railway spur, providing a means of shipping out a very important commodity collected at the pond: ice. An icehouse stood on the south shore of Round Pond from the 1840s to 1911, when it was destroyed by fire. Not far from this intersection is another trail, marked with a sign proclaiming it Sprig Tree Path, veering off to the left (2). Take this and enjoy its meander through a pleasant oak–hickory forest.

Just before Sprig Tree Path reaches the north end of Long Pond, it comes within sight of the southern end of Ligonee Brook. A short side trail on the left leads to an overgrown concrete bridge (3) spanning the brook which, in August of 1998, was flowing quite well but in many Augusts is completely dry. Just upstream from this bridge is another concrete structure, a dam built in 1889 which was part of Sag Harbor's waterworks. The waterworks provided drinking water to sections of Sag Harbor Village through a series of pipes originating on Ligonee Brook (at the site marked on the map as "old waterworks").

Continuing on Sprig Tree Path, beautiful views are afforded across the northern end of Long Pond and its extensive emergent marsh full of pond lilies, pickerelweed, and a variety of rushes and sedges. A stand of phragmites, an aggressive tall grass that grows well overhead and out-competes many native shoreline plants, has become establishes here. Although an attractive species, biologists are concerned about its rapid spread here in the rare coastal plain pond plant community shoreline. TNC staff have attempted to eradicate it by various means, some of which have been controversial. Along with its habitat restoration efforts, TNC constructed a wooden fence along the trail here, as well as a bench on which to rest and enjoy the view.

During my early August visit, a large flock of tree swallows flew just inches over the marsh busily catching insects. Against the distant shoreline, some tupelos had already begun to show their brilliant scarlet autumn colors. This section of trail, completely underwater for most of the spring and early summer, should probably be relocated to pass around the Long Pond wetland, not through it. On the right or upland side of the trail are patches of wetland shrubs such as buttonbush and sweet pepperbush, the latter unmistakable in August with its sweet-smelling white clusters of flowers in full bloom. Enjoy this stretch of trail, with several views out over the pond to the left. At (4), see if you can pick out the poison ivy plants growing thirty feet up into the oak canopy and overhanging the trail. Take a close look at its stem with its characteristic hair-like, aerial roots, a distinctive feature which may enable you to identify it in the winter.

Veer left off Sprig Tree Path at the next trail junction to view Long Pond's middle and southern sections. Here, the pond is deeper and the emergent marsh plants give way to open water. Try scanning the pond for waterfowl and muskrat and, as you walk along the trail, look for evidence of turtle nesting. At (5), a large, open sandy area near the pond, several turtle nests had been dug up and the eggs eaten with only the white, curled shell fragments remaining. Five turtle species have been documented in Long Pond area: stinkpot, painted, red-bellied, snapping, and box. All are subject to heavy egg predation by foxes and raccoons, but because of their relative longevity (30 to 75 years depending on the species) these losses are not a problem. Of more concern to biologists is the heavy mortality suffered by adults interacting with automobiles as they move to and from nesting areas bisected by roads.

The trail narrows significantly as it swings back toward the railway. On the left is a pretty view into a cove of the pond showing another stage of ecological succession of a pond: a red maple swamp. In 1998, these maples had already taken on their brilliant fall colors as early as July 28. Turn left onto the Old Railway Trail for a short distance before making another left back onto Sprig Tree Path. At (6) you will pass through another swamp community, this one dominated by tupelo, which is draining across the trail toward the pond. At the LIPA powerlines, turn right and climb up to the Old Railway Trail, this time turning right (north) on it for the return trip. On your left is a great view of a red maple swamp (7): with time accumulating leaves, branches, and silt will fill in the swamp, allowing other trees, such as oaks and hickories, to become established: a dynamic process of change called ecological succession.

Take the next left (Toll House Road) and a quick right for a close view of Little Long Pond. A short spur trail (8) takes you right to the pond's southern edge. There are several nice views overlooking this pond further along the trail before intersecting the Old Railway Trail and proceeding north once again. One more side trip to Little Long Pond is worth making: a boat-launching area at the next left, before hiking the mile back along the oddly corrugated railway trail to the Turnpike.

Directions: Approximately 200 yards south of the Bridgehampton Turnpike–Jermain Avenue intersection, on the east shoulder of the Turnpike, is a dirt parking area (adjacent to a children's playground). This provides a good access point to the greenbelt via the old abandoned railway.

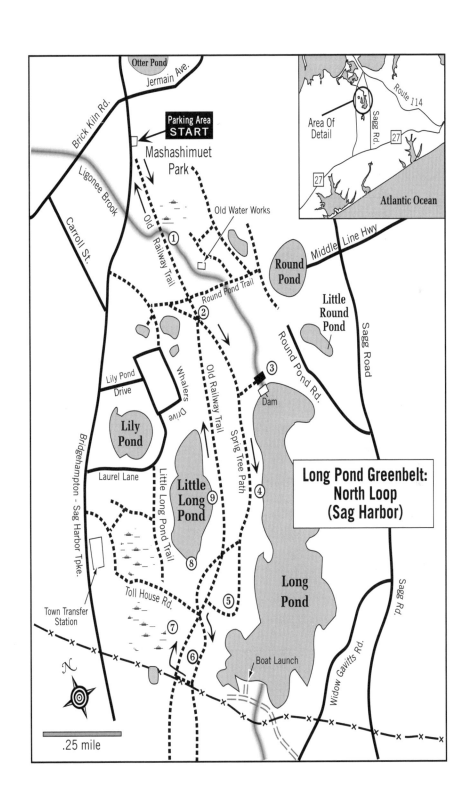

Long Pond Greenbelt:
North Loop
(Sag Harbor)

Long Pond Greenbelt:

South Loop

Although the Long Pond Greenbelt is characterized by a north-to-south trending string of ponds, vernal pools, swamps, and marshes, this 3.5-mile trail loop begins and ends with a traverse of the largest dry section of the entire greenbelt. Shortly after leaving Haines Path, the trail (Old Farm Road) passes through a pitch pine forest, with some very large specimens on either side of the trail. This tree has evolved several important adaptations to surviving in fire prone areas: an extremely thick outer bark which insulates the sensitive xylem and phloem inner bark from the damaging heat of fire; the ability to resprout needles from adventitious buds hidden beneath the outer bark, after fire has scorched all the existing needles; and the development (on some specimens) of a few serotinous cones which won't release their seeds until after the heat of a forest fire has unsealed their protective scales. Another fire-adapted tree, the scrub oak, is very common along the first half mile of this trail. It can resprout from its underground root collar following even the most severe forest fires. As the name implies, it has a very scrubby appearance and is the smallest member of the *Quercus* (oak) genus in our area: generally less than ten feet tall. The small acorns are distinctive in that the cup nearly covers the entire nut. Both of these species, although well-adapted to periodic fires, may be prevalent here due to the fact that they are also well-suited to the extremely dry, nutrient-poor sandy soils found in this section of the greenbelt.

At the first trail intersection, turn right onto Widow Gavitt's Path. Note that the forest in this next section is composed of fairly small oaks, including the white oak which can live over 200 years and grow to over 80 feet tall, with a trunk girth exceeding three feet. One such specimen grows near Black Pond, a half mile to the west. It is tempting to assume that these are all very young trees. However, tree size is a function of growing conditions as well as age, with slow growth being a reflection of poor site conditions. Many of our morainal forests have small, stunted trees due to the porous Carver-Plymouth soils and drying effects of the prevailing southwesterly winds, a situation not unlike the stunted growth found among tiny but old trees of the alpine, or "krummholz," zone in mountainous areas.

The trail narrows and swings left of a depression (1) which seems to contain mostly scrub oak and low-growing shrubs. Another such depression with similar vegetation is found on a section of the Old Farm Road (7). Generally, these depressions accumulate fine sediments and develop richer soils, and often have some of the largest tree specimens in the immediate area. Why this is not the case here is a mystery to me.

Back in a closed canopy forest, take the next trail (a narrow footpath) on your left, leaving Widow Gavitt's Path and diagonaling toward the southwest corner of Crooked Pond. The trail intersection at (2) affords a nice view of the pond. Continue straight ahead to the next trail intersection and turn right onto Crooked Pond Trail, which weaves in and out of stands of mountain laurel and has several vantage points from which to scan the pond's waters for wildlife. Crooked Pond, with tiny islands, coves, and peninsulas, is my favorite greenbelt pond. It is also the best example of the coastal plain pond shore ecological community in the greenbelt, and possibly the state, with a variety of rare and unusual species adapted to life on a shoreline which might be underwater one year and on terra firma the next.

On the left side of the trail the land rises steeply to the old railway, the slopes providing an attractive challenge to dirt bike enthusiasts who have caused much unsightly erosion here. Keep to the right at all the trail junctions and eventually the Crooked Pond Trail begins to swing away from the railway embankment. At (3) is another nice pond view; you might be surprised to learn this is still Crooked Pond. The oak trees in this section of the greenbelt are substantially larger (but not necessarily older!) than those seen along Widow Gavitt's Path, a reflection of the better growing conditions here. It would be interesting to age a sample from each area with a wood corer.

Before turning left onto Sprig tree Path, take some time to visit Deer Drink. A bench (5), placed in memory of greenbelt and trail advocate Ted Griffin, is a good place to stop and enjoy the sights and sounds of this late successional wetland. Ted used Deer Drink to illustrate to people what all the ponds of the greenbelt would eventually become through a long process called ecological succession: wooded swamps. You can see that this waterbody has very little open water; accumulated sediment, leaves, and other organic matter have slowly filled in areas such that they can support various wetland shrubs such as highbush blueberry, leatherleaf, inkberry, sweet pepperbush, and staggerbush. Scattered about the shrub swamp are several red maple saplings, an indication of the next successional stage: a wooded swamp.

Back at the Sprig Tree Path–Crooked Pond Trail intersection (4), head north on Sprig Tree toward the powerlines, the halfway point. Turn left onto the powerline road and left again onto the Old Railway Trail. In the warm months the powerline is a good place to look for butterflies. Yellow-flowered goldenrods and orange-flowered butterfly weed are favorite sources of nectar for these beautiful insects.

The Old Railway Trail was an actual railway connection from the Bridgehampton train station to Sag Harbor's Long Wharf between 1870 and 1939. At (6) a trail connection comes down on the right from the Bridgehampton Turnpike near Scuttlehole Road. Nearby is a fenced-in sump, the formidable cyclone fencing topped with barbed wire. Perhaps this unsightly affair will someday provide some useful data as a deer exclosure.

The railway embankment here, 50 feet above Crooked Pond, provides several nice overlooks of the pond. A series of fences has attempted to stem erosion caused mainly by dirt bikes. The first left after the split rail fence is Old Farm Road. This leads directly back to Haines Path, passing the new homes in the Bridgewoods subdivision on the right, and continuing straight through two trail intersections: the Crooked Pond Trail and Widow Gavitt's Path. En route note a similar landscape to what was viewed earlier at (1): a large area of low growing plants inhabiting a shallow kettlehole (7). As at (1), one of the dominant plant seems to be scrub oak.

Directions: The trailhead is well-marked at the intersection of Old Farm Road and Haines Path. From Montauk Highway (Rte. 27), turn north at the Sagg Main Street traffic light onto Sagg Road. Take the first left after the wooden bridge (which spans the LIRR track) onto Narrow Lane, and the next right onto Old Farm Road. The paved portion of Old Farm Road ends at its intersection with Haines Path, and the trail (actually the unpaved Old Farm Road right of way) begins directly across Haines Path.

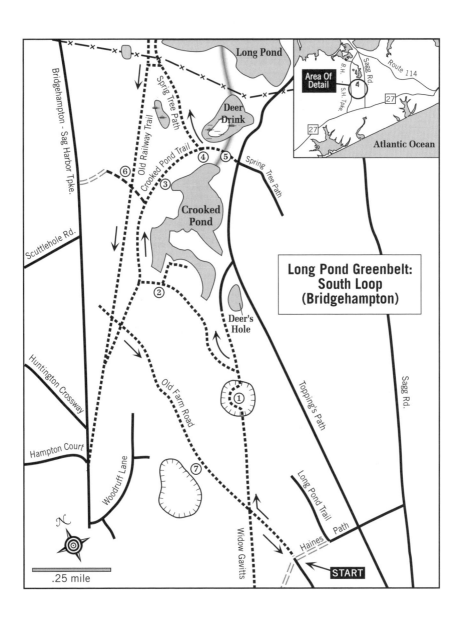

Long Pond

Area Of Detail

B.H. - S.H. Tpke.
Sagg Rd.
Route 114
4
27
27
Atlantic Ocean

Bridgehampton - Sag Harbor Tpke.

Old Railway Trail

Spring Tree Path

Deer Drink

Crooked Pond Trail

6

4 5

3

Spring Tree Path

Crooked Pond

Long Pond Greenbelt: South Loop (Bridgehampton)

Scuttlehole Rd.

2

Deer's Hole

Huntington Crossway

Old Farm Road

Hampton Court

Woodruff Lane

1

Topping's Path

Sagg Rd.

7

N

Long Pond Trail Path

Widow Gavitts

Haines

START

.25 mile

POXABOGUE PRESERVE

Situated between the LIRR tracks and Montauk Highway, just west of Old Farm Road, Poxabogue Preserve is a small but diverse package of natural resources, and well worth a visit. Approximately half of the preserve is wetlands: two freshwater ponds and their adjacent marshes and tupelo–red maple swamps. The other half is a mix of oak and pitch pine forest and old field vegetation. The cornerstone of the preserve is the 40-acre Poxabogue Pond, the southernmost of a string of coastal plain ponds extending north to Sag Harbor and comprising the Long Pond Greenbelt System, an area of outstanding natural diversity of statewide significance.

Connected to the main pond is what I consider the gem of the preserve: Little Poxabogue Pond. This small pond is surrounded by a mature tupelo–red maple and oak-hickory forest, and it is not hard to imagine that it has remained largely unchanged since the first white settlers arrived in this area three centuries ago.

Most of the upland portion of the preserve, 20 acres owned by the county, is comprised of an old field community that forms a striking mosaic of little bluestem grasses, lichens, bayberry and winged sumac shrubs, and red cedar and pitch pine evergreens.

Many naturalists and artists are drawn to this part of the preserve. Birders may come for a glimpse of the orchard oriole or willow flycatcher, which are known to nest here, or to observe the courtship flight of the American woodcock. Other naturalists may come for the challenge of observing and identifying one of the species of butterflies that reside here, including the cobweb skipper, eastern tailed blue, American copper, coral hairstreak, and wild indigo duskywing. Steve Biasetti, an avid bird and butterfly watcher, estimates that 32 butterfly species can be found here. Artists, inspired by the setting of field, pond, and woodlands, seek the challenge of capturing this scene on canvas or film.

From the parking area off Old Farm Road (1), follow the dirt road which parallels the LIRR tracks, just off to the right. This road, which eventually curves south towards the pond, was to become a fully paved subdivision road providing access to choice pondfront lots. Fortunately, through the combined efforts of the Group for the South Fork, The Nature Conservancy, and town and county officials, the subdivision never came to fruition. The roadbed now provides an excellent surface to look for animal tracks: deer, fox, cottontail rabbits, and raccoon are a few of the common creatures that often leave footprints here. South of the gate (2) is a band of mature pitch pine and eastern red cedar which, as evergreens, provides cover in an otherwise open meadow area for migrating and nesting birds throughout the year.

Just before the gate, a narrow footpath (3) leads south (left) and cuts across the field. Despite its close proximity to farmland and rich soils, this area's soil resembles the sandy morainal soil to the north rather than the prime agricultural soils of the outwash plain a stone's throw to the south. The dominant groundcover in the old field community are reindeer lichen, several types of moss, a short-leaved, clumpy grass called Pennsylvania sedge, and a taller, clumpy grass called little bluestem—all well-adapted to the dry, nutrient-poor, sandy soils found here. According to Robert F. Tillotson, this area was once used for grazing back when it was owned by Fred "Page" Topping.

Several bluebird boxes have been installed and maintained in the preserve by the South Fork Natural History Society. Although designed and located specifically to attract our state bird, the beautiful eastern bluebird, most of these boxes are apparently used by other cavity nesters, tree swallows and house wrens.

Another birdhouse, a large multi-family affair mounted on a tall pole, is designed to attract our largest member of the swallow family, a colonial cavity nester and acrobatic flyer well-suited for catching insects on the wing: the purple martin. Martins are not easy to attract to these nesting structures and, although the surrounding field and nearby pond and farmland provide excellent martin habitat, none have been seen nesting here.

The footpath reconnects with the old roadbed (4), where the old field herbaceous community has been shaded out by a variety of shrubs: bayberry, winged sumac, and black cherry being predominant (although one of the larger woody specimens here is some type of crab apple). This slow and steady conversion of old field to shrub thicket and eventually the original oak-hickory forest is called ecological succession. Should a preserve management plan call for maintaining the old field vegetation, some type of disturbance (e.g., burning or mowing) will have to be introduced.

Another footpath leads through the shrub thicket down to the phragmites-lined edge of Poxabogue Pond (5). The derivation of "Poxabogue," according to William Tooker's book of Indian place names, is "a pond that opens up or widens out." This is an appropriate description of a pond that has, at times, shrunken in size to a mere puddle and, at others, flooded over its banks and even overtopped Montauk Highway. Mr. Tillotson has seen both in his lifetime: the former resulting in a puddle brimming over with snapping turtles, and the latter associated with alewives swimming through Sagg Swamp to the edge of Montauk Highway.

According to a 1989 town study of this groundwater fed pond, it is extremely shallow (a maximum depth of four feet was estimated) as evidenced by the water lilies (*Nymphaea odorata*) growing in the middle. An analysis of the pond water found it to be highly enriched with nutrients, a condition called hyper-eutrophic. As with other groundwater fed, coastal plain ponds, water levels fluctuate dramatically seasonally and from year to year. Due to its shallowness, a six-inch drop in its water level can expose a large area of formerly submerged shoreline. Several species of plants have adapted to this unique situation, or niche, by developing seeds that can remain buried in the nearshore sediments for several years until the water level drops and the shoreline sediments are re-exposed, triggering the seeds to finally germinate.

As with the old field, the pond is slowly but constantly changing: accumulating organic matter and sediment, gradually filling in, and enabling rooted aquatic plants to move ever further out into the pond until it will resemble a marsh more than a pond and, with time, a swamp more than a marsh: another example of ecological succession.

Retrace your steps a short distance back toward the road, and make a left turn onto another footpath. This narrow path cuts through a band of oak-hickory woods, and close by some large black cherries, en route to Little Poxabogue Pond. Just as Little Poxabogue comes into view, turn left (6) and follow a trail onto a peninsula between the two ponds. This short but sweet section of trail provides a nice view over both ponds (7). Proceed quietly and you may be rewarded with a glimpse of the secretive wood duck, a black racer sunning itself on a leafless shrub, or a muskrat busily enjoying meal of fresh greens.

Back at the intersection (6), proceed northward where the footpath becomes less discernible for a short while before widening into what appears to be an old woods roadbed. Eventually the trail enters a grove of pitch pine (8), with a beautiful stand of mature, open hardwoods leading down to Little Poxabogue on the left. As the trail approaches the LIRR tracks, it swings right into a thicket of sumac and bayberry before reaching the roadbed (9).

I recommend that you schedule your spring visit here for early evening, perhaps after work, such that you reach the knoll (10) at sunset to witness the unusual courtship flight of the American woodcock. This event takes place from mid-March through May, in the twilight hours just after sunset and just before sunrise (on bright moonlit nights, courtship flights may occur on and off throughout the night). The flight begins with the bird taking off from the ground, quietly flying in wide circles until it reaches about 50 feet in height, after which its wings begin to make a loud, twittering sound as it continues to ascend in ever diminishing circles. This noise is caused by air rushing through the outer three primary feathers of the wing, which are narrowed in such a way as to produce a variety of whistling and twittering sounds. At a height of several hundred feet, the wing-twitter stops abruptly and the bird begins a zig-zag descent accompanied by a few musical chirps. Back on terra firma, the woodcock gives a very loud and distinctive call, best described as a buzzy "peent!"

It is possible, but difficult, to follow the bird through most of this erratic flight. However, I always lose sight of it as it approaches the ground, and I can never be sure of even the approximate area where it may have landed. The purpose of this extravagant air show is to attract mates. The males fly while the females watch; if impressed, a female will wander over to the male's mating territory and put a brief end to his flying antics before heading off to build a nest, not much more than a scrape on the ground. The male, meanwhile, resumes the display flight in hopes of attracting other females; there does not seem to be any lasting bond between mates and the male has no role in nesting or raising the young.

This interesting bird has several unusual adaptations worth noting. Its main food source is the earthworm, which the woodcock captures by probing the soil with its long bill. The upper tip of the bill is flexible and can open to grasp an underground worm without having to open the entire three inch long bill. Another adaptation involves its eyes. While moving along the ground with its head down, probing for worms, the woodcock is quite vulnerable to predation. Birds rely heavily on vision for predator avoidance; it is their most highly developed sense. The position of the eyes on the head determines an animal's range of monocular versus binocular vision. At one end of the spectrum are the owls, with eyes located in the front of the head such that they have maximum binocular vision (important for judging distances) but minimum range of vision. The latter is compensated for by the fact that owls can turn their heads completely backwards. At the other extreme end of the spectrum is the woodcock, whose eyes are located on opposite sides of its head such that it has limited binocular vision but an amazingly large field of vision: 360 degrees!

Directions: From Montauk Highway (Rte. 27) just east of Bridgehampton, turn north at the traffic light onto Sagg Road. Take the first left onto Hildreth Lane and bear right onto Old Farm Lane. The entrance to the park is an unmarked dirt road on the left, just before the stone overpass for the LIRR.

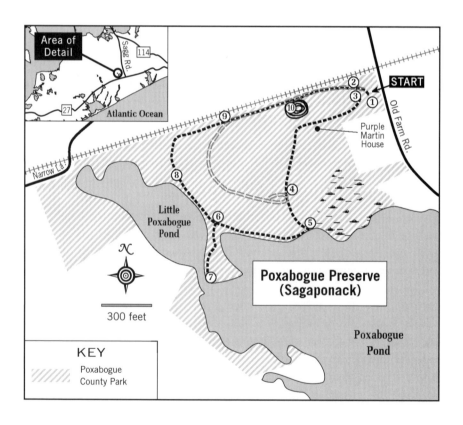

SAGG SWAMP PRESERVE

Sagg Swamp is a 95-acre preserve owned by The Nature Conservancy and situated between Montauk Highway and Sagg Road. The swamp's freshwater supply originates largely from groundwater moving slowly but steadily southward from as far away as Crooked Pond, two miles to the north. The water supply is augmented, at times, by overland runoff flowing south from Poxabogue Pond, under Montauk Highway (just east of Poxabogue Lane) and into the swamp via a small creek which can be followed much easier on a topography map than in the field. I have not actually seen water flowing under the highway but, according to Richard Hendrickson, Sr., back in the "good old days" the dip in the road there provided a convenient place for wooden-wheeled wagons to sit and soak up water, ensuring a snug fit among rim, spokes and hub, and a relatively smooth ride.

Several small creeks and numerous man-made ditches criss-cross the swamp, eventually spilling into one another to form a 10–15-foot-wide creek at the south end of the swamp. Assuming this small creek would be named Sagg "something," I was surprised to learn that it's called Solomon's Creek. The creek continues southward into a culvert under the Sagg Road bridge, called White Walls, and into Sagg Pond.

Together with Sagg Pond, Sagg Swamp represents the southern end of the Long Pond Greenbelt, a linear chain of ponds, marshes, swamps, and streams extending north to the bays and coves of Sag Harbor. An approximately 0.5-mile long trail traverses the southern half of the Sagg Swamp preserve, culminating in a long stretch of boardwalk which provides an interesting, close look at a normally inaccessible part of the swamp.

The trail begins on Sagg Road approximately 150 yards west of White Walls, a small concrete bridge, and is well-marked with a large sign (1). The first two hundred yards of the trail hug the preserve's western border and the edge of the swamp where several exotic shrubs have established themselves. One, known as burning bush or winged spindle tree (*Euonymus alatus*), has very noticeable corky ridges, or wings, along its stem and twigs. I'm not sure what the function these odd growths have, but this popular ornamental, which hails from China and Japan, competes very well with our native shrubs in this wet, shaded habitat.

After turning right and picking up what appears to be an old, well-worn roadbed (2), the trail heads deeper into the preserve. Off to the left was the site of a late 1990s proposal to build on a very wet five-acre lot that would have adversely impacted the trail, among other things. After much acrimonious debate at Town Hall hearings, TNC managed to package a deal that sent the prospective swamp resident elsewhere, and the lot was added to the preserve.

The old roadbed crosses several man-made drainage ditches and swings quite close to the main creek. Although this stretch of trail seems flat, there are subtle changes in elevation between 20 and 10 feet above mean sea level. Because the forest here is so close to the water table, these subtle changes in topography have a profound impact on the vegetation with pockets of oaks dominating the higher ground and pepperidge (or tupelo) and red maple in the lower, wetter sites. Take a close look at one of the several downed red maples near the trail: this shallow-rooted tree is obviously very susceptible to windthrow but, despite the loss of most of its root system, more often than not manages to survive and quickly sends up new shoots to replace the fallen trunk and crown.

At the trail junction (3) take the right fork, staying on the old roadbed, to the Solomon's Creek weir (4). As with many other "natural" areas on the South Fork, Sagg Swamp has a long and interesting history of human use, some of which I was able to piece together with the help of several knowledgeable residents of the area and a Nature Conservancy publication authored by William T. Griffith. Although I haven't been able to pin down the exact date when the small dam was first constructed here, Richard G. Hendrickson is certain it dates back to at least the turn of the 20th century when a group of avid duck hunters decided to enhance the swamp's waterfowl habitat by impounding the creek and creating more, and deeper, standing water. Among the group was a Mr. Mathews who, in addition to becoming the superintendent of schools in the area, stocked the creek with trout, probably browns trout. Years later, around 1923–24, a 1.75-pounder was caught in the creek near the Sagg Road bridge.

According to John White, the quarter-mile stretch of creek downstream of the weir to Sagg Road was once navigable by canoe; today the journey is made by eels, alewives, and huge carp making their way up from the pond. John added that for many years, tucked in a discreet spot northeast of the weir, was a home-brewing operation. Predating the still and weir was a water mill located at the site of the bridge on Sagg Road. This was last operated in the mid-1800s by one of a long line of John White's living in the area. Richard Hendrickson surmises that the flow rate and height of the water at this location were not quite enough for a successful mill. Richard also pointed out that, predating even the mill, he has found much evidence of occupation of this area by Native Americans, probably drawn to the nearby game, shell and fin fish resources in the pond, and ample fresh water supply.

Continuing along the trail, it winds as a narrow footpath through a grove of large pepperidge or tupelo (5) before reaching the eastern edge of the boardwalk. The first thing most visitors notice when they reach the boardwalk is the openness of the swamp here. The dominant groundcover, sphagnum moss, is able to absorb and hold an incredible amount of water, like a living sponge, creating a very unstable platform for large trees to grow on. In fact, it appears that the water-loving pepperidge can't even get its seeds to germinate on this spongy, acidic medium, while the red maple, although the dominant tree here, is very stunted in size. The lack of a well-established forest canopy allows sunlight to penetrate through to the surface of the swamp, enabling shade intolerant plants such as cattails to thrive (6). Take your time walking along the boardwalk, as this is where you are likely to see the most wildlife: woodpeckers among the numerous snags and a variety of waterfowl in the standing water or flying among the several holes of deeper water. Off in the distance you may notice a grove of evergreen trees: this is one of three stands of Atlantic white cedars in the preserve that unfortunately are not easily accessible from the trail. These groves are regular roosting spots for great horned owls. Another interesting feature of the preserve, Jeremy's Hole, is just north of the boardwalk, a short but difficult 100 yards away. Mr. Hendrickson related an incredible encounter he had near the edge of this tiny pond in early to mid-summer: more than a hundred snakes were massed together, weaving in and out of the sphagnum, over and around each other!

My wildlife encounter on a winter visit was a bit more mundane: on the eastern end of the boardwalk is a bridge spanning some deep water where I watched a muskrat fattening up for the winter months. Nearby, growing in the shallows, was a large patch of watercress (*Nasturtium officinale*), still a striking green even in mid-December. This aquatic mustard is edible and often used to spice up a fresh salad.

The boardwalk ends a short distance from the trail intersection (3); turn right and backtrack to exit the preserve.

DIRECTIONS: The entrance to the Sagg Swamp Preserve is on Sagaponack Road, at the north end of Sagg Pond, 0.5 mile west of the Sagaponack School in, of course, Sagaponack. From Montauk Highway (Rte. 27) in Bridgehampton turn south onto Ocean Avenue and take the second left onto Sagaponack Road. The trail is on the north side (your left) of Sagaponack Road, just west of a small concrete bridge at the north end of Sagg Pond.

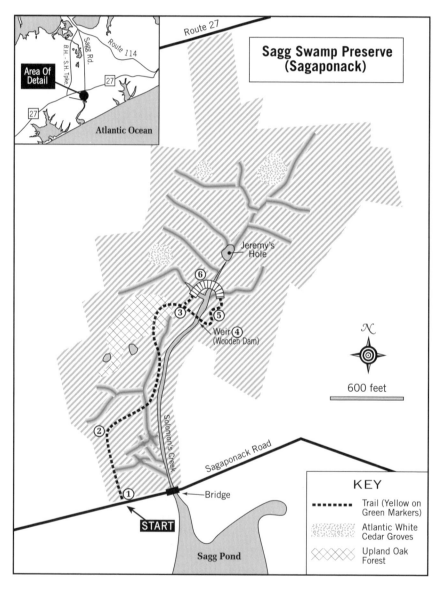

East Hampton

Village

Wainscott

East Hampton Village

Nature Preserve

The footpath closely follows the meanderings of a silent, slow-moving brook, past ancient, gnarled swamp maples and dense thickets of arrowwood and sweet pepperbush. Small patches of watercress, a deep green amidst the stark winter landscape, cling to the edges of the brook, swathed in its relatively warm waters, while higher up on the steep-sided banks, the spikes of skunk cabbage flowers protrude from the snow.

On a winter afternoon a frigid stillness hangs over the swamp, its quiet broken only by a chattering wren, scolding me for intruding, and a downy woodpecker busily chipping away on a snag in search of dormant insects. A catbird quietly works over a nearby wild rose, deftly plucking red fruits from its branches, unconcerned about my approach. Further upstream a snipe, a larger but much more wary bird, stealthily probes the unfrozen mud of the shallow brook with its oversized bill, barely enabling me to catch a glance before taking flight.

These birds were only a small segment of the diverse community of year-round and seasonal residents of the swamp. Evidence of other inhabitants and their daily activities is clearly written in the snow: the tracks of gray squirrel, cottontail rabbit, raccoon, deer, red fox, white-footed mouse, great blue heron, and pheasant.

Where was all this wildlife activity taking place? The vast wooded swamps of Montauk? That diverse ecological treasure known as the Long Pond Greenbelt? The secluded Great Swamp of Bridgehampton? No, this was the East Hampton Village Nature Trail and Wildlife Sanctuary, a narrow belt of wetlands a mere stone's throw from the hustle and bustle of Main Street.

This Village greenbelt courses through lowlands adjacent to the Hook Pond Dreen, a narrow band of red maple and tupelo swamp and cattail and phragmites marshes, between David's Lane and Fithian Lane, which flows southward into Hook Pond and eventually the Atlantic Ocean. These lowlands are, in turn, the southern part of a six-mile-long alluvial valley, spanning from the Atlantic Ocean to Gardiner's Bay, which can be easily traced on a topographic map northward to Round Swamp, Tanbark Creek, Soak Hides Dreen, and Three Mile Harbor.

The highest point in this valley is found on the east side of Three Mile Harbor Road, in the vicinity of Round Swamp Farm, at a mere 35 feet above mean sea level. This location, a watershed divide, correlates closely to the groundwater divide since the latter is so close to the surface. North of this point, groundwater and surface water move towards the bay; south of this point, both move towards the ocean, filling the Hook Pond Dreen in the process.

Of note is the fact that this is one of only three north-south alluvial valleys found on the South Fork, remnants of glacial meltwater carving channels through the ridge of morainal sands. One of the other two valleys connects Northwest Harbor and Sagaponack Pond, is riddled with small ponds, and is referred to as the Long Pond Greenbelt; the other is a somewhat less linear system which includes North Sea Harbor, the Alewife Dreen, Big and Little Fresh Ponds, and various coastal ponds and marshes in Southampton Village.

The history of the Nature Trail area is as unique and interesting as its ecology and wildlife. At the turn of the century, the swamps and marshes between what is now Fithian Lane and David's Lane were owned by three families: Huntting, Fithian, and Woodhouse. Jonathan Fithian's homestead farm included the northern half of the wetlands between Huntting and Fithian Lanes, and extended westward to Main Street. Lorenzo G. and Emma Woodhouse owned the three acres west of the Dreen and immediately south of Huntting Lane (3 on the map), which was adjacent to their residence called Greycroft, built in 1894. In 1901, Emma converted this wetland area into a Japanese water garden with a series of bridges over small streams and ponds and two tea houses. Although no evidence of the structures remain, some Asian plants, such as bamboo, can still be found.

The remainder of the wetlands, some 20 acres, were part of the David H. Huntting Estate, which included the farmland extending westward to Main Street. A remnant of the original private road which connected the Huntting Estate farm buildings and Egypt Lane is now part of the trail system (the path parallel to David's Lane and leading to the statue of St. Francis). Where this roadway bridged the Dreen is now the duck feeding area. David H. died in 1893, at which time Huntting Lane was opened and named for him; David's Lane was not constructed until sometime after 1910.

In a 1984 East Hampton Historical Society publication entitled "East Hampton Invents The Culture of Summer: The Legacy of the Woodhouse Family of Huntting Lane," author Ellen R. Samuels details the land transactions involving what is now the Village's Nature Trail and Bird Sanctuary, the various parties involved, and the corresponding dates. Between 1910 and 1920, the Huntting and Fithian properties were subdivided and sold. In 1934, the wife of East Hampton artist G. Ruger Donoho acquired eight acres of the Fithian wetlands and donated them to the Village as a wildlife sanctuary in memory of her husband, who drew inspiration from the seasonal changes and colors of that area.

Much of the Huntting property ended up in the ownership of Lorenzo G. Woodhouse and his nephew, Lorenzo E. This family, particularly Lorenzo E. and his wife Mary, were responsible for the construction of many important community facilities still in use today: the East Hampton Library (1912), the restoration of the Clinton Academy (1921), and Guild Hall (1931). By 1935, Mary Woodhouse had inherited the family lands and, with the help of the East Hampton Garden Club, created a system of paths and bridges through the wetlands and opened the area to the public. In 1950, she deeded this area to the Village.

Two other smaller additions were made to round out the Village's Nature Trail holdings: an eighth of an acre donation just downstream of Fithian Lane, made by Miss May Rogers in 1978, which enables visitors to walk out to Fithian Lane; and a 2.5-acre donation in 1992 by Mrs. Ronald V. Christie on the north side of David's Lane.

Another transaction in the 1990s was the sale of Village property at the north end of the Dreen to a local developer, enabling the construction of a larger commercial building (now CVS pharmacy) than was possible with the Village parcel in public ownership. This was an unfortunate and unexplained transaction on the part of Village officials.

An interesting sideline to the history of this swamp in one of America's most beautiful villages: in 1938, the Village Board put forward a proposal to clear, fill, and plant flowers in the Donoho portion of the Nature Trail, off Fithian Lane, in order to "make it one of the showplaces of Long Island." The community response was firm and eloquent.

> Do you know this lot? Have you watched it through the seasons? It is beautiful beyond words! In the spring and especially in the fall, it shows forth a glory that no hand of man could create!... The way it changes from season to season through spring and summer, always with some new

enchantment, until it reaches its high climax for the year in late September and October. Then it takes on the most marvelous colors, from soft, tender hues to the rich and flaming reds of autumn. Moreover, the pattern of its growth is matchless. No gardener could achieve such harmony of line and color.

The lot, jut as it is, has rare perfection, without any trouble or upkeep… People travel miles all over the country to see beauty like this wherever Nature paints such pictures, but they are becoming more and more rare in this part of the world. Lucky is the village that has it in her midst!

So why not let us enjoy and appreciate it, keeping it unchanged, and be deeply thankful that in this tumultuous world of today there is this place of serene beauty, always waiting and ready to give to any who care to stop and look, a quiet moment of inspiration and peace.

—Hildreth King

Today, the caretakers and managers of this greenbelt face many of the same issues being grappled with at preserves and refuges elsewhere: the impacts of its popularity and the practice of feeding "wildlife." As the number of visitors has increased each year, wear and tear on the trails has prompted a more formal and erosion-resistant stone path along the Dreen's banks. And, as the number of loaves of bread being thrown into the Dreen increases exponentially, the down-side of feeding ducks is becoming more and more evident.

Still, a walk into the northern reaches of this sanctuary will most likely find you alone amidst a beautiful landscape.

Directions: Entering the Village eastbound on Rte. 27, continue up Main Street past the flagpole and Guild Hall. Turn right onto David's Lane (a large white church is on the corner). The well-marked main entrance to the Nature Trail is at the far end of David's Lane, just before Egypt Lane.

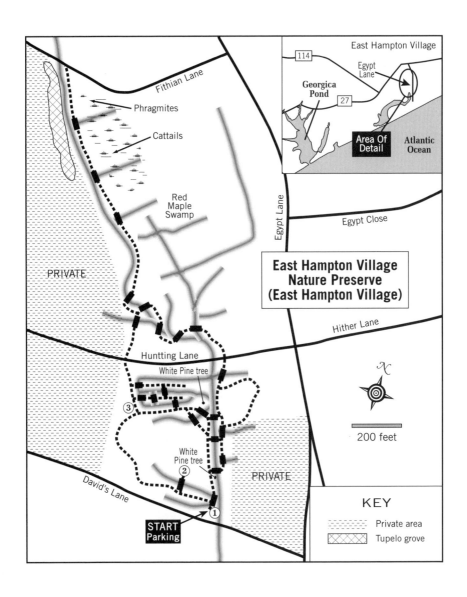

East Hampton Village
Nature Preserve
(East Hampton Village)

KEY

Private area
Tupelo grove

Paumanok Path:

Wainscott Section

The Paumanok Path is a proposed trail system designed to traverse the east end of Long Island, linking federal, state, county, and town greenbelts and private preserves owned by various conservation organizations and individuals. From Rocky Point State Preserve on the west to Montauk Point State Park on the east, the trail will eventually span over 130 miles. The Paumanok Path is marked with a white rectangular blaze. In many places the route overlaps other marked trail systems; in those cases the route may be marked with other symbols in addition to the white rectangular blaze. To date, approximately 45 continuous miles in the pine barrens west of the Shinnecock Canal, and another 45 continuous miles traversing the entire length of the Town of East Hampton, are complete.

The Paumanok Path enters East Hampton Township high on the moraine, north of the town airport, in an area known as Miller's Ground. From the intersection of Denise Street and Town Line Road, head south on Town Line Road. Within sight of the power lines, look for a well-worn trail and the white rectangular blazes on the right (1).

If you have the time and inclination, following the white blazes from here will, 45 or so miles later, take you along the bluffs within sight and sound of the Montauk Point lighthouse... amazing! Keep a sharp eye on those blazes: within the first 200 yards the trail forks four times, although each intersection and fork is well-marked.

The East Hampton section of the Paumanok Path was completed in October 1998, the year the township celebrated its 350th anniversary. I first learned of the idea of a trail spanning the entire town from trails advocate and local historian Rick Whalen. That was in 1988, but Rick had obviously been thinking about the idea for some time before then. I credit Rick for not only having the vision, but working to keep it alive over the next decade and making it a reality.

At (2), the trail turns sharply to the right onto an old woods road that connects the powerline and Merchants Path. This well-worn path, three feet below grade in some places, may date back to the horse-drawn wagon cart era. It follows a fairly level line through otherwise gently rolling terrain dom-

110

inated by a canopy of the black oak species and an understory carpet of huckleberry and lowbush blueberry. This mosaic is periodically punctuated by stands of mountain laurel, providing a beautiful burst of showy flowers in June and some welcome greenery through the winter months.

Be careful not to miss the sharp left off this pleasant woods road (continuing straight leads to the Switchback Trail) and onto a narrow, winding footpath at (3). Here the trail winds over the knob-and-kettle topography so typical of the morainal ridge and makes a long, gradual descent to a small but unusual kettlehole (4). Take some time to note the dramatic shift in the vegetation in this small depression: the forest canopy has opened up, letting in more sunlight, and the trees appear much smaller in girth and height, with some resembling shrubs more closely than trees.

A closer examination of the plants in this area reveals an abundance of a short, wiry, tufted grass, called Pennsylvania sedge, clumps of reindeer lichen, and a shrub-like species of the black oak group aptly named scrub oak (*Quercus illicifolia*). These are all plants common to the dry, sandy, nutrient-poor soils of the pine barrens, and may indicate that this particular kettle was "disturbed" in the not too distant past… perhaps burned.

Just over the rise, another small depression is likewise somewhat different: the dominant oaks here are white oaks (*Quercus alba*), one of the few oaks that I feel comfortable identifying to species. The understory composition has also shifted with the lower-growing lowbush blueberry much more prevalent than the taller huckleberry. Both the sparse and low-growing shrub layer, and the light-colored bark of the white oaks, combine to accentuate the growth of dark green mosses on the base of each tree trunk.

Leaving this depression, the forest cover reverts quickly back to a mix of black oak species and huckleberry re-enters the understory. A steep descent to a vernal wetland (5) provides a closeup of highbush blueberry and maleberry, two tall shrubs related to the ubiquitous lowbush blueberry–huckleberry mix, but with a competitive edge in the wetter soils here. Also of note here are the large pitch pines rimming the wetland: one trailside specimen has a girth exceeding two feet.

This wetland, called "vernal" as in "of or occurring in the season of spring," is often dry during the summer months but usually filled with freshwater during the spring, coinciding with the egg-laying season of various forest dwelling salamanders, tree frogs, and toads. Thus, while of a small and temporary nature, these vernal wetlands play a very important ecological role in the grand scheme of things.

Being sure to take the right fork as you leave the wetland (left leads to the Six Pole Highway Trail); climb onto a low ridge vegetated with stunted white oaks and more of the lichen–Pennsylvania sedge understory association. Note that many of these oaks have multiple trunks: two to four stems growing from a single root collar. This clumped growth form indicates that the area was either cleared or burned in the not too distant past. The prevalence of Pennsylvania sedge and reindeer lichen, both pioneer or early successional plants, also supports the notion that some type of disturbance took place in this limited area.

The trail descends into another kettlehole with many large pitch pines, stands of mountain laurel and several old fox dens before climbing up to the shoulder of Wainscott–Northwest Road. The trail continues directly across the road, skirting the edge of two shallow kettleholes before climbing past a large (eight-foot-high) boulder, technically called a glacial erratic (6), covered with several species of crustose lichens that resemble splashes of paint.

The trail continues to climb, winding up onto a low ridge and crossing a stretch of level terrain (7). Someday it may be possible to create a trail link south from here to the Buckskill Preserve Trails.

Contouring around the flank of a high hill with a house sitting on its top, the trail comes to a T intersection (8). Left (unmarked) was the original Paumanok Path route; the section you just hiked from Wainscott–Northwest Road is a re-route still being worked on during the winter of 2003. The re-route was made possible by a recent town open space acquisition that, in turn, was made possible by funds generated via the 2% Land Transfer Tax. Much of the Miller's Ground area was acquired in the 1990s due to its location atop the largest freshwater resource in the Town of East Hampton.

Follow the white blazes to the right, along a common driveway and down to the intersection of Route 114 and Edwards Hole Road. Directly across route 114, the Paumanok Path continues as part of the Northwest Path (9).

Directions to Start of Trail: To start from Montauk Highway (Rte. 27), turn north onto Sagg Road heading into Sag Harbor. Just before entering the Village limits, turn right onto Mt. Misery Drive. At the first stop sign, turn right onto Denise Street, following it as it climbs and winds around Mt. Misery until the intersection with Town Line Road, and park there. Although you can drive south along Town Line Road, there isn't much of a shoulder to park on and turning around can be difficult.

Directions to End of Trail: See the starting point directions for the Paumanok Path: Northwest Section.

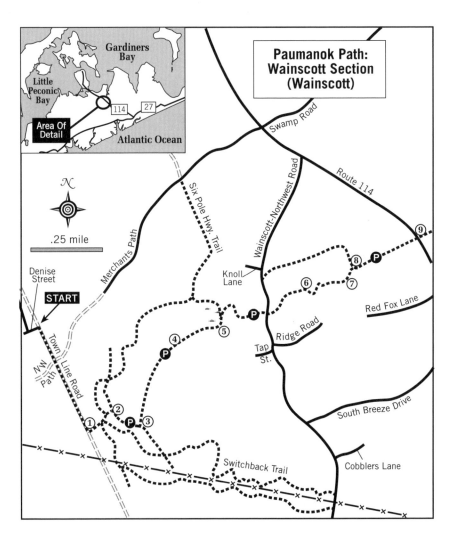

MILLER'S GROUND PRESERVE

A little-used trail on the south side of the powerline road in Miller's Ground, along with the popular Switchback Trail, close by but on the powerline's opposite side, creates a long, narrow trail loop of approximately 2.5 miles in length. The route winds its way over dramatic knob-and-kettle topography throughout the entire loop, providing a challenging workout for hikers, mountain bikers, and runners.

Unfortunately, the unknown trail designer's focus on challenging terrain has created an all-together different and most likely unforeseen challenge: trail maintenance. Designing a functional switchback is not as easy at one would think. Several portions of the Switchback Trail have been reconfigured in recent years, and a few sections on the southern portion of the loop should probably be re-routed to avoid steep, unstable slopes and the unsightly communication tower area.

In addition to the interesting topography, the loop passes through some magnificent stands of mountain laurel, as noted on the accompanying map. This slow-growing native shrub thrives in our morainal forests for several reasons. It is very shade-tolerant and well-adapted to the acidic, dry, nutrient-poor soils found there. As a relatively large-leaved evergreen, its presence adds some color to an otherwise monotonous winter landscape of grays and browns. In mid-June, its showy flower clusters add even more beauty to the oak forest; a visit at that time of the year is well-advised.

As a result of some recent land purchases by the town and county, the entire route is now publicly owned. The acquisitions received high priority due to their groundwater recharge importance. In addition to being on or near the groundwater divide and in a deep recharge area, Miller's Ground lies atop the thickest freshwater portion (350 feet thick) of the Magothy Aquifer in the entire Town of East Hampton.

The little-used trail on the south side of the powerline road is not marked but easy to find. From the powerline road, walk south along the pavement for approximately 100 feet and turn right (west) onto an unpaved road (1) that provides access to a communications tower. Walk 75 feet along the access road and look for the narrow footpath that forks off to the left.

The trail veers away from the road and powerlines through a mixed forest of mostly white oak but with scattered tall pitch pines (2). Many of the oak boles, or trunks, are covered in a velvet layer of emerald green moss. The presence of the moss is not unusual, but the height it attains is. Generally limited to the lower three to five feet of the tree trunk, these trees have moss growing as high as 15 feet above ground. Why? I'm not sure, but I first noticed this after a severe defoliation of the forest canopy by gypsy moths.

A small wetland is visible through the forest off to the left. This vernal wetland, called Daniel's Hole, often has no standing water but its soggy soils retain enough moisture to support a variety of sedges and other wetland plants, including a ring of highbush blueberry around its edge. At 15 feet above mean sea level, Daniel's Hole is most likely intercepting the top of the water table in this area, and not a perched wetland.

The trail soon swings north and intercepts the access road, which you follow right up to the communication tower. Pick up the trail again on the embankment to the right (north) of the tower. This section of the trail should be re-routed to the south to avoid the road and tower area altogether.

Beyond the tower the trail climbs two quite steep areas; the second ascends a prominent knoll at 120 feet higher than Daniel's Hole and the start of the hike. Crossing a swale at (4) you might detect the faint outline of an old woods roadbed, one of many that crisscross the Miller's Ground forest.

Beyond the next knoll, in a mountain laurel stand, look for a well-worn trail veering off to the left (5). This eventually crosses Town Line Road and leads to what mountain bikers refer to as Toyland, a series of obstacles set along the trail. Don't worry if you miss the intersection. Continue straight, cross under the powerlines, and wind your way to the intersection of the Paumanok Path (6).

The Paumanok Path is a marked trail (white rectangular blazes) that extends from this point east to the Montauk Lighthouse, approximately 45 miles. Part of a regional trail system, it will eventually link westward with the 50-mile-long Pine Barrens Trail on the west side of the Shinnecock Canal. Much of the trail between here and the Canal is in place, but there are still many pieces of the puzzle unprotected and in private ownership.

Turn right and follow the Paumanok Path for approximately 75 feet to the next intersection, and turn right again onto an unmarked trail that continues through the oak-dominated forest dotted with stands of mountain laurel. At (7) the trail descends into a shallow kettlehole or swale where hickories far outnumber the oaks.

The trail next ascends a steep-sided knoll where mountain bikers have made a tight loop to test their climbing skills. The erosion-prone Carver-Plymouth soils here have not held up well; once the bikes cut through the root zone and expose the sandy soils beneath, gullies form quick and deep.

Cross an old roadbed at (9), a continuation of the one crossed earlier at (4). The trail begins a gradual ascent to the highest point in the area, passing by a large glacial erratic en route (10). The high point (11) is 162 feet above mean sea level. Due to its height, the trees here are subject to consistent winds no matter the direction. This fact, along with the sandy soils that do not retain moisture well, stresses the plants and stunts their growth, not unlike the "krummholz" zone of mountaintops around the world. The water-related stress is severe enough here to greatly reduce the ratio of white oak to other, more drought-resistant oaks. Water stress has also enabled a few scrub oaks (*Quercus illicifolia*) to become established here.

Most of the oaks growing on the hilltop are less than 15 feet in height, while the same species growing just a short distance down slope exceed 30 feet. The short, sparse crown allows for a glimpse of the ocean in the distance.

Not far from the knoll (12), the trail begins a series of twists and turns, called switchbacks, to descend the 140 feet in elevation to Wainscott–Northwest Road. Mountain laurel seems to grow best on north-facing, steep-sided slopes, and there is a lot of that terrain between (12) and (13). This section of the trail has some of the largest stands of laurel in Miller's Ground, and is quite a beautiful sight during the third week of June when its showy blooms usually peak.

Directions: Park on road shoulder where high tension powerlines cross Daniel's Hole Road / Wainscott Northwest Road (the road changes names just north of the East Hampton Airport). From Rte. 27 (Montauk Highway) head north on Daniel's Hole Road; from Rte. 114 head south on Wainscott Northwest Road. Start on the unpaved dirt road adjacent to (south side of) the powerline road. Trail begins seventy five feet in from pavement as a left fork off of the unpaved road.

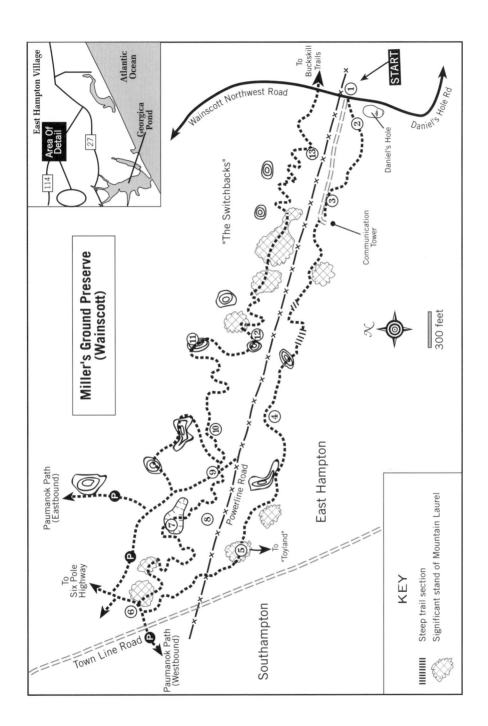

Miller's Ground Preserve (Wainscott)

East Hampton Village

Atlantic Ocean

Georgica Pond

Area Of Detail

27

114

START

To Buckskill Trails

Wainscott Northwest Road

Daniel's Hole

Daniel's Hole Rd

"The Switchbacks"

Communication Tower

Paumanok Path (Eastbound)

Paumanok Path (Westbound)

To Six Pole Highway

Town Line Road

Powerline Road

To "Toyland"

East Hampton

Southampton

300 feet

KEY

Steep trail section

Significant stand of Mountain Laurel

117

BUCKSKILL PRESERVE

Within the area bounded by Route 114, South Breeze Drive, Wainscott–Northwest Road, Daniel's Hole Road, the LIRR and Stephen Hands Path is a 700-acre woodland known as Buckskill. Over half this acreage was preserved in 1998, most of it by way of a creative deal involving the town, county, and Rosenthal Estate, and brokered by Paul Rabinovitch of The Nature Conservancy. Another 110 acres were already owned by the town, part of their undeveloped airport property along Daniel's Hole Road, and the final significant parcel, approximately 130 acres, is part of a site plan being reviewed by the Town Planning Board: the Ross School expansion.

Although there are over 13 miles of trails in the Buckskill area, a large trail segment crosses the privately owned Ross School property for which a trail easement has yet to be worked out. Another very small trail section crosses onto private property that the town is negotiating to buy for open space. Here I've described a the three-mile-long loop through the Buckskill area that is all within the public portion of the preserve. Start near the intersection of Stephen Hands Path and Route 114. The trail, blazed with yellow-on-green markers, is easily found almost directly across Rte. 114 from the Hardscrabble Farmstand and named, appropriately, the Hardscrabble Loop.

The trail traverses a forest of typical pine barrens species: a canopy of oaks and pitch pine and an understory of low-growing, woody shrubs composed of two species of lowbush blueberry (*Vaccinium angustifolium* and *V. pallidum*) and huckleberry (*Gaylussacia baccata*). However, within 100 feet of the start you might notice a small mound vegetated with early successional plants indicative of some type of disturbance: black cherry, eastern red cedar, black locust, bittersweet, and Virginia creeper, among others. While taking notes there I met Henry Schwenk and his beautiful husky out for a late afternoon stroll on the trail. Mr. Schwenk, a long-time farmer of the nearby Long Lane farmland known as Hardscrabble, offered some insight into the mystery of the mounds and its atypical pine barrens vegetation. The Schwenks had a dairy herd as part of their farm operation; the manure was periodically gathered up and dumped in the woods here.

As far back as Henry can recall, these woods were never completely cleared. From there the conversation ranged over a wide variety of topics from traffic and supermarkets to property rights and the inequities of farmland preservation programs, with quite a few criticisms leveled at the town and the Group for the South Fork. We parted company agreeing that in this imperfect, sometimes insane world, the South Fork was still a pretty good spot to call home.

En route to the first trail intersection (1), notice that the trees are mostly oaks (white, scarlet, and black, or *Quercus alba, Q. coccinea,* and *Q. velutina* respectively, according to a town report) with very few pines. If you look carefully at the lower end of the oak trunks, you will see that many of them are actually connected to two or three other trunks at ground level. Multi-trunked trees are often the result of fire or logging which kills the above-ground portion of the tree, but leaves the root system intact. The uppermost section of the root system, called the root collar, contains adventitious buds which sprout in response to the death or removal of the main trunk. These coppice sprouts all compete with one another for the limited supply of nutrients and water from the roots and the limited sunlight above. Until many of the slower-growing sprouts are shaded out by better positioned ones, the oaks resemble a shrub more than a tree. Eventually, the sprouts develop into new trunks and, over time, only one to four generally survive.

Roughly halfway between the start and the first intersection at (1), the trail crosses over the top of a small but noticeable knoll where another oak species, scrub oak (*Quercus ilicifolia*), is found. This species, the best-adapted among the oaks for surviving frequent fires and dry, sterile soils, never grows out of the small shrub stage and is the most common oak found in the core of Long Island's fire-prone pine barrens west of the canal.

At (1) turn right and follow the trail through one of several pure stands of pitch pine (*Pinus rigida*) currently found in the Buckskill area. This three-needled conifer is extremely well adapted to fire prone areas. In fact, its tiny, winged seeds (a striking contrast to the large, heavy seeds of the oaks) require contact with bare soil to germinate: a condition created after a forest fire has swept through and consumed all the leaf litter and organic humus. Knowing this, it is tempting to conclude that the pitch pine stands here are evidence of periodic fire. However, a quick look at an aerial photograph of the Buckskill area shows that the most dense stands of pine are unnaturally regular-shaped. In this case, a bird's-eye view of the pine stand reveals a sharply defined trapezoid shape and, adjacent to a portion of the LIPA powerlines, a perfect long rectangle. In both cases, it appears that the pine seeds sprouted on soils laid bare by bulldozers. According to Henry Schwenk, this area adjacent to Rte. 114 might have been cleared for fill to create the turnpike.

As the trail swings north and comes within view of Route 114, look for an opening off to the right, just beyond the pines, where small herds of deer feed in a small meadow at dawn and dusk. From this point to the intersection with Buckskill Road, one mile from the start, the trail stays quite close to Rte. 114. In 2001, an ATV user residing on the north side of Rte. 114 near here began accessing the preserve (illegally) and made a mess of the trail system in a short span of time.

Buckskill Road is a narrow, unpaved roadway which now marks the boundary between town and county preserves. Turn right onto the dirt road for a short distance (200 feet) and take the first left turn onto another footpath. The most abundant herbaceous plant in this area is bracken fern; its change from green to a yellow-brown is one of the earliest signs of autumn in this forest.

Take the next trail heading off to the left (2). This trail link was created in 1999 to avoid the construction (and private property) at Goodfriend Drive, visible in the west. The link goes a short distance (800 feet) to another intersection (3) at which you make another left.

Note that since the shrubs on the forest floor rarely grow taller than three feet, and the trees tend to self-prune, or lose their lower, shaded branches as they grow in height; one can look quite far off into this forest. The effect, particularly in the low-angle light of early morning or late afternoon, is quite special: one of those magical, natural scenes that would be difficult to capture on film.

At several points along this stretch of forest—a mix of oaks and pitch pines, with the largest trees being pines—the trail weaves among small stands of mountain laurel. Many rank our oak forests as a dull fall foliage show. I disagree. The huckleberry and blueberry shrubs turn a dazzling array of yellow, orange, and red; that alone is a pretty good show.

Roughly three-quarters of a mile from (3) the trail ends at a T intersection (4): right takes you to the powerline road and a town trail (5) that links westward to Wainscott–Northwest Road, connecting to trails in the Miller's Ground area, the Paumanok Path, and the Sagaponack greenbelt. To complete the Hardscrabble Loop, turn left, cross Buckskill Road again (unpaved), and continue for three-quarters of a mile (passing 1) back to the starting point at Rte. 114.

Along the stretch between 4 and 1, see if you can find any pattern to the orientation of the moss growing at the base of many of the white oaks. Woods lore states that the moss grows thickest and highest on the north side of tree trunks, where it is less likely to face the drying rays of the sun. Unfortunately, it's not quite that simple. The proximity of other trees, which block the sun, creates so many exceptions to this rule that anyone relying on moss growth to walk an approximate compass course could spend several days wandering around the Buckskill forest.

Directions: From (Rte. 27 travel east through Wainscott; turn left onto Stephen Hands Path and left again at the traffic light onto Route 114. Park on the shoulder of Rte. 114, just past the Hardscrabble Farmstand.

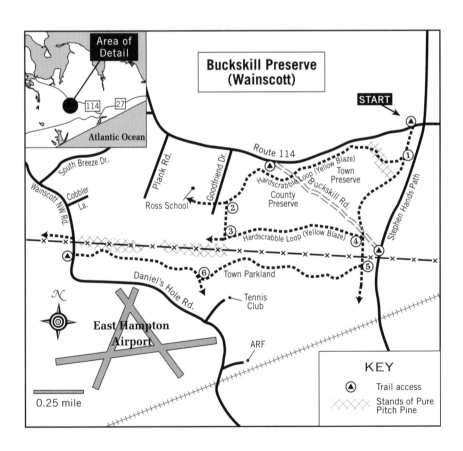

NORTHWEST

BARCELONA NECK PRESERVE

Steeped in history, rich in ecological resources, and with scenic panoramas atop 80-foot-tall bluffs, Barcelona Neck is a wonderful place to explore. The Neck juts northward from Swamp Road out into Northwest Harbor with the tidal creeks Little Northwest and Northwest completing its western and eastern edges respectively. The nearly 700 acre preserve includes state, county, and town holdings and encompasses extensive tidal wetlands, wooded swamps (including an unusual white pine swamp at its southern end), and a large oak and hickory forest.

Once known as Little Northwest Neck and Russell's Neck, the latter being the name of the family who farmed here in the early 1700s, the present name, Barcelona Neck, dates back to the 1840s. At that time, nearby Sag Harbor was an important port for whaling ships that spent several years at sea visiting ports on both sides of the Atlantic. Sailors returning from such voyages noted the resemblance between the sandy bluffs marking the entrance to Sag Harbor and those marking the entrance to the port of Barcelona, Spain, and the name survived the next 150 years.

Most of the seven miles of trails in Barcelona are old Trustee roads, some dating back to the 1700s. Some of the northernmost trails were cut by developers to show prospective home buyers the bluff top water views over Northwest Harbor. Around 1992–93, New York State Department of Environmental Conservation staff cut several new sections of trail, much of it in the swampy southern portion of the preserve, to connect existing trails into a large loop marked with blue disks. Beginning at the clubhouse, a three-mile loop through the northern two-thirds of the preserve is described as follows.

At the clubhouse, the paved entrance road terminates and leads to two dirt roads forming a fork. After parking, take the right fork, which wraps round the back of the clubhouse and enters the forest. Within several hundred feet, turn right (2) onto a smaller dirt road (Note: this eventually leads out to Swamp Road and, by way of Edwards Hole Road, to the Paumanok Path, a mile and a half to the south). Take this another several hundred feet to the second sharp bend and turn left onto a narrower old woods road (3).

Off to the right is a tupelo swamp with an understory of tall, dense woody shrubs including sweet pepperbush, chokeberry, and swamp azalea. You are now on a section of trail marked with blue disks, which you should notice nailed to trees. Continue along this old woods road, passing through a section lined on both sides with bayberry. Notice that the plants here lack the typical wax-coated berries; I have found that bayberries growing in the shade of the forest rarely flower and produce fruit.

The trail, actually the original East Side Road, skirts along the edge of the wetlands, marking the transition between the drier soils of the upland oak-hickory forest and water-saturated soils of the tupelo swamp. Off to the east, or trail-right, the tupelos eventually give way to the marsh and waters of Northwest Creek, barely visible over the trailside thicket of sweet pepper-bush. Approaching the remnants of the old Connors house, a sturdy, two story affair built in the 1920s, the trail passes alongside a row of cedar fence posts, still in good condition. Here, the trail leaves the old roadbed and, passing close by a dilapidated outbuilding, becomes a narrow footpath winding back out to the current East Side Road (4)near the intersection with the road to Cuffee's Landing.

The short detour down to Cuffee's Landing is well worthwhile: the vista over the Northwest Creek marshes is spectacular. With few exceptions the entire creek, its substantial marshland, and a significant woodland fringe are protected from development. Ironically, this small, well-protected estuary suffers from water quality problems which have closed its waters to shellfishing.

The landing is named for Wickham Cuffee, a Shinnecock Indian and whaler. According to local historian Norton Daniels, Wickham was the last member of the Shinnecock and Montaukett tribes who could speak in all the dialects of both tribes. Before leaving, note the large white oaks and the unusual post oaks near the edge of the forest. In the vicinity are a cellar hole and rock-lined well, the remnants of an old homestead.

Back at East Side Road, turn right and follow this well-maintained road. This road now serves as a driveway to the one and only private home on the entire neck, in addition to providing vehicular access to NYS DEC hunting stations. After climbing a slight hill on a curve, with a view to the right of marshland and an osprey pole, look for a left turn where the blue trail leaves East Side Road. This is Second Crossing Road (5), which is closed to vehicles. Look for trailing arbutus, a low-growing evergreen, along the edge of the trail, and the distinctive scalloped-edged leaves of the chestnut oak, very common in this forest. Follow Second Crossing Road for about 250 yards, where the blue trail turns right onto a narrow footpath (6).

At this point, the trail gradually climbs, crossing over three knolls with elevations of 90, 95, and 100 feet respectively. Before reaching the highest point, the trail skirts a small pit; in the immediate vicinity are over 100 pitch pines, most less than 15 feet in height. Growing in the shade of the oaks, these spindly specimens hardly resemble the towering pines of Buckskill or the spreading form found throughout Napeague. In the words of East Hampton naturalist Jim Ash, *Pinus rigida* is a very "plastic" species, showing great variation in its form depending upon the habitat it is found in.

Once over the highest knoll, the trail turns left onto a moss-covered woods road (7) and descends steeply to the Third Crossing Road. At this intersection, make a right and a quick left into a wooded area draped with catbriar (8). This traverses the northern edge of the neck where northerly winds drive sand up the eighty foot bluffs and into the forest, in places obliterating the footpath. Although the trail avoids the unstable edge of the bluff, there are several places where you can hike out to the edge for a spectacular 180-degree view over Northwest Harbor. In sight, from west to east, are North Haven, Shelter Island (with Mashomack Point and Ram Head clearly discernible), Cedar Point, and the Grace Estate. Of note is the amount of protected land within this view.

On a clear day, Orient Point is visible and, from the height of eighty feet, the hills of Connecticut and Rhode Island stand out. Closer at hand on a calm day, look down through the clear waters of the harbor where rocks and eelgrass beds are visible even in depths of six feet. At this point its easy to linger and turn the short three-mile hike into a half-day outing.

Moving on, still following the blue trail markers, turn onto Third Crossing Road again and follow it down to West Side Road. Here, the blue markers direct you south along the road but I recommend walking out past the salt pond and onto the beach (9). Follow the beach south for a third of a mile to the next access point (10), near First Crossing Road. Enjoy the sights and sounds of the beach along the way. In the distance is the waterfront of Sag Harbor.

On an autumn visit, seaside goldenrod was in full bloom and fiddler crabs scurried about on the edge of the marsh. A recent storm had deposited eelgrass along the high tide line, in places nearly a foot thick. The leafy portion of this seagrass dies back each fall, accumulating on our shorelines as a significant part of the wrack line. Rich in nutrients and minerals, this was once an important harvest among local subsistence farmers, who relied on it to restore fertility to their gardens. So important, in fact, that a disagreement over collection rights at a nearby beach resulted in a lawsuit!

Turning back in to the West Side Road, note the gradual changes in vegetation reflecting degrees of salt intolerance: beachgrass, groundsel, red cedar, post oak, and finally white oak. Follow the blue trail markers south on West Side Road, and stay on the road to return to the clubhouse parking area. Just before exiting the forest and reaching the fairways, the blue trail veers off to the right on a little used footpath (11). This turn is not well-marked. From that point the blue trail winds through wetlands and the trail is not well-maintained.

Directions: The main entrance to Barcelona Neck Preserve is off the Sag Harbor Turnpike (Rte. 114) between Sag Harbor Village and Swamp Road. The paved entrance road is marked by large wooden NYS DEC and golf course signs; follow the road for 0.7 mile to a building (the golf clubhouse) where the pavement ends. There is a gravel parking area next to the clubhouse and a grass parking area nearby; if using the latter, pull up to the edge of the woods before parking.

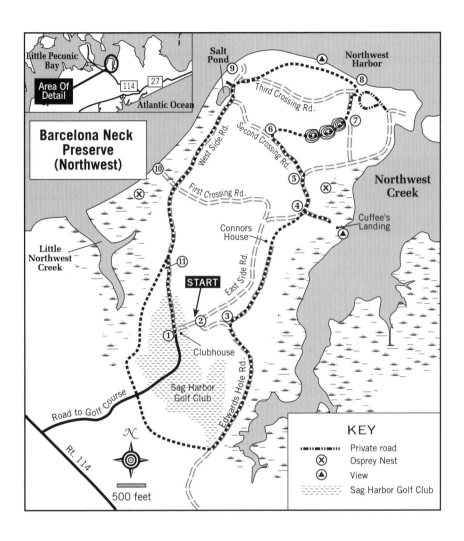

Barcelona Neck Preserve (Northwest)

Little Peconic Bay

Area Of Detail

114   27

Atlantic Ocean

Salt Pond

Northwest Harbor

Third Crossing Rd.

⑨

⑧

West Side Rd.

Second Crossing Rd.

⑥

⑦

⑩

⑤

First Crossing Rd.

⊗

⊗

Northwest Creek

④

Cuffee's Landing

Little Northwest Creek

Connors House

East Side Rd.

⑪

START

②   ③

①

Clubhouse

Sag Harbor Golf Club

Edwards Hole Rd.

Road to Golf Course

Rt. 114

N

500 feet

KEY

━━━━ Private road
⊗ Osprey Nest
▲ View
∷∷∷ Sag Harbor Golf Club

Paumanok Path:

Northwest Section I

This section of the Paumanok Path piggybacks on one of the South Fork's most popular trails, the Northwest Path, blazed with yellow triangles and extending between Route 114 and Cedar Point County Park, six miles to the north. The Northwest Path was designed by Rick Whalen and formally opened in 1989. Although much of the route was newly cut to link existing public parks and greenbelts, in several places, notably the Grace Estate Preserve, the trail follows old roadbeds that date back to the 1600s when the town was first settled.

Before heading off, it should be noted that the unpaved Edwards Hole Road provides a trail connection between the Paumanok Path and the trail system of Barcelona State Preserve, three-quarters of a mile away.

Following both the white rectangular blaze of the Paumanok Path and the yellow triangular symbol of the Northwest Path, hike through an oak forest sprinkled with both of Long Island's native pines: pitch and white. After a short distance along an old woods road, the trail turns left onto a narrow footpath and climbs Winter Harbor Hill (1), so named because its ninety foot-high, leafless winter view includes a glimpse of Northwest Harbor, two miles away.

Crossing Two Holes of Water Road, the trail enters another town park whose centerpiece is a beautiful freshwater wetland called Chatfield's Hole, visible on the left. The term "hole" often refers to small water-filled depressions, while a "hollow" is normally dry. Together with many of our South Fork ponds, these often share a similar origin: large fragments of glacial ice calved from the receding glacier and buried by the debris-laden meltwater to form kettleholes.

You may wonder, as I did when first exploring this area, why Two Holes of Water Road swings by Chatfield's Hole and not the Two Holes of Water designated on the map. I suspect that the map maker was looking for a less subtle "two holes" than actually exists along the road, and labeled the obvious, but quarter-mile distant, two holes as such. Actually, Chatfield's Hole is more often than not two holes of water: every so often the water level in

Chatfield's drops to the point that a narrow land bridge forms between its two deepest sections, creating the appropriately named two holes.

The intersection of the Paumanok Path and Foster's Path (red/orange blazes) is a large sandy area that, in June, attracts female snapping and painted turtles from the pond looking to deposit their leathery eggs (2). Foster's Path is named in honor of Debra Foster, one of several Town Planning Board Chairs who was a staunch advocate of open space and greenbelt trails, and without whom the Paumanok Path and other trails would not exist today. (Note: Foster's Path re-intersects and overlaps the Paumanok Path again in the vicinity of Grassy Hollow, creating a nine-mile loop with the Northwest Path.)

Crossing Foster's Path, there are several places where you can make a short and worthwhile detour down to the pond's edge. Take some time to enjoy both the panoramic view, particularly the brilliant fall foliage of the wetland edge vegetation, and a close-up examination of the plants found along the shoreline. Between the water and the closest woody shrubs and trees is band of herbaceous plants adapted to the seasonal changes in the pond's water level. This zone reflects groundwater fluctuations and contains many rare and unusual plants, including sundews: small, easily overlooked and interesting insectivorous plants.

Leaving Chatfield's Hole, the path soon crosses Lone Grave Road (3). To the left this old road connects with the Hubbard grave site (hence its name) in Northwest County Park. To the right it intersects Foster's Path.

Beyond Lone Grave Road, the trail climbs a short hill (elev. 86 feet) at the top of which is a lopped tree and an old well lined with stones (4). It is curious that someone spent the time and energy to construct a well at the top of a hill, more than 60 feet above the water table. From this point, across Bull Path and on to the intersection of Old Northwest Road, the trail traverses a breathtaking grove of white pine, apparently the largest native white pine forest on Long Island.

Unfortunately, very little of this magnificent forest has been protected. Before reaching Bull Path, the trail follows the perimeter of narrow easements through a residential subdivision (5). This section of trail clearly illustrates the shortcomings of relying solely on large lot zoning to protect natural resources: the homesites are scattered throughout the forest, destroying its visual character and ecological integrity.

Ironically, the most spectacular section of the white pine forest is privately owned. Found in a large shallow kettlehole between Bull Path and Old Northwest Road, this section of the white pine forest is known as "Wilson's

Grove" (6) for its owner, Marilyn Wilson. The towering pines and thick carpet of needles tend to mute sounds, including the wind, and filter the sunlight in such a way as to create a somewhat solemn and sacred atmosphere.

At a time when many South Fork estate owners are barricading their properties with fencing and state of the art security systems, we are incredibly fortunate to have such a generous steward of this natural treasure, one who has allowed a public footpath to be cut across her property. The public trail permission came with one minor restriction: no mountain bikes. Please respect the owner's request and follow the mountain bike bypass (7) to the Grace Estate Preserve.

While Wilson's Grove has a forest primeval feel about it, you may be surprised to learn that no tree here is older than sixty years, the number of years since the 1938 hurricane when the forest was completely leveled. White pine is a fast-growing, sun-loving species which can gain two to three feet in altitude over the course of a single year and, when full grown, is the tallest conifer east of the Mississippi.

Notice that where the pines are most dense and form a uniform grove, the understory is quite barren. This tall evergreen creates too much year-round shade on the forest floor for most plants to survive, including its own seedlings. The only areas where pine seeds have germinated are where shafts of sunlight penetrate through the canopy, such as where a large white pine has toppled over.

Upon reaching Old Northwest Road, turn left and cross the road: the trail continues between the intersection of Northwest Landing Road and Northwest Road. Here you have once again entered onto town parkland, a 500-acre preserve called the Grace Estate, named for W. R. Grace who purchased the land in 1910. Plans for the development of a summer community of several hundred condominium units, tennis courts, swimming pools, polo field, and a golf course, filed with the town in 1982, rallied residents to approve a 1985 town referendum which enabled most of it to be preserved.

As you approach the dramatic kettlehole named Samp Mortar Hollow (8), note that the forest canopy is largely composed of oaks, yet there are many white pine saplings growing in the understory. This is unusual, as white pines are very shade-intolerant trees. It appears that the pines are actually expanding the range in this area, and may one day replace the oaks in the forest canopy. My guess is that the successful germination and growth of white pines in this area is related to several severe gypsy moth defoliations, which stripped the oak leaf cover, over the past fifteen years.

Along the steep sides of Samp Mortar Hollow, the tall pines once again prevail. At the bottom, which usually has water, the swamp maple rules. Toppling over with age and exposing most of its root system to the killing air, the hardy swamp or red maple survives and sends an array of new shoots up from the now horizontal main trunk. The elevated mass of root and soil provides a micro-environment for other plants to colonize, such as several species of moss that lend a year-round tint of emerald green to the swamp backdrop.

Beyond Samp Hollow we begin to see evidence that this area was once cleared for farming and grazing. A line of old, wide-spreading oaks is visible to the right of the trail, in the vicinity of the buffalo waller (9). Their squat, wide-spreading growth form indicates that they once grew in an open field. Within a forest, the growth of trees is largely vertical as each individual competes with its nearby neighbors in a race to the sunlit sky. The more densely packed the trees, the more intense the competition; this can result in a forest of tall, thin trunks and minimal branching. On the other hand, growing out in the open away from other trees there is a competitive advantage to extending sideways with long, spreading branches. This strategy allows the tree to maximize its exposure to sunlight and shade out potential future competitors. Such trees are referred to as "wolf trees" since, like the wolf, they often stand alone.

One hundred years ago, the fields surrounding the wolf trees were grazed by bison or buffalo, collected out west and brought here by David Gardiner, and "cattalo," the offspring which resulted from his experiments in cross breeding with domestic cattle.

At a sharp right turn in the trail is a large piece of granite, Standing Rock (10). Plucked off a mountaintop north of here and deposited by the last glacier, the process of transportation is part of the origin of its geological name: glacial erratic. Not much further along is the Five Corners, a major trail intersection.

Most of the existing trails in the Grace Estate are actually old roadbeds dating back several hundred years to when Northwest was the main port for the town, predating Sag Harbor. Ships navigated their way into Northwest Harbor between Mashomack Point, Shelter Island and Cedar Island (now the western tip of Cedar Point), unloading provisions from as far away as the Caribbean. All that remains of this bustling center of commerce are a few cellar holes, old wells and several cemeteries.

Between Five Corners and Scoy's Pond Road are more wolf trees and several stands of eastern red cedar growing amidst the reestablished oak-hickory forest. Red cedar seeds will not germinate unless exposed to a substantial amount of sunlight. Here again is evidence that this area was once cleared of much of its forest cover.

Unless you are planning to camp overnight at Cedar Point County Park, leave the Northwest Path and the yellow triangular blazes by turning right onto Scoy's Pond Road, following the white Paumanok Path blazes. A short side trip to Scoy's Pond is worth the time; take the first trail on the left after leaving the Northwest Path (11). This pond is the headwaters of Alewife Brook, which flows through nearby Cedar Point County Park and into Northwest Harbor.

Back on Scoy's Pond Road, it is a short hike out to the pavement of Northwest Road. Scoy's Pond Road runs from the shoreline of Northwest Harbor, in the vicinity of Whalebone Landing and Kirk's Place, to the Van Scoy homestead and old schoolhouse at Grassy Hollow. Crossing Northwest Road, the Paumanok Path intersects and parallels the northern end of Foster's Path; its orange/red blazes can be followed back to Two Holes of Water Road via Jason's Rock.

Directions to Start of Trail: The start is at the intersection of Route 114 and Edwards Hole Road. From Montauk Highway, turn north onto Daniel's Hole Road (the exit for the East Hampton Airport), wind your way around the airport and, without turning, onto Wainscott Northwest Road. Continue on the latter to the stop sign, turn right onto Route 114 and travel 0.5 mile to Edwards Hole Road, a nondescript unpaved road on your left marked with one of those difficult to read, white vertical posts. Pull off Route 114 and park.

Directions to End of Trail: See directions to the start of Paumanok Path: Northwest Section II.

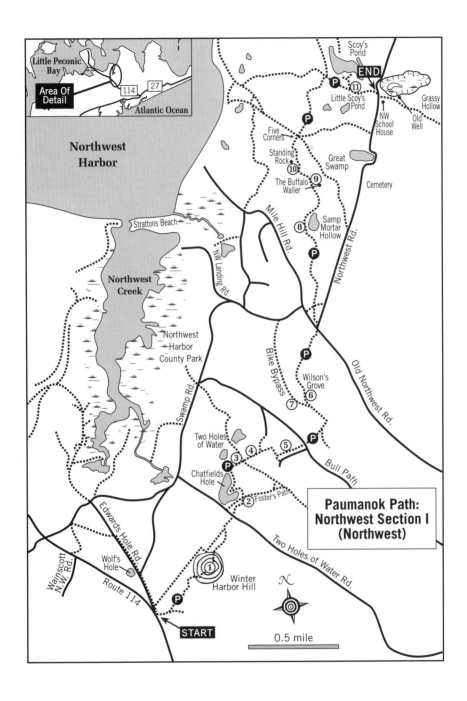

Paumanok Path:
Northwest Section I
(Northwest)

135

GRACE ESTATE PRESERVE

This three mile-long loop incorporates a beach walk along scenic Northwest Harbor, a seldom-visited corner of Cedar Point County Park, a portion of the Paumanok Path, and an old, unpaved roadway dating back to the 1600s. In addition, the route provides a glimpse into the early history of the town, parallels a beautiful tidal creek, crosses a freshwater brook, and overlooks a remote pond. I think you'll enjoy it.

From the "A" entrance to the Grace Estate Preserve (see map and directions) hike along an unpaved but fairly wide roadbed that follows a ridge of pitch pines to the northern shore of Scoy's Pond (2). The pine ridge separates two large freshwater marshes, both marked by tall plumes of phragmites visible through the forest. Both marshes also have mosquito control ditches that connect the freshwaters of Scoy's Pond (whose average surface elevation is listed as four feet above mean sea level) with the estuarine waters of Alewife Pond, at mean sea level.

After a look at Scoy's Pond, hike back to the turn marked with yellow triangular trail blazes, which leads onto a narrow footpath. These yellow blazes identify this trail as the Northwest Path, a popular six-mile-long route from Rte. 114 to Cedar Point County Park. Designed by Rick Whalen and officially opened in 1989, the route follows several old woods roads that date back as many as 300 years. The loop described here incorporates the little-used northern section of the Northwest Path that is not part of the regional Paumanok Path route.

At (3) the trail crosses Scoy's Run, the main outlet of Scoy's Pond. Shallow, narrow, and steep-sided, the brook here is pinched between two ridges of upland pine-oak forest, a perfect site to easily bridge the waterway. Elsewhere the quarter-mile-long brook courses through flat marshland, and most of it has the appearance of an artificial, improved vector control ditch.

Not far beyond the footbridge the Northwest Path turns left onto another old roadbed called Old Alewife Brook Road (4). Most likely the original roadway linking Northwest Road and Alewife Brook Landing, the older route not only follows more level ground, it avoided wetlands (unlike the paved Alewife Brook Road which crosses through two). These practical considerations were incorporated into road layout long before there were any wetland protection regulations.

At the next intersection, leave the Northwest Path by turning right onto an unmarked, unpaved, wide roadbed called Scoy's Pond Road. Note several gray birch trees in the woods on either side of the trail; its bark color sometimes resembles the bright white of the paper, or white, birch with which it can sometimes be confused. But gray birches tend to grow in multi-stemmed clumps whose trunks age quickly, die, and are replaced by dozens of new trunk shoots, a growth characteristic not unlike the shadbush. I don't think there are any native paper birches found on the South Fork, but if in doubt check the leaves during the growing season: the gray birch's triangular-shaped leaf is quite distinctive from the oval shape of the white birch's.

The eastern red cedars, black locusts, and thickets of catbriar found here are evidence of disturbance to the original forest many years ago, as their seeds require open, sunlit areas to germinate. A more recent disturbance to the forest is the proliferation of deer fencing along the northern border of the Grace Preserve. Aesthetically displeasing, some would like the trail rerouted out of sight of the fencing and landscaping. There is also growing concern about the ecological impact of the now ubiquitous plastic fencing. One town biologist has pointed out that the fencing is not species-specific and may be impacting more than the white-tailed deer; he claimed to have found an alarming number of dead owls along these fences.

Approaching Northwest Harbor and Kirk's Place, more evidence of clearing and disturbance to the original oak-hickory forest is visible, including a large area of little bluestem grass and reindeer lichen off to the left. Both of these plants specialize in colonizing cleared areas whose soils lack nutrients and organic material, and their presence here may reflect farming and grazing impacts to the soil.

The Northwest area was East Hampton's main port from 1653 until the first wharf was built at Sag Harbor in 1761. Whale oil and whalebone were carted from whaling stations at Sagaponack and Mecox, via Merchant's Path (cut in 1712), to shipping wharves at Northwest. There, along with furs and horses, they were loaded on ships bound for England and the West Indies; ships bound for the latter would return with holds full of rum and molasses.

Ship building, wood cutting, farming, and fishing further developed the area; there was even a fish factory built to extract oil from menhaden, and an oyster aquaculture enterprise. Kirk's Place is named for Josiah Kirk, an "obstinate Irishman" according to Harry Sleight, editor of the early Town Trustee Journals. He settled here in the early 1860s on 390 acres of land, and for eleven years battled in court and on his beachfront to keep his fellow townsmen from gathering eelgrass that washed ashore on his property. In that day, eelgrass was a valuable commodity used for insulation, fertilizer, and cattle bedding. The following is from his obituary in a 1901 issue of the *East Hampton Star*:

> With the death of Josiah Kirk at the age of 83 years, which occurred at the Suffolk County Almshouse at Yaphank, Oct. 21, a man once prominent at the East End and in the county courts passed away. Mr. Kirk settled at Northwest about 30 years ago, and his farm was one of the finest in this section, well stocked with choice herds of animals, high stepping and spirited horses in particular, being well remembered. Mr. Kirk's dwelling at Northwest faced the bay, but a short distance from the beach, and his fertile acres bordered on the water for a long distance. It was on this strip of beach that the controversy arose which resulted in the famous East Hampton seaweed litigation which was waged for a number of years and which finally wrecked him financially. The case was tried many times, and appealed and re-appealed, Kirk losing in most instances, until his once fine property fell into decay and his princely fortune went to pay the costs of court proceedings and to the lawyers.

The most obvious remains of the Kirk homestead are the large basswood, or linden, trees on the shore. This time of the year, their bright red buds make them easy to identify. The old cellar hole, well and the foundation of the barn (5) are well hidden among the honeysuckle, catbriar, bittersweet, and poison ivy vines and shrubs.

Follow the path out onto the beach. Facing the water, the high sandy bluffs of Barcelona Neck State Preserve are visible to the left, as is the Village of Sag Harbor. Straight ahead is North Haven; right of that is Mashomack Preserve on Shelter Island and, continuing further to the right is the Cedar Point lighthouse (built in 1839 and recently slated for restoration) and Cedar Point County Park. Combined with the 500-acre Grace Estate Preserve, there are over 4,000 acres of preserved land bordering Northwest Harbor. This reflects the commitment of several levels of government, and organizations such as the Group for the South Fork, The Nature Conservancy, and the Northwest Alliance towards protecting this historic and productive waterway. None of these initiatives would have succeeded without a strong commitment from the local citizenry that persevered through years of meetings, letter writing campaigns and other lobbying efforts.

Head north along the beach (passing close by an osprey pole) to Alewife Brook Landing, turn right, and walk up Alewife Brook Road a short distance to gate #3 on your left (6 on the map). You are back on the Northwest Path following its yellow blazes through Cedar Point County Park.

The trail hugs the edge of the oak forest with several outstanding views over the tidal waters and marshes of Alewife Brook, one of the prettiest creeks on Long Island in spite of the ugly cyclone fencing (a trademark of County Parks) at its outlet. If you have the time, take advantage of the bench overlooking the brook (7) and relax.

The Northwest Path exits the County Park (8) at gate #2 and follows the road to cross Scoy's Run (9). I haven't seen anyone fishing for alewives here as they once did; nor have I seen any evidence that Scoy's Run is still being utilized by spawning alewives. Alewives, for whom the brook, road, and nearby pond are named, begin their spawning runs in mid-March which, not coincidentally, is the time of year when the osprey, or fish-hawks, return from their overwintering grounds as far away as the Amazon Basin.

The alewife, a member of the herring family that travels in large schools, prefers to migrate upstream to its spawning grounds under the cover of darkness. Those that choose to swim the shallow upper sections of the brook in daylight are easy prey for a wide-assortment of hungry piscivores: egrets, herons, osprey, and even man. Although a bony, oily fish not particularly good for eating, the females carry a large sack of eggs in their bellies during the spawning season, as many as 100,000 per female, and the roe is quite tasty.

Another 200 yards up the road is the trail where you began the hike (A).

Directions: Heading east on Montauk Highway (Rte. 27), pass through Wainscott and turn left onto Stephen Hands Path. Follow the signs for Cedar Point County Park at all the major intersections: straight across Rte. 114; left onto Old Northwest Road; right onto Northwest Road; and left onto Alewife Brook Road. Travel 0.4 mile on Alewife Brook Road, passing the entrance to Cedar Point Park on the right, and park at the intersection of an unpaved road in a clump of pines on the left. This entrance point to the Grace Estate is labeled "A" on a signpost.

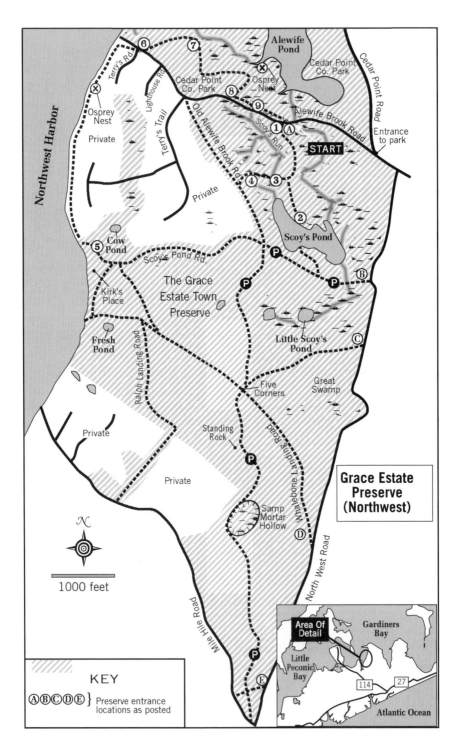

Grace Estate Preserve (Northwest)

Alewife Pond

Cedar Point Co. Park

Cedar Point Road

Northwest Harbor

Terry's Rd

Lighthouse Rd

Osprey Nest

Private

Cedar Point Co. Park

Osprey Nest

Terry's Trail

Old Alewife Brook Rd

Alewife Brook Road

Entrance to park

Scoy's Run

START

Private

Scoy's Pond

Cow Pond

Scoy's Pond Rd

The Grace Estate Town Preserve

Little Scoy's Pond

Kirk's Place

Fresh Pond

Ralph Landing Road

Five Corners

Great Swamp

Private

Standing Rock

Whalebone Landing Road

Grace Estate Preserve (Northwest)

Samp Mortar Hollow

Private

Mille Hile Road

North West Road

N

1000 feet

Area Of Detail

Gardiners Bay

Little Peconic Bay

114   27

Atlantic Ocean

KEY

Ⓐ Ⓑ Ⓒ Ⓓ Ⓔ } Preserve entrance locations as posted

CEDAR POINT COUNTY PARK

Purchased by Suffolk County in 1965 from a private owner who was using the area as a hunting preserve, Cedar Point County Park is a 600 acre tract located in the extreme northwestern corner of East Hampton Town. The majority of the park is forested, most of that being the oak-hickory forest community, but a tidal creek, salt pond, freshwater pond, and several deep kettleholes containing vernal ponds, swamps, and freshwater marshes add to the park's diversity of flora and fauna. Over four miles of shoreline border Northwest Harbor and Gardiner's Bay, including sandy beaches, tall north-facing bluffs, and a mile-long sand spit separating the two bays.

Best known for its camping facilities, the park's physical characteristics also make it a popular destination for saltwater fishermen, sea kayakers, and duck hunters. Less well-known are its hiking trails, totaling five miles, which provide access to all the various ecological communities and several out-standing scenic view points over the bays. The most popular hike is a two-mile loop through the park's wooded interior to the best of several scenic overlooks atop the Hedges Banks bluffs. The first leg, approximately one mile from the parking area to the bluff lookout, follows the park's "Nature Trail" for which there is an interpretive guidebook available and numbered posts (1–14) at intervals alongside the path. At the time I visited the Nature Trail, several numbered posts were missing. These (1,3, and 6) are not located on the accompanying map.

Beginning at the parking area, the trail winds through a mature forest dominated by oaks, with chestnut oak (*Quercus prinoides*) being the main oak species represented. Not far from the start the trail passes close to several white pines, the largest and oldest being approximately 25 years of age. White pines can be aged by counting the number of whorled lateral branches along the main trunk, since each cluster of branches usually repre-sents one growing season. I say usually because, under certain conditions, white pines will sprout two sets of lateral whorls in one season. But generally speaking, a close approximation of age can be made by this method.

Although considered a shade-intolerant species whose seeds will only germinate on soil exposed to sunlight, white pines seem to be expanding their range into the oak forest in the Northwest area of East Hampton. In fact, the understory of some areas of the nearby Grace Estate is dominated by white pine seedlings, which are thriving under the oak canopy. Over time, it appears that the fast growing and long-lived pines may replace the oaks, converting the deciduous hardwood forest into an evergreen, coniferous one. Perhaps this unusual example of ecological succession is possible due to the South Fork's long growing season. This may enable the pines to capture and store direct sunlight energy in the spring and fall when the oaks are bare of leaves.

The Nature Trail's interpretive stops are marked by short 4" x 4" wooden posts, painted dark brown, with a number corresponding to numbered sections in the park's Nature Trail Guidebook. Stop 2 is a cluster of glacial erratics plucked from the bedrock of New England and deposited here by a slow-moving ice sheet, or glacier, during the last ice age. Stop 3 discusses the chestnut oak, which is well represented all along this section of trail.

The oak genus is divided into two main groups: the white oaks, whose leaves have rounded tips and whose fruit (acorns) matures in one year; and the red or black oaks, whose leaves have pointed or bristle tips and whose acorns take two years to mature. Unlike many of our common oak species which are difficult to identify based solely on leaf characteristics, the chestnut oak has a distinctive, easily recognizable leaf shape. Look around the forest floor for its elliptically shaped, regular- and coarsely-toothed leaves with fairly evenly spaced and prominent veins which somewhat resemble the American chestnut leaf; hence the similar name. Being a member of the white oak group, the tips of the chestnut oak lobes or teeth are rounded, unlike the American chestnut's sharply pointed tips.

Chestnut oak grows slower than most other oaks and is less tolerant of shade; therefore it does not compete well with its relatives on most sites. Its dominance on a particular site is usually an indication of poor, dry soil conditions for which it is well-adapted and competitive. Take a close look at its thick and heavily furrowed bark, a distinctive characteristic which enables identification in the leafless months of the year. The bark was considered the best source of oak tannin, an acidic compound used to process hides into leather.

At stop 4 (mosses and lichens), the Nature Trail veers left onto another trail for a short distance before turning right and continuing northward. Nearing stop 5, the trail begins a steep descent into an elongated kettlehole, one of three such formations that extend westward to Cedar Pond and Northwest Harbor. The interpretive guide uses this vantage point to discuss the various layers of a forest: canopy trees, understory trees, shrubs, groundcover, and leaf litter. Each layer is unique in terms of light, temperature, humidity, and moisture, a feature that allows for variation and diversity in the forest as an ecological community.

As mentioned earlier, the canopy is largely one of oaks. The next layer is composed of tree species too small in height, even at maturity, to reach the canopy, and therefore well-adapted to capture the limited sunlight filtering through the canopy leaves. These include flowering dogwood, sassafras, and shadbush. The shrub layer is a mix of lowbush and highbush blueberry, huckleberry, and bayberry. In areas clear of these shrubs, for example along the edges of the trail, are examples of the ground layer: trailing arbutus, Pennsylvania sedge, spotted pipsissewa, and wintergreen.

Over the thousands of years since the ice sheet receded, rain and snow melt has washed finer sediments down into the kettlehole creating a soil base better able to hold moisture than the surrounding area. This, in turn, has enabled red maple (*Acer rubrum*) to compete with the oaks, and here in the kettlehole it forms a significant portion of the forest canopy.

The presence of red maple could be interpreted to mean that the bottom of the kettlehole is intercepting, or close to, the water table. This is true of another deep kettlehole adjacent to the campground, whose bottom elevation is listed as one to four feet above mean sea level (AMSL). But the lowest elevation in this kettlehole is 27 feet AMSL, far above the water table (between two and three feet AMSL).

The route back up the other side of the kettlehole is badly eroded, a function of poor trail design as much as anything else. Most of the park's trail system was laid out utilizing old woods roads, providing a functional, but not necessarily an interesting or aesthetically pleasing, hiking experience.

I failed to locate station 6 (decomposition of leaves and logs as a form of nutrient recycling), one of two stations I couldn't find in the field. At station 7 (a red cedar browsed by deer) the trail begins a traverse of fairly level terrain through 13 and the bluff overlook.

As you approach station 9 and are within 500 feet of the bay, the size and the structure of the forest begins to change. The canopy trees are diminished in size and a thorny vine, catbriar (*Smilax sp.*), dominates the groundcover and shrub layers, even reaching high into the understory. Both features could be the result of the area's close proximity to the bay. The stunted trees are most likely due to the salt-laden northwesterly winds regularly pruning back any trees that reach too tall. Station 10 highlights several features of catbriar. Catbriar usually indicates the area was subject to some type of disturbance in the past which removed much of the forest canopy. In this case, even though elevated high above any flood waters, a severe Nor'easter could do quite a bit of damage to this coastal forest by drenching its leaves and buds with salt water carried aloft via gale-force winds.

Stations 11, 12 and 13 highlight the three common understory trees: sassafras (*Sassafras albidum*), shadbush (*Amelanchier canadensis*), and flowering dogwood (*Cornus florida*). Just beyond 13, the Nature Trail intersects another path; turn right for the short walk out to the Hedges Banks overlook.

Remnants of the observation platform (14) constructed here not long ago are reminders that coastal areas, even these tall bluffs, are unstable zones subject to the erosive forces of nature: wind, water, wave and currents. A variety of new plants are found here: those that can withstand the periodic salt spray and sand burial associated with this blowout, such as American beachgrass and beach heather; and others that can't compete in the shade of the oak forest but thrive in full sun conditions, such as little bluestem and switchgrass (both grasses), black cherry, and several species of vine (honeysuckle, bittersweet, and catbriar).

On a clear day, the hills of Connecticut are visible on the northern horizon; closer at hand (from west, or left, to east) are Ram's Head (Shelter Island), Orient Point, Plum Island (marked by a water tower), Gardiner's Island (whose white windmill is discernible), and the sandy bluffs of Camp Blue Bay in springs.

From the overlook, the hiker has several choices for the return trip. By continuing west on the Hedges Banks Trail (along the bluff) to Cedar Pond, and then back by Cedar Point Road (paved), the return route is a little over two miles. That distance can be doubled by continuing west from Cedar Pond to the Cedar Point lighthouse and back. This can be a beautiful walk with views over Northwest Harbor towards Barcelona Neck, the Grace Estate, Sag Harbor, North Haven and Mashomack Preserve on Shelter Island. The long sandy spit is a popular waterfowl hunting area, so don't plan that loop in the fall or early winter.

The most direct route back is the unmarked trail running south to Cedar Point Road. At the pavement, turn left onto the hiking-only trail and follow this to the intersection with the Nature Trail at station 4. Turn right and backtrack on the Nature Trail to the parking area, completing a two mile hike.

Directions: Cedar Point County Park is located deep in the Northwest Woods, as far from the main highway (Rte. 27) as you can be and still be in the Town of East Hampton. Fortunately for those unfamiliar with the maze of roads in

Northwest Woods, all the key turns and intersections are marked with signs "to Cedar Point Park." From Montauk Highway just east of Wainscott, turn north (left if eastbound) onto Stephen Hands Path, left onto Old Northwest Road, right onto Northwest Road, left onto Alewife Brook Road and right onto Cedar Point Road, which leads into the park. Once in the park, look for the park office building (a log cabin) on the right; the trailhead parking area is clearly marked nearby.

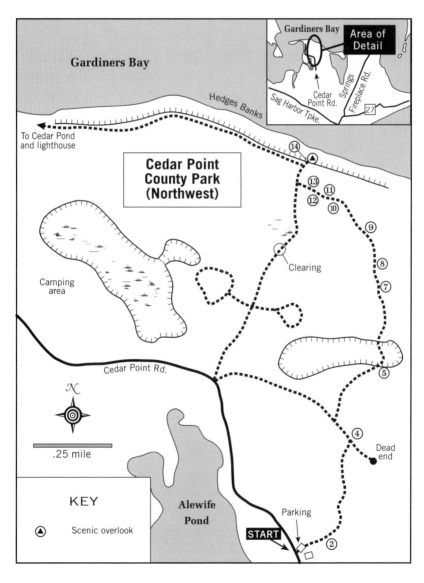

Paumanok Path:

Northwest Section II

This five-mile section of the Paumanok Path begins in an area rich in post-European settlement artifacts and ends in an area rich in Native American artifacts. Another interesting feature of this section of trail is the fact that, with the exception of the last quarter-mile, it traverses greenbelts created through the land subdivision process as opposed to land acquisitions. Armed with a tax map of this area, one sees first-hand the evolution of residential subdivision design in East Hampton, from sprawling developments and narrow, ribbon-like greenbelts with little, if any, ecological value, to large blocks of preserved forest, a pleasure to hike through, adjacent to clusters of residential development. In several places, the limitations of this land use planning tool are quite evident to the hiker: the encroachment of homesites, lawns, tennis courts, swimming pools, paved roads, and driveways on the thin band of preserved forest through which the trail is woven. However, overall this section of the Paumanok Path provides a nice mixture of deep forest and neighborhood trail experiences, and connects several important points in East Hampton's history.

From Northwest Road, walk up the unpaved road toward the fenced-in cemetery on the left (1). This is the Van Scoy cemetery, and a bit further up the road, the cellar hole of Isaac Van Scoy's house, built in the 1760s and apparently the first farmhouse in Northwest. Before that time, from 1653–1761, Northwest's importance lay in the fact that it was East Hampton's principal port. Ships bringing goods from as far away as the Caribbean pulled into Northwest Harbor to unload their wares. In 1761, a wharf was built at Sag Harbor and, in 1770, Long Wharf was completed which enabled deeper draft ships to pull right up to shore for transferring cargo, marking the decline of Northwest as a port of call and the beginning of its farming community. For a more detailed history of this area, I recommend reading the "Memories of Old Northwest" series written by Jeannette Edwards Rattray for the East Hampton Star in 1973.

By 1792, Northwest had enough families to warrant establishing their own school district and building a schoolhouse. Directly across from the cemetery you can still see the outline of the newer schoolhouse constructed in 1827. Take some time to wander around what East Hampton Trails Society founder Lee Dion refers to as a ghost town, a farming community until the 1890s and now reverted back to forest.

Under a large flat rock, part of the schoolhouse foundation, I found one of our common woodland salamanders, the red-back salamander (note: the South Fork only has the gray phase of this species; no red coloration is visible). An important inhabitant of the forest community, this creature is a predator of small insects; part of the system of checks and balances in the leaf litter and soil micro-environment. Later, while poking around near the cellar hole, a woodcock burst out from under an old apple tree, breaking the woodland silence and startling me.

The trees in this area are simply awesome: in addition to some unusual specimens, such as apples and hawthorns associated with the homestead, there are many big flowering dogwoods and huge oaks and hickories. One oak, on the right side of the roadway just before the trail turns sharply to the right and becomes a footpath, is a monster—between three and four feet in diameter.

Speaking of sharp turns, watch for this one which is only 200 yards from the start. Note that the route here is blazed with two colors: white for the Paumanok Path, and an orange/red blaze signifying Foster's Path. Once on the footpath, the trail winds its way in a southerly direction for a half-mile, passing a red maple swamp on the right, joining an old woods roadbed for a stretch, and entering a grove of pitch pines (2). Here the trail intersects a well-worn and wide dirt road: to the left the road connects to Alewife Brook Road, to the right it runs down to the old John Hand Peach Farm. Go right and follow the road for 250 yards where the Paumanok Path makes a sharp left turn (3) and becomes a footpath through old field vegetation: bayberry (a woody shrub often keeping its green leaves through the winter, although not a true evergreen), sumac (with brilliant red berries that persist through much of the winter), red cedars, and little bluestem grass. This was part of the adjacent Peach Farm, an unsuccessful operation in terms of peach production, but the last remaining Northwest farm operation, producing landscaping material today. Up until 1962, Salvatore Criscione ran a horse farm there, complete with a quarter-mile racetrack which is still visible today.

Reentering the forest, the trail winds its way down into a slight depression (4) where two big white pines loom. From here the trail climbs very gradually for a quarter mile to a paved driveway, which it crosses (5). At this point, you have traveled 1.5 miles through a fairly significant block of forest protected in the 1990s by the town's subdivision review process. Over much of the distance to Springy Banks Road the character of the trail changes somewhat: while the forest type is similar, the greenbelt reserve areas were created in the 1970s and early 1980s and are barely wide enough to accommodate the trail. In places, nature clearly takes a back seat to suburbia.

After crossing a paved driveway, the trail winds up and down some hilly terrain before intersecting a very wide trail spanning between Cordwood Lane and Timber Lane (6). A right turn here, toward Timber Lane, will take you on a trail back to Northwest Road, a mile further south than where you started but near to a Grace Estate trail called Whalebone Landing Road, enabling you to loop back to the Van Scoy homestead.

Continuing on the Paumanok Path, the trail makes a sharp left turn onto what appears to be an old woods road and passes through an area where the oak forest's understory contains many white pine seedlings; in time, the quick-growing pines may replace the oaks and turn this section into another white pine grove. A future trail link heading off to the right into a mature white pine forest will someday link back to the Grace Estate near the Old Northwest Road–Northwest Road intersection.

Just beyond the pine seedlings, the trail climbs onto a small ridge and Foster's Path (orange/red blazes) turns right (7), leaving the Paumanok Path en route to Jason's Rock another intersection with the Paumanok Path at Chatfield's Hole and Two Holes of Water Road.

This section of the Paumanok Path is used by horseback riders who have set up log obstacles for jumping practice. It should be noted that there are two parcels between here and Hands Creek Road which, if acquired, would greatly improve this trail corridor. Hands Creek Road (8) marks the halfway point: 2.5 miles.

Between Hands Creek Road and Middle Highway, the trail swings eastward and parallels the cul-de-sacs Van Scoy Path West and East, a subdivision which preserved two small sections of forest in addition to the trail linkage. At the far end, cross Van Scoy Path East and diagonal over to the paved portion of Middle Highway, crossing it as well and head back into the forest before turning south (9). Middle Highway is an old town right-of-way which is paved in sections, unpaved but drivable in places, and little more than a narrow horse trail in other areas.

Over the years, the town's Planning Board managed to secure several narrow greenbelts on either side of this section of the right-of-way, creating a woodland buffer from adjacent development as wide as 400 feet in some places. However, after only about 200 yards through the woods, the green-belt narrows and the trail is forced out onto the cleared right-of-way. At this point, you are at elevation 150 feet, the highest point between Old Northwest Road and Three Mile Harbor.

Continue southward along the cleared but unpaved roadway until it ends at its intersection with Trail's End Road, a paved road on the right. The Paumanok Path continues straight ahead (south) into the woods as a narrow horse trail and swings close to a dead-end road on the left, which is Bucks Path.

From here the trail enters a beautiful and well buffered forest, and begins to descend into a large swale. This section of trail is well worn in from horse use, and could use some maintenance work.

The next trail intersection (10) is easy to miss: as you begin climbing out of the swale, look for a narrow footpath on your left and take it. Although the intersection is marked, the new trail is much less worn in than the section of horse trail and there is a tendency to look down as you trudge up the slope, often resulting in missing the white painted blaze signaling a turn.

The trail meanders eastward through the Rivers Road development, crossing the pavement twice and dropping down into another pretty swale before reaching Springy Banks Road near its intersection with Soak Hides Road. The Paumanok Path crosses Springy Banks Road and enters a 17-acre waterfront parcel recently acquired by the town (11).

This property, overlooking the south end of the harbor, is rich in Native American artifacts. Nearing the creek at the south end of Three Mile Harbor, the trail is improved with boardwalking to span the soft wet soils of the adjacent tupelo-red maple swamp. This, in turn, lead to a stand of phragmites where the boardwalk is raised to form a bridge over the marsh and creek bed.

The creek's headwater is Round Swamp, a half-mile to the south on the east side of Three Mile Harbor Road in the vicinity of Round Swamp Farm. The two common names for the creek, Tanbark Creek and Soak Hides Dreen, reflect its historic use by Native Americans in preserving and tanning animal skins. Its close proximity to shellfish beds and freshwater made it prime real estate for the area's earliest inhabitants, and today it provides a beautiful destination for hikers on the Paumanok Path.

On the opposite shoreline, the trail meanders through another town preserve to Gardiner's Cove Road. Walk to the end of Gardiner's Cove Road, and cross Three Mile Harbor Road. The route continues in the woods on the east side of Three Mile Harbor Road, diagonaling northeast to Karlsruhe/Cross Highway, where the Stony Hill section of the Paumanok Path begins.

Directions to Start of Trail: From Montauk Highway (Rte. 27), turn north onto Stephen Hands Path and follow the signs to Cedar Point County Park across Route 114, onto Old Northwest Road and then Northwest Road. One mile down Northwest Road is a tight bend in the road to accommodate a swamp on the left. A half-mile further, the trail (a fairly wide unpaved road) crosses Northwest Road. Park at the pull off on the right.

Directions to End of Trail: See directions to the start of Paumanok Path: Stony Hill Section.

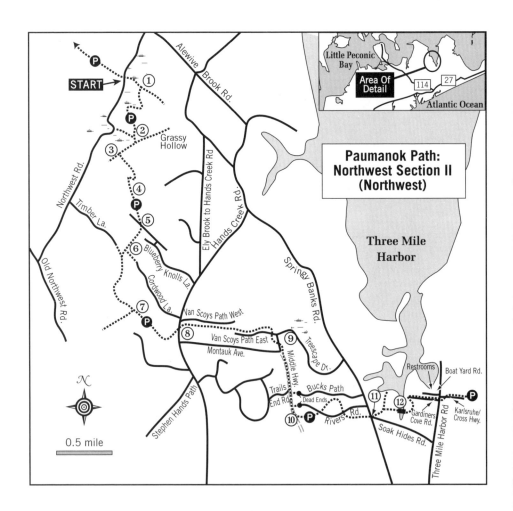

SAMMY'S BEACH PRESERVE

There are many coastal sand spits located along the South Fork's northern or bayside shoreline, providing many of our coves and harbors with various degrees of protection from the wind-generated waves of the Peconic and Gardiner's Bays. In this way they function as barrier beaches, an important coastal feature that allows cordgrass (*Spartina alterniflora*), a salt marsh pioneer plant, to become established in its lee and, over time, develop into a diverse salt marsh community. One such sand spit, separating Gardiner's Bay from Three Mile Harbor, is called Sammy's (sometimes spelled on maps as "Sammis") Beach. While all these coastal spits are similar in form and function, few can match Sammy's Beach in size, diversity, and sheer beauty.

Ironically, it is the bay's wave action, along with tidal currents, that establishes these spits. Through a process called littoral drift, waves move sand along the beach until they hit an obstruction (e.g., a jetty) or deep water (such as an inlet). Sammy's Beach formed as a result of sand being transported from the bluffs of Hedges Banks (to the west) eastward across the mouth of Three Mile Harbor. The opposite is true at Cedar Point, on the west side of Hedges Banks, where net littoral drift is westward and has created (and continues to add to) a 1.5-mile-long sand spit out of Hedges Banks material.

This process also continues at Sammy's Beach, although it is much altered by the presence of shoreline bulkheads, rock jetties, and periodic dredging of the inlet. Coastal management policies and decisions have long been a matter of heated debate, and the 1998–99 inlet dredging was no exception. Many people were outraged to see bulldozers preparing most of the upland area of the Sammy's Beach Nature Preserve to receive the inlet's dredge spoils. Since then, in no small part to hard-working volunteers, the area has completely re-vegetated.

Sammy's Beach, a mile-long, over a half-mile wide at its eastern end, and encompassing several hundred acres, is largely undeveloped. As with many sand spits, this one curves inward at its eastern extremity, forming a hook that reaches far into Three Mile Harbor. The hook, and a very narrow sliver of beach sand along the harborside, shelters an intricate labyrinth of tidal creeks, salt ponds, salt meadows, and mosquito ditches equal in size to one-half the sand barrier itself. Called Goose Creek and often referred to as "the maze," it is an outstanding feature of the Nature Preserve.

A two-mile-long loop, including the section of trail along Goose Creek, can be hiked from the parking area on Sammy's Beach Road, with the option of returning via the interior four-wheel drive road or hiking along the bay beach. The latter choice provides an opportunity to view shorebirds, such as the small flock of ruddy turnstones I watched in the fall, feeding along the beach's wrack line. During the tern and plover nesting season (April through July), portions of the preserve may be closed to visitors.

From the parking area at the end of Sammy's Beach Road, there is a wide dirt road heading east which soon forks: left leads a short distance to the bay beach; right is the main east-west four wheel drive roadway leading to the inlet. The most interesting hiking route along the peninsula is the southern route. From the parking area, walk back along the pavement to the sharp curve at (1), where a sandy road provides four-wheel access to the north end of the Harbor. The hiking-only footpath is a left turn off this water access road.

Between (1) and (5) the path follows along the edge of the Goose Creek marsh, with some of the upper marsh plants growing right in the trail. This reflects the fact that, on a high spring tide, these portions of the trail may be flooded. One of the best times to visit the preserve is August through October. Many of the salt marsh plants are in flower at this time of year, including most of the marsh grasses, and the numerous biting insects are gone. I brought along Newcomb's *Wildflower Guide*, *Beachcombers Botany* by Loren Petry, and *Grasses* by Lauren Brown and searched the trailside flora for unfamiliar specimens.

Sea lavender (*Limonium carolinianum*), with its sprays of tiny light purple flowers, puts on quite a show. Less numerous but as showy are the salt marsh asters (*Aster tenuifolius*), whose white flowers have just a hint of purple to contrast with the numerous cluster of bright yellow stamens in their centers, and the pink, somewhat funnel-shaped flowers of seaside gerardia (*Gerardia maritima*). Another form of pale purple flower can be seen on sea rocket (*Cakile edentula*), and a hand lens is useful for finding the small, inconspicuous flowers on the glassworts (*Salicornia* spp.).

For those naturalists who would like to learn to distinguish the various upper marsh grasses from one another, early autumn is a good time. Flowers or seeds can be found on all the four dominant marsh grasses: cordgrass (*Spartina alterniflora*); salt hay (*Spartina patens*); black grass (*Juncus gerardi*); and spike grass (*Distichlis spicata*). The wide-bladed cordgrass is easy to pick out any time of year. It's the other three, growing in the high marsh or salt meadow area, that can be tricky to distinguish. Black grass, actually a rush, has very dark seeds. Salt hay's seeds are arranged like the teeth on a comb. Spike grass can be picked out from quite a distance by its yellowish flowers. When you have identified each, examine their leaves and other aspects of the plant to aid in identification at other times of the year.

There are other interesting plants in the upland area on your left to look for. Beach plum, Virginia rose, red cedar, the ubiquitous poison ivy, and cat briar can be found, as well as a species of oak best-suited for life on the edge of the sea: post oak (*Quercus stellata*). The sprawling post oak specimen at (2) is twice as wide as it is tall, a growth strategy to minimize exposure to salt-laden and desiccating winds.

Along your hike, look for evidence of the marsh grasses trying to colonize the path. As with beach grass, these grasses (and the rush) rely mostly on horizontal rhizomes, not seeds, to reproduce and invade new areas. Note that many of the specimens growing into the path from the adjacent marsh form a straight line. Digging down into the sand between two plants will reveal a horizontal rhizome: these are all connected.

At (3), where the footpath ends, continue to follow the edge of the marsh along a sandy road, passing a clump of one of our largest grasses at (4). This is phragmites, or common reed grass, distinguishable from a distance by its height and large, attractive plumes of purplish flowers. An aggressive grass, it can spread via horizontal rhizomes at a rate that is measured in meters, not inches, per year. Tanbark Creek, at the far south end of the harbor, is choked with this plant, yet Goose Creek remains relatively phragmites-free.

You may have noticed small, quarter-sized holes in the path. These become quite numerous as you approach the tip of the spit's hook (5) near the eastern inlet of Goose Creek (there's a western inlet not far from the osprey pole). These are the burrows of the fiddler crab (*Uca* spp.), an important, year-round resident of the salt marsh. Their first pair of legs end in a spoon-like structure specifically designed for scraping algae and nutritious bacteria off the surface off plants, detritus, mud, and sand. Male fiddlers have to make do with one feeding structure, the other of the pair having developed into an impressively oversized claw whose sole function is to attract mates. These air-breathing crabs retreat to their burrows and are generally inactive during the high tide cycle, but I have seen them moving about underwater.

Between (5) and (7) the path gradually leaves the salt marsh and enters the dune community. Look for some unusual, out-of-place shrubs, including a dogwood (6) and several smooth sumacs. And don't miss the large patch of prickly pear cactus (*Opuntia humifusa*), our only native representative of this group of desert specialists. Low growth habit, large water storage capacity, low surface-area-to-volume, and no leaves (photosynthesis occurs in the chlorophyll-filled stems) are all adaptations for living in dry, sandy soil. Their stem joints also tend orient their flat surfaces to the east or west, anything but an intense southern exposure. These special adaptations come at a cost: this plant grows very slowly. (Note: its low growth habit has enabled it to thrive along the mowed shoulder of Sammy's Beach Road.)

At (7), turn left to return via the inland route, which passes through the middle of the old dredge spoil area and the beach grass plantings. Or continue straight and return via the bay beach to enjoy views north to Orient Point, Plum Island, and beyond to Connecticut.

Directions: From Rte. 27 in East Hampton Village, travel north on North Main Street, bearing left at its intersection of Springs Fireplace Road and Three Mile Harbor Road. Continue north on the latter for a mile and turn left onto Springy Banks Road. Follow Springy Banks, a winding road that changes (without making any obvious turns) into Hands Creek Road, Alewive Brook Road, and Old House Landing Road over the course of approximately 3 miles from Three Mile Harbor Road. Travel another 0.75 mile and turn right onto Sammy's Beach Road. Follow this until it ends in a small parking area on Gardiner's Bay.

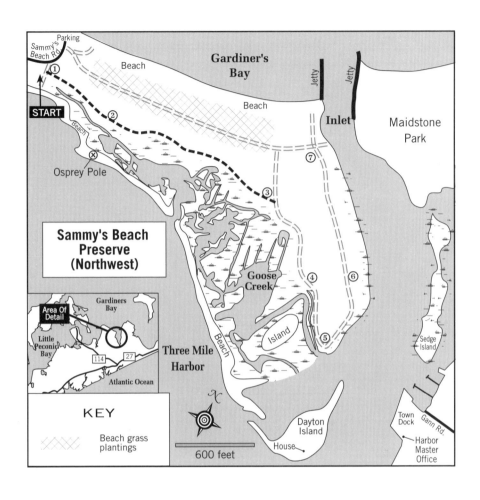

Sammy's Beach Preserve (Northwest)

Gardiner's Bay

Parking

Sammy's Beach Rd.

① Beach

START

Beach

② Beach

Osprey Pole ⊗

Jetty Jetty

Inlet

Maidstone Park

⑦

③

Gardiners Bay

Area Of Detail

Little Peconic Bay

114 27

Atlantic Ocean

Three Mile Harbor

Beach

Goose Creek ④ ⑥

Island

⑤

Sedge Island

Dayton Island

House

Town Dock

Gann Rd.

Harbor Master Office

KEY

Beach grass plantings

600 feet

SPRINGS

AMAGANSETT

Paumanok Path:

Stony Hill Section

From the town parking area near Boat Yard Road–East Hampton Marina, walk south on Three Mile Harbor Road and turn left onto Karlsruhe/Cross Highway (1). This road is anything but a highway. Although this town trustee road technically extends clear across to Springs Fireplace Road, after 200 yards the pavement ends and the "highway" looks no different than the adjacent oak–hickory forest. At this point the trail, a narrow footpath, meanders along the wooded right-of-way with houses to the left and right, crossing Mashie Drive and continuing out to Springs Fireplace Road as a well buffered trail.

Within sight of Springs Fireplace Road the trail swings left and parallels the busy road just inside the woods to Shadom Lane. Cross Springs Fireplace Road and turn left (north) following the Paumanok Path blazes along the asphalt sidewalk for approximately 250 yards to a footpath that enters the woods on the right (2). This is the Peconic Land Trust's Accabonac Preserve, whose trail system is described in detail elsewhere in the book.

The Paumanok Path intersects with several other well worn trails in the preserve; a left at the first one (3) leads to an old brush dump partly revegetated with an assortment of non-native vegetation. The open area here is a good place to spot a red-tailed hawk soaring overhead. At (4) the trail winds through a nearly pure stand of American beech. Note this trees shallow root system which you can often feel underfoot, and the number of small saplings under larger trees. A careful look at the saplings reveals that many are clones growing out of the root systems of larger trees, a common reproductive strategy employed by beeches.

The beech grove ends at an old woods roadbed which the trail briefly follows (5). A portion of the roadbed may have been excavated at one time for fill; the sandy soil in this area is being colonized by pitch pine, beach heather, bearberry, and reindeer lichen. Leaving the roadbed, follow the blazes onto a narrow footpath that links to another old woods road, one of many established in the Stony Hill area to harvest wood. Woodcutting was an important commercial activity here dating back to the 1700s when cordwood was transported onto sailing vessels at landings on Gardiner's Bay and shipped to New York City and Connecticut.

Leaving the woods road, the trail winds its way down into a kettlehole and by a large American holly before reaching Accabonac Road. Cross the road and walk 0.5 mile along unpaved Stony Hill Road to a trail entrance on the left (6). This is the old Archery Trail which traverses the largest privately-owned forest east of Route 114. Permission was secured from the landowners to allow public access on the 0.8-mile-long Archery Trail, which derives its name from its use as a kind of par course with archery targets set up at intervals along the trail. The mixed hardwood forest here includes many American beech trees, and is as pleasant an area to hike through as any on the South Fork. Keep in mind that the trail and surrounding forest remain private property, and enjoy!

The Paumanok Path leaves the Archery Trail with an abrupt right turn (7), and skirts around the top of the spectacular Baker kettlehole before entering a narrow (30-foot wide) subdivision reserve area for the remaining 0.5 mile to Old Stone Highway. This section of the trail, although still meandering through the beautiful Stony Hill forest, has been severely comprised by the lack of a suitable buffer from adjacent residential development, particularly a hideous, ten-foot-high cyclone fence.

In addition to being part of the Paumanok Path, this is the westernmost section of the two mile long George Sid Miller, Jr. Trail. George Sid was an avid horseback rider and, among many other things, chaired the town's Planning Board in the early 1980s. In this capacity, he was an early advocate of protecting trail linkages from residential subdivision developments. Without his efforts, particularly his diplomatic persuasiveness, it might not have been possible to route the Paumanok Path through sections of East Hampton Town.

Further along the trail, look for the white oak lop or boundary tree near the top of a slight rise (8) and, not far from there on the right side of the trail, an old fox den. In the hollow just this side of Old Stone Highway is a large black (or sweet) birch, unusual for the Stony Hill area.

On the east side of Old Stone Highway, the trail climbs up and then drops down into a clay pit (9), one of three along the trail in this area. The clay pits were dug in soils containing a high percentage of clay material, enough to enable a craftsman to form loaves which were baked in kilns to create bricks. The resulting excavation somewhat resembles one-half of a kettlehole, so much so that a hiker may think they are passing by a natural formation dating back 10,000 years! According to town records the clay pits were dug in the early 1700s, allegedly by an Isaac Barnes for whom Barnes Hole Road and Barnes Landing are named, and the brick kilns here created material for building Clinton Academy in East Hampton Village. Very likely, for hundreds of years before Mr. Barnes, the Montauketts collected a limited amount of clay for their pottery: eating, drinking, cooking, and storage vessels. A monument about the brick kilns, and two chunks of rejected bricks, can be found on Fresh Pond Road, a short distance west (right) of where the trail crosses (18).

Crossing the old Bell Estate driveway (10), now closed to vehicles, the trail passes between two huge sassafras trees and through a small field of New York ferns before climbing up and around the edge of the second clay pit (11). Here, set among a beautiful grove of American beech trees, the hiker is rewarded with a dramatic view down into the now reforested pit.

After crossing Albert's Landing Road, the trail passes by a large birch tree (12) whose exact species is a matter of debate. Our common whitish-barked birch is the gray birch (*Betula populifolia*), a smallish many-trunked tree growing in wet soils and old fields, with a triangular-shaped leaf and lacking the distinctive peeling bark of the paper or white birch (*Betula papyrifera*), not common to the east end. This specimen has the leaf characteristics and growth form of a paper birch yet the bark, although it is peeling, does not form the large, loose sheets of bark for which this species is renowned. At any rate, it's definitely not a gray birch. I've been calling it a paper birch but I wouldn't be surprised if a knowledgeable botanist keyed it out as a European white birch (*Betula pendula*) which apparently has some characteristics of both. Given the stature of this specimen, we had Ray Smith, a local arborist, cable the two trunks together to keep it around longer.

Just after the birch, the trail joins an old woods road and winds through a pleasant oak–beech forest with scattered American hollies adding some greenery in the winter months. Don't miss the sharp left turn at a junction of three trails (13): continuing straight will take you out to Fresh Pond Road not far from the South Fork Golf Course. Just beyond a large patch of ground pines (14), a lycopodium or clubmoss resembling a small Christmas tree, the trail crosses one of the many roads named "Cross Highway" in East Hampton and enters Fresh Pond Town Park. The 130-acre park is comprised of forest, swamp, marsh, creek, sandy bayfront beach, and tidal (not fresh) pond. A view of the phragmites-choked head of the pond can be had through the leafless trees (15). The third of the clay pits (16), this one frequented by red foxes seeking denning sites along the steeply sloped edges, is encountered before another woods road leads you out to Fresh Pond Road. Just before reaching the road, note a footpath to the left (17) that leads to the picnic area and restrooms at Fresh Pond Park. Be sure to walk the hundred or so feet west along the paved road to the brick kiln monument (18) before continuing on.

Directions to Start of Trail: From Montauk Highway in East Hampton Village, turn north onto North Main Street, through the traffic light at Cedar Street, and take the left fork where North Main turns into Three Mile Harbor Road. Continue north on Three Mile Harbor Road for 1.8 miles and look for a marina/boat basin on your left; turn left there (Boatyard Road) and park. Town restroom facilities are nearby. The trail begins at the intersection of Three Mile Harbor Road and Karlsruhe/Cross Highway, just a short walk south of the marina.

Directions to End of Trail: See directions to the start of Paumanok Path: Napeague Section.

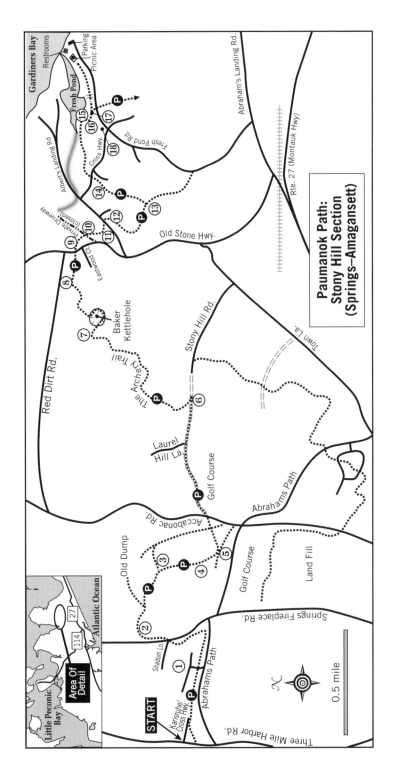

**Paumanok Path:
Stony Hill Section
(Springs–Amagansett)**

Gardiners Bay

Restrooms

Parking

Picnic Area

Fresh Pond

Alberts Landing Rd.

Private Driveway (closed)

Easswood Ct.

Cross Hwy.

Fresh Pond Rd.

Abraham's Landing Rd.

Rte. 27 (Montauk Hwy)

Old Stone Hwy.

Red Dirt Rd.

Baker Kettlehole

The Archery Trail

Stony Hill Rd.

Town La.

Laurel Hill La.

Golf Course

Abrahams Path

Accabonac Rd.

Golf Course

Land Fill

Old Dump

Springs Fireplace Rd.

Shadom Ln.

Abrahams Path

Karlsruhel Cross Hwy.

Three Mile Harbor Rd.

START

0.5 mile

Little Peconic Bay

114

27

Atlantic Ocean

Area Of Detail

163

Springs Woodblock Preserve

Deep in the heart of the Springs, nearly completely surrounded by dense residential development, lies a mosaic of woods and fields dotted with cedars. One of the few remnants of Springs' rural past, the 75-acre block of open space is the centerpiece of a system of greenbelt trails totaling three miles in length. Until the mid-1990s this small gem and its unmarked trails, visited mostly by adjacent neighbors, were little known to local environmental groups, town planners, and even most Springs residents.

Fortunately, that situation has changed. Two neighbors, not willing to wait until a development proposal threatened the area, took a proactive approach to its protection. Krae van Sickle and Nancy Kane, both trail enthusiasts and open space advocates, worked with the Group for the South Fork to produce the Springs Woodblock Study. The study mapped the trails and vacant land and outlined two alternative strategies for their long-term preservation. The study, along with endorsements from a variety of organizations, was presented to the town and eventually adopted as a town planning goal.

Subsequently, 40 acres were preserved through public acquisition with another 30 targeted for purchase. The effort had another equally important but unforeseen consequence: a broadening of preservation efforts in the Springs area. For many years, preservation and acquisition efforts in the Springs focused on wetlands and waterfront parcels. The Springs Woodblock project became the catalyst for other woodland preservation initiatives in the hamlet, such as Jacobs Farm and the Lassaw property.

One other interesting item pertaining to the Woodblock Study is worth mentioning. Krae is a successful local realtor and Nancy's family is in the construction business. Some readers might find this ironic and surprising, but those familiar with open space preservation in East Hampton will not. This is one of many examples, large and small, where the environmental and business interests have successfully worked together for the good of the broader community. The local business community has been one of our best allies in open space protection efforts, including the real estate transfer tax and Peconic Estuary Program.

There are a half-dozen places to access the Springs Woodblock trail system. One of the most convenient is the access off of Three Mile Harbor

Road–Hog Creek Highway near the Maidstone Market (1). In fact, the trail continues along the road shoulder to link with the Market, where hikers can quench a thirst and enjoy a bite to eat.

Head into the woods on a well-worn path that was protected by the Town Planning Board many years ago as part of the Talmage Farm subdivision. At the time, little emphasis was placed on protecting wildlife habitat, and the preserved greenbelts that crisscross the subdivision are barely wide enough to accommodate the trail. In many areas the greenbelt is only 20 feet wide, yet the trail system, directly accessible to all seventy lots in the subdivision, is a nice feature of the neighborhood.

According to several members of the East Hampton Trails Preservation Society who have checked the deeds, not all the trails that were protected from development are open to the general public; some have access limited to residents of the adjacent area. Turn left at the first trail intersection to continue on the public portion (2), and skirt the edge of an old field to the left. This is one of two vacant parcels in the area that has been targeted for public acquisition and preservation.

The trail soon turns right and the greenbelt widens considerably. Look for lopped trees on the left between here (3) and (5). These are easy to pick out: two or three from the ground the trunk veers off to one side, grows parallel to the ground for a few feet, and then makes another right angle to grow straight upwards again. Also called "boundary trees" because they mark the edge of different properties, lopped trees are not uncommon sights on the South Fork.

The unusual growth form is man-made. Young, pliable saplings were simply bent over and pinned to the ground; larger trees were apparently notched on one side to facilitate bending the trunk parallel to the ground. I'm not sure how large a tree this could be done to. Over time, since plants have a habit of growing toward sunlight, the trunk will curve upward perpendicular to the ground once again (or one of the larger lateral branches will take over as the main trunk). Wait a few decades and, providing the tree survives the abuse, you'll have a genuine lopped tree.

Why was this done? In the fall 2001 issue of the *Long Island Botanical Society* newsletter, author Philip Marshall sheds some light on the matter. In pre-colonial times, Native Americans in the midwest did this to mark trails, but apparently there is no documentation of the practice among the Montaukett or Shinnecock. Early settlers adopted the practice from the British tradition of farm hedges, creating a form of living, inexpensive livestock fencing. Small trees, saplings, and shrubs were bent over and their branches and trunks woven together to make a thick, impenetrable fence. Eastern Long Island, as was the case with Great Britain earlier, was largely cleared of forest by mid-1700. Wood for post and rail fencing was expensive!

At (4) continue straight ahead. The trail to the left, although well used, traverses private property. The acquisition of an easement would allow a trail link to the Wildflower subdivision greenbelt. At the next intersection (5) again continue straight along the edge of an old hedgerow to the T intersection at (6). A right turn here leads out to Talmage Farm Lane but could someday provide a link to The Nature Conservancy's Merrill-Lake Preserve and Accabonac Harbor. It is currently just one easement and 250 feet shy!

For now, turn left and follow the narrow, winding trail that loops through an old pasture slowly reverting back to forest. Turn left at (7). Note the clumps of little bluestem grasses, a very attractive native grass and an excellent forage for livestock, interspersed among the early successional woody plants. Bayberry, black cherry, and eastern red cedar are the pioneers that begin the process of changing the herbaceous field to woody forest. Already, a number of oaks have invaded from the nearby forest.

Back at (5), retrace your steps to the start. Directly across Three Mile Harbor Road from the starting point is the 372-acre Camp Blue Jay property owned by the Girl Scouts of Nassau County. This is now the largest developable parcel in the Town of East Hampton. With large wooded areas and extensive bluffs bordering Gardiner's Bay, this would make an excellent addition to the town's park system. Its acquisition would also allow the Woodblock Trail system to connect west to Gardiner's Bay, Maidstone Park, and Three Mile Harbor.

Although much work remains to be done, trails and open space advocates are hopeful that the existing Woodblock Trail will someday be expanded to traverse the entire Springs peninsula: from Accabonac to Gardiner's Bay and Three Mile Harbor.

Directions: From East Hampton Village, head north on North Main Street, which after bearing left soon becomes Three Mile Harbor Road. Continue straight for approximately four miles. Look for Fort Pond Blvd. and the Maidstone Market on the right. Park on the shoulder just past the Maidstone Market and follow a path along the shoulder to where the foot path makes a right turn, leaves the road, and enters the woods (1 on the accompanying map).

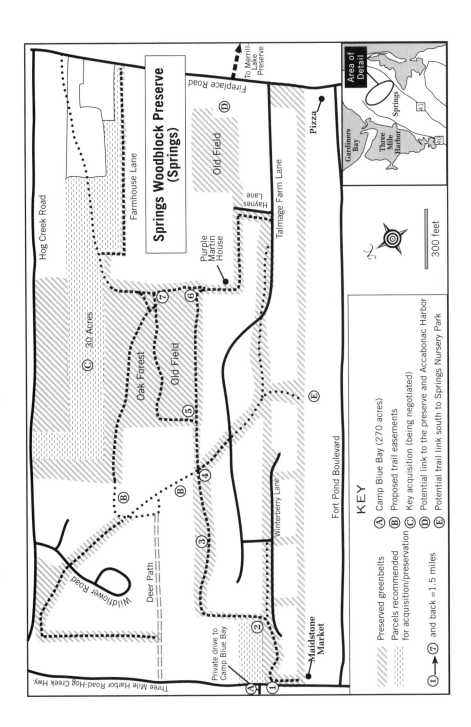

Springs Woodblock Preserve
(Springs)

Hog Creek Road

Farmhouse Lane

Old Field

To Merrill-
Lake
Preserve

Fireplace Road

Pizza

Haynes Lane

Talmage Farm Lane

Purple Martin House

30 Acres

Oak Forest

Old Field

© C

⑦

⑥

⑤

Fort Pond Boulevard

Ⓔ

Ⓑ

Ⓑ

④

③

Winterberry Lane

Deer Path

Wildflower Road

Private drive to Camp Blue Bay

②

Maidstone Market

Three Mile Harbor–Hog Creek Hwy.

Ⓐ

①

Area of Detail

Gardiners Bay

Three Mile Harbor

Springs

41

Accabonac Harbor

KEY

Preserved greenbelts

Parcels recommended for acquisition/preservation

Ⓐ Camp Blue Bay (270 acres)

Ⓑ Proposed trail easements

Ⓒ Key acquisition (being negotiated)

Ⓓ Potential link to the preserve and Accabonac Harbor

Ⓔ Potential trail link south to Springs Nursery Park

①⟶⑦ and back =1.5 miles

300 feet

167

ACCABONAC PRESERVE

To those familiar with the area, the words "Accabonac Preserve" generally conjure up images of salt marshes dotted with oak hummocks, long vistas over placid embayments, and osprey, herons, and terns seeking their scaly prey on wing and foot.

Wedged between Springs–Fireplace and Accabonac Roads at the southern border of the Springs, the Peconic Land Trust's Accabonac Preserve is actually quite far removed from the coastal scene described above. With the exception of an occasional gull passing overhead en route to the nearby landfill, first time visitors to this woodland preserve might be disappointed to find no easily viewed marsh wildlife or waterfront vistas over the beautiful harbor that bears the same name. Even in winter, with its forested landscape stripped of leaves, the distant harbor is out of view.

Yet with its classic knob-and-kettle topography and extensive trail system, the preserve is definitely worth visiting. Two miles of trails criss-cross the oak-dominated forest; stands of American beech, red maples, pitch pines, and mountain laurel add some interesting diversity for the hiker.

Nestled on the northern flank of the Ronkonkoma moraine, the 90-acre preserve is part of a larger assemblage of morainal woodlands and trails extending eastward to Old Stone Highway and referred to as Stony Hill. Much of the easternmost portion of Stony Hill was once part of the Bell Estate. It was subdivided into large residential lots, destroying much of the ecological integrity of the forest as the parcels were cleared and built, although a series of narrow greenbelt trail corridors were preserved in the planning review process.

The bulk of the remaining forest is being protected by a few dedicated and generous landowners working with the Peconic Land Trust. Funding to acquire the Accabonac Preserve property was made available by one such generous landowner who wishes to remain anonymous. The sellers, the Potter family, certainly deserve thanks for enabling the preservation plan to move forward. The deal, which closed just a few years ago, added a significant forest preserve at no public cost to the Springs hamlet, an area whose residents are becoming increasingly concerned about residential sprawl.

Other than moving a house that was slated for demolition onto the preserve's northwestern corner (to provide housing for staff working at the Land Trust's nearby Quail Hill organic farm), it appears that the Land Trust is intent on keeping the remainder of the property undeveloped. The Group for the South Fork, working with the East Hampton Trails Preservation Society, contacted the Land Trust soon after the acquisition was made public to seek permission to establish a public trail system on the property. The request was received favorably, and GSF staff began mapping and inventorying the network of old woods roads, and footpaths. A mile-long loop trail and mile-long section of the Paumanok Path were opened in the spring of 2002.

For those wishing to take a hike on the Preserve, I suggest parking near the intersection of Stony Hill Road and Accabonac Road, and beginning your walk there (1). The one-mile-long loop is easily followed and showcases some of the more interesting aspects of the Preserve.

Look for the footpath, marked with the white rectangular blazes of the Paumanok Path, directly across Accabonac Road from Stony Hill Road. A short distance into the woods the route veers right and works its way down into a deep kettlehole, passing close by a large American holly before ascending the far end of the kettle. A hundred yards further, as you approach the intersection with a wide woods road (2), look for a small, inconspicuous evergreen shrub called sheep laurel. Turn left onto the road, continuing to follow the white blazes.

Approximately 150 yards along the old road the trail turns right onto a narrow footpath (3) and down into another kettlehole. As you begin climbing again, you might notice a small pit on the left. Although the Stony Hill area was a popular spot for digging clay to make bricks many years ago, my guess is this was a sandpit. Foxes have made use of the embankments of these pits to excavate their dens.

Passing under a large sprawling pitch pine, the trail leads onto another wide roadbed, this one not shaded by the adjacent forest canopy but open to the sunlight. Its loose sandy soils have been colonized by a variety of sun-loving plants commonly found in the back dune community of our bay and ocean beaches: beach heather, bearberry, and reindeer lichen (4).

Many of these old roads traversing the Stony Hill forest were created by woodcutters. The forest was divided up into small woodlots that provided the early residents of Amagansett and Springs with fuel. Later, sometime in the 1700s, commercial harvesting began with cutters using draft horses to harvest wood during the winter months. Cordwood was piled up at landings along Gardiner's Bay to be shipped by boat to New York City and Connecticut. The last commercial woodcutter in the Stony Hill area, Bart Hadell, sold his woodlot (located just east of here) to Evan Frankel in the 1950s.

Heading west, the forest edge quickly closes in on the narrowing road-bed, and the route swings right into a beautiful grove of American beech (5). Beech leaves are extremely shade-tolerant, so these trees have no need to self-prune, or lose their lower branches as oaks, hickories, and pines do. Therefore, beech trees have many layers of leaf-bearing branches that cast a dark shadow on the forest floor. As a result of this and the beech's surface-feeding roots, the forest floor beneath a grove of beeches is largely devoid of a shrub or herbaceous layer. This makes for easy walking on or off a trail, as is the case here.

The trail soon emerges from the beech grove and reenters the oak forest. Another trail is intersected at (6). The Paumanok Path swings left and eventually leads to Springs–Fireplace Road (8). Halfway there is another unmarked but well-worn trail (9) that leads to the edge of the old town brush dump (10), recently dubbed Accabonac Meadows by the neighbors.

To complete the loop, leave the Paumanok Path at (6) by turning right onto the unmarked trail. It gradually ascends a hill, turns north, then descends to the old woods road you were on earlier (7). Turn right on the road and follow it back to the spur trail (2) that leads to Stony Hill Road and your starting point.

Directions: Take Rte. 27 into East Hampton Village. Turn north (left if east-bound) at the traffic light near the East Hampton Post Office onto Accabonac Road. Follow Accabonac Road, passing the landfill and a golf course on the left, and across Abraham's Path. The first right after Abraham's Path is Stony Hill Road; turn right on this dirt road and park on the road shoulder.

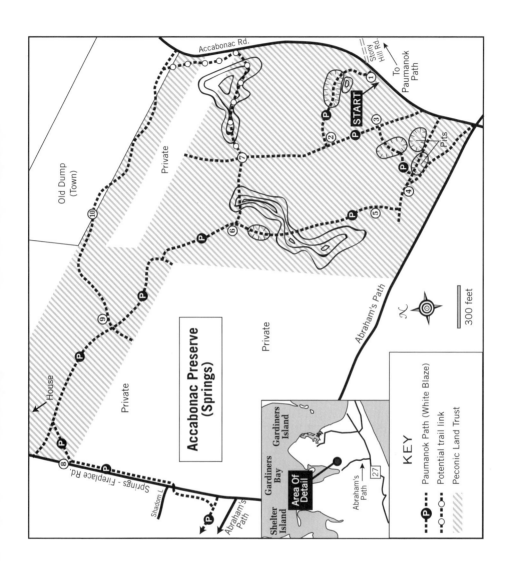

Accabonac Preserve (Springs)

KEY

- ▪▪▪P▪▪▪ Paumanok Path (White Blaze)
- ▪▪O▪▪O▪ Potential trail link
- ░░░ Peconic Land Trust

Abraham's Path

27

Gardiners Island

Gardiners Bay

Shelter Island

Area Of Detail

300 feet

N

Accabonac Rd.

Stony Hill Rd.

To Paumanok Path

START

Pits

Abraham's Path

Old Dump (Town)

Private

Private

Private

House

Springs - Fireplace Rd.

Shadom L.

Abraham's Path

NAPEAGUE

MONTAUK

Paumanok Path:

Napeague Section

This six-mile section of the Paumanok Path begins at Fresh Pond Park, traverses the eastern flank of the Stony Hill forest, and then descends the moraine onto the Napeague isthmus. Crossing Napeague, a low-lying spit of sand connecting Amagansett and Montauk, the route winds its way among pitch pine forests, dunes, and cranberry bogs to the extensive salt marshes on the southern shore of Napeague Harbor, and ends at the entrance to the famous walking dunes area of Hither Hills State Park: quite a diverse and interesting section of trail!

Starting from the parking area at Fresh Pond Park, walk along the dirt road separating the shaded picnic area from an open field. The trail is a link to the Paumanok Path and therefore not blazed with the white rectangular markers. Look for the trail at the far end of the dirt road, close to the latter's intersection with Fresh Pond Road, where it enters a thicket on your right (1). Much of this link trail hugs the edge of a wide band of wetland shrubs that effectively screen the nearby pond from view, but there are several glimpses over portions of the pond. The trail crosses a dirt road (2) that provides access to the pond's southwestern end, a short 100-yard diversion that you might consider.

The 129-acre Fresh Pond Park was once part of the Dennistoun M. Bell estate, a spread of 685 acres. The park was established by Mr. Bell in 1952, with the provision the town maintain an open channel between Fresh Pond and Gardiner's Bay. Fresh Pond is actually brackish, and a small salt marsh can be found at its eastern end where an osprey nest is located.

At the intersection with the Paumanok Path, turn left and cross Fresh Pond Road. A short distance further, the trail leads up to a cemetery with a single grave marked by two stones (a headstone and a footstone), that of Isaac Conkling, buried in 1744 at age 32 (3). The next 0.5 mile of trail winds through a wooded reserve area and over a paved cul-de-sac created as part of the Fresh Pond at Devon subdivision.

The narrow forest trail joins the unpaved section of Cross Highway to Devon (4) over a quarter-mile stretch to Abraham's Landing Road. Crossing the pavement, the trail continues over another unopened section of Cross

Highway for a short distance to where the road bearing that name is paved (5). There, a third of a mile of road walking is necessary along Cross Highway to Cranberry Hole Road. Turn left onto the latter, being sure to hug the shoulder as this is a dangerous section of roadway with very limited sight distance. Within fifty yards of Cross Highway, on the right (south) side of Cranberry Hole Road, the trail turns right onto a narrow, rough, dirt road which is actually the original wagon route across Napeague—Old Montauk Highway (6).

The Paumanok Path essentially follows the historic Old Montauk Highway route for the next 2.5 miles. Prior to 1911, what is now the Paumanok Path and the eastern portion of Napeague Meadow Road was in fact Old Montauk Highway. Diagonaling down the face of what was once the ocean bluffs or Amagansett headland, the trail levels off in a forest of pitch pines on the low-lying Napeague isthmus.

After the glacial ice sheet receded from this area a line of glacial deposits, stretching from present-day Brooklyn northeast to Cape Cod, was left behind. Known as the Ronkonkoma moraine, it had several extensive low points which, as the ice continued to melt and sea level rose, became submerged, creating several islands along the morainal chain: Montauk, Block, Martha's Vineyard, and Nantucket. The latter three remain islands to this day; Montauk, of course, is not. As a result of three thousand years of shoreline currents (littoral drift) at work, sandy spits grew eastward from Amagansett and westward from Montauk, eventually connecting the two and creating a three-square-mile area of dunes, cranberry bogs, freshwater marshes and swamps, extensive salt meadows, and a shallow estuary (Napeague Harbor). Perhaps in acknowledgement of its mosaic of marshes and dunes, the Montaukett Indians named the area Napeague, which roughly translates as "waterland."

The first evidence of this waterland is found a half-mile from Cranberry Hole Road, where the surface of Old Montauk Highway is so close to the water table that cranberries flourish in the roadbed. Over the next quarter mile, a variety of freshwater wetland plants are found in and alongside the roadbed: star and sphagnum mosses, switch grass and Canada rush, highbush blueberry, sweet pepperbush, swamp azalea, and inkberry. This section of trail can be quite wet in the spring. On your right, several openings in the shrub thicket (mostly deer trails) overlook an even lower marsh area. A close examination of this marsh reveals it to be a sharp-edged, linear wetland with a striking resemblance in width and orientation to the Old Montauk Highway roadbed, which it parallels. Actually, the marsh was the old roadbed:

sometime in the 1960s the town highway superintendent took a bulldozer through the area to open up the overgrown roadbed, removing enough soil in the process to expose the water table and create perfect conditions for a bog to develop. Since the old roadbed was now underwater most of the year, vehicles traveling through steered a course over the relatively drier area on the north side of the impassable wetland; this reroute is the trail we are using today.

A similar situation is found at (7), where the trail/road swings north to avoid a bog, complete with insectivorous plants and rare orchids, created compliments of the highway department. Here the trail is forced up onto the flank of the northernmost of the two relic dune systems found in the interior of Napeague. In the distant past, each of these dune ridges (clearly visible on aerial photos even today) were the primary dunes marking the ocean shoreline. This relic oceanfront dune is now more than a half-mile inland from the Atlantic Ocean and the current primary dune. The dune's soft sands make for tiring hiking, but the open landscape, covered with low-growing beach heather, bearberry, and reindeer lichen, and dotted with pitch pines, is quite beautiful.

At the point where the trail crosses an abandoned railway (8), you are standing in the middle of the 1500-acre Napeague State Park, roughly equidistant from the ocean and the bay. The LIRR was extended through Napeague to Montauk in 1895. This spur railway connected the main LIRR line with several fish factories located at an area of Napeague that became known as the Promised Land. By the late 1800s, there were ten fish factories operating in the Napeague area. The factories rendered menhaden, a bony and oily fish once found in huge schools in this area, into a valuable oil used in paints, cosmetics, and lubricants. The rendering process also produced a powerful odor that prompted passers by to exclaim that the area "stank to high heaven" and that led to the biblical place name "Promised Land."

The last of the fish processing plants closed in 1968, and in 1976 The Nature Conservancy negotiated the acquisition of most of the Smith Meal Company and Hanson Trust Ltd. holdings. TNC held the property for a year until the state could come up with funding; in 1977 the 1,364 acres became Napeague State Park.

East of the railway, the trailside scenery reverses itself with the upland pine forest to the right (south) and freshwater wetlands largely to the left. At (9) the Paumanok Path leaves the roadbed to avoid a stretch that is often wet and follows a narrow foot trail winding through the pitch pines, across the LIPA substation access driveway, and onto an overgrown unpaved powerline service road (10), which becomes less and less distinct as you head east through duneland. A series of old utility poles cut off 3–4 feet above ground act as unattractive but sturdy trail markers.

There is a short (0.2 mile) section of road walking along Napeague Meadow Road: look for kestrels, our smallest falcons, often perched on the telephone lines nearby, and red tailed hawks, often soaring above the salt meadows. These birds of prey are around all year while another aerial predator, the osprey, is visible from April to August. See if you can pick out the latter's nest built on the steel radio tower.

Turn down the driveway towards the Art Barge, a landmark on the south shore of Napeague Harbor where classes in painting and photography are held during the summer. Just before reaching its parking area, turn right onto a foot path through the dunes and onto the harbor beach. The next half mile is a delightful beach stroll along one of the prettiest embayments on the east end, with two simple bridges spanning small tidal creeks that empty into the harbor. The winds and tides are constantly changing the face of the beach, and each visit has at least one new surprise in store. On one visit, the shore was littered with thousands of small horseshoe crab shells, castoffs from a recent molt.

Approximately 100 yards after the second bridge, leave the beach via an unpaved road used by baymen to access fishing and hunting areas along the harbor (11). Follow this road out to Napeague Harbor Road, where the trail crosses and enters Hither Hills State Park.

Directions to Start of Trail: From Rte. 27 just east of the Amagansett Train Station, turn onto Abraham's Landing Rd., cross over the train tracks and continue straight, passing a lumber yard on the right. Take the first left onto Fresh Pond Rd. and follow this winding road for 1.5 miles to a parking area overlooking Gardiner's Bay. (During the summer, visitors lacking a Town of East Hampton parking permit should park on the shoulder of Fresh Pond Rd. where it intersects the Paumanok Path... approximately 0.4 mile further back., where you will see three boulders on your right)

Directions to End of Trail: See directions to the start of Paumanok Path: Hither Woods Section.

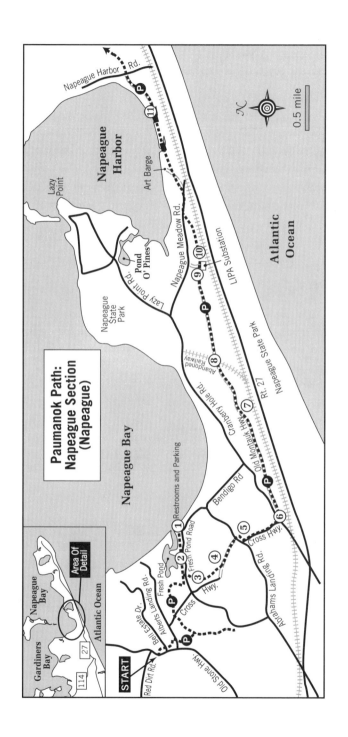

179

WALKING DUNES

This one-mile loop trail has something for everyone to enjoy: fascinating landforms, a wide variety of plant communities, animal tracks, and exceptional scenic vistas. It is also my favorite area for nature interpretation—that is, figuring out why certain plants are growing where they are and what the area might look like in the near future. Dune, freshwater wetland, forest, and coastal shrub plant communities all interact and are rapidly changing in a very compact area. But before we describe the interesting sights along the trail, let's first discuss the walking dunes in general.

This area contains three parabolic dunes, each similarly shaped, yet due to varying degrees of stabilization, with a very distinct character. The southernmost dune can be seen from Montauk Highway just west of the Old Montauk Highway intersection. Lying north of the railroad, and nearly spilling onto the tracks, this and the middle parabolic dune have extensive forest cover and are fairly well-stabilized. We will traverse the northernmost dune, which is least stabilized, has large areas lacking any plant cover at all, and is still moving or "walking" towards the southeast.

All three dunes were formed of the same ingredients and are driven by the same forces, namely:

- a tremendous quantity of sand, readily supplied by the eroding bluffs of Hither Woods' north shore and transported to Goff Point by the longshore currents of Gardiner's Bay;
- brisk northwesterly winds which carry the sands at Goff Point further inland; and
- vegetation which intercepts the wind-blown sand, causing it to pile up into a dune.

These parabolic dunes are only about 100 years old. U.S. Coastal Survey maps dated 1842 show this area as being relatively flat and wooded. Although we have uncovered many of the ingredients of a walking dune, Mother Nature has yet to reveal the entire recipe. It remains a mystery as to why three dunes were formed—no more, no less—and what catalysts started the whole dune-building process in motion. One theory is that these were originally typical linear coastal dunes located along the Gardiner's Bay and Napeague Harbor shorelines and were set in motion by wood cutting and clearing activities associated with the old fish factories in this area. Fish factories consumed large quantities of wood in the process of rendering oil from bunker or menhaden. (The first fish factory in the area was built at Goff Point in 1858. Twenty years later there were three operating on the east shore of Napeague Harbor.) Another theory maintains that each parabolic dune represents the sand of a former beach. This follows the concept that the Goff Point area was built by a succession of beaches, each one representing a recurved spit pointed west. Interestingly, while all the ingredients and forces identified above are evident today, a fourth walking dune has yet to form.

The trail begins on the opposite side of the parking lot from the water. The numbered points in the text and on the map correspond to numbered trail markers; lettered points (A through D) correspond to interesting points along the trail that are not identified with trail markers. Within the first 100 feet you should be able to find poison ivy, a good plant to know by sight, and two similar species easily distinguished by even the novice botanist (1).

Poison ivy (*Rhus radicans*) is best identified by its compound leaves which bear three shiny smooth-edged leaflets. All parts of the plant (roots, leaves, berries, and stems) contain the poisonous oil which is long-lived and difficult to remove. People are often infected by handling articles of clothing on which the oil has collected. There have even been cases of botanists contracting a rash after handling dried herbarium specimens that were 100 years old! If you think you may have come in contact with this plant, wash your skin (and clothing) with a strong soap. Be sure to scrub under the fingernails, a place where the oil can collect and spread while scratching.

Poison ivy is adaptable to many soil conditions. Its seeds are distributed by flickers and other birds that eat its small grayish-white berries. Once established, it persists even in deep shade. Shaded plants rarely produce berries; rather, they spread extensively by underground runners.

Similar to poison ivy, and often found growing with it, Virginia creeper (*Parthenocissus quinquefolia*) is a very common vine in sandy coastal areas and turns a striking crimson-red in late August. However, Virginia creeper has five leaflets while poison ivy has only three. Common dewberry (*Rubus flagellaris*) resembles poison ivy in that it has three leaflets. But these leaflets are serrated and its stem has thorns. Both the stem and leaf-edge on poison ivy are smooth.

The trail soon enters a shrub community typical of sandy coastal areas. The soil here is very dry, sterile, and nutrient-poor, and lacks a humus layer. The plant community that can survive in these harsh conditions is dominated by three hardy species: black cherry, beach plum, and bayberry. They are easily identified by their leaves. Bayberry (*Myrica pennsylvanica*) leaves have a distinct spicy odor when crushed. Although they can be used to flavor soups and stews, this is not the plant which produces commercial bay leaves. Commercial use of this plant is limited to its waxy gray-blue berries which, when boiled, yield the waxy substance from which bayberry candles are made. Black cherry (*Prunus serotina*) has shiny, oblong, fine-toothed leaves. By mid-summer, a close look at the underside of a large leaf will reveal orange fuzz growing along the midrib. This tree is very striking in May and June, when in blossom, and also in autumn, when its leaves turn a brilliant orange-yellow; hence its popular use as an ornamental by landscapers. In good soils, black cherry can reach heights of 60 feet; here the poor soil limits its growth to that of a large shrub. Beach plum (*Prunus maritima*) is closely related to the black cherry. Its leaves are smaller, more oval, duller, and lack the orange fuzz along the midrib. The two shrubs can also be distinguished by the way their leaves appear from a distance. Black cherry has a longer leaf stalk (petiole) which causes the leaves to droop on their twigs. All these shrubs and vines produce fruit which is eaten by over 70 species of birds. The ripening of these fruits coincides with the fall migration and provides an excellent source of energy for the birds' long journey south.

Entering a more open area (2), look for bearberry (*Arctostaphylos uvaursi*), a low-growing, mat-like plant. This evergreen has small, shiny, leathery leaves and "hairs" growing along its twigs. These characteristics are adaptations common among plants in windy dry environments such as deserts, coastal dunes, arctic tundra, and alpine mountaintops. This slow-growing, long-lived, hardy plant is actually most abundant in the far north, but its range extends south where extremely dry windy environments (such as here) give it a competitive edge.

The path here, once quite narrow, has been widened by the wind undermining the bearberry's roots, creating a blowout. The major force behind this restructuring of plants and sand is the northwest winds. Our prevailing wind, averaged over the entire year, is from the southwest. However, the northwesterly winds blow hardest, and during the winter months they are the prevailing winds. Here, the northwest wind blows directly across the path from left to right, making the right side of the path more susceptible to undermining. As the sand is blown away and the roots are exposed to the air the stabilizing plants are killed, enabling the wind to carry away even more sand, eventually creating a blowout. As you enter the pine-oak forest ahead, you will see where some of the sand from this blowout has ended up. Also, look for an unusual pitch pine specimen on the right side of the trail (A).

At first glance, this pitch pine does not stand out from the others around it. Look more closely and notice how it has grown. A compass would reveal that the trunk of this old-timer is oriented to the southeast. Another example of the effect of the northwesterly wind? One theory is that since most of the shrubs growing between here and Napeague Harbor were not present during this trees younger days, it was more exposed to salt-spray generated by the northwesterlies blowing across the harbor. During the winter months, salt-spray damaged the buds on the trees windward side, while the leeward, sheltered buds survived and were able to sprout in the spring. What you see now is the result of many years of repeating this process. Did you notice the poison ivy growing in the shade of the pines and oaks here?

Emerging from the forest, a well-worn footpath straight ahead ascends very steeply to a lookout atop the ridge of the walking dune (3). Please heed the "keep off the dunes" sign and follow the flank of the dune to the right. You are now traversing around the outside edge of the northernmost walking dune, which lies to your left. Between (3) and (6) along the dune's outer flank, several distinct plant communities are visible. A plant community is a natural grouping of plant species living under similar environmental conditions. Environmental conditions include such things as climate, soil, moisture, wind exposure, sand burial, and salt-spray, and the dominant ones at work here are the rate of sand burial and moisture. The plant community on the dune's ridgetop and upper slopes is dominated by American beachgrass. There, the high rate of sand burial would be intolerable for most plants, but beachgrass thrives in this. Immediately to your left, at the foot of the dune where sand movement is much less, the dominant plant is a low-growing woody plant called beach heather.

Beach heather (*Hudsonia tomentosa*) can tolerate some degree of sand burial, although not nearly to the extent that beachgrass can. This plant is the needle-leaved plant whose branches grow low to the ground and outward such that it resembles a round cushion. As with beachgrass, over time each can eventually help stabilize the area of shifting sand and, in doing so, bring about its own demise. Both begin to die when sand burial ceases. Can you find the dead stalks of beachgrass among the heather?

Once beach heather has stabilized the sand, bearberry can begin to grow. Its woody branches also radiate out and form a mat-like circle. Should larger shrubs establish themselves, such as the black cherries seen here, they will shade out and eventually kill the sun-loving bearberry and beach heather plants.

On the far right is the pine-oak forest community, part of which you traversed earlier. This community covers most of the area from here south to Montauk Highway. Adjacent to the forest, but closer to the trail is yet another plant community comprised of several different shrubs not usually found in a sandy, dry environment; these are actually considered wetland indicator plants. Speckled alder (*Alnus rugosa*), so named because its bark is covered with light speckles, is the large shrub with the deeply veined leaves and cone-like structures at the tips of its branches. Avid canoeists might recognize this common wetland shrub which often forms impenetrable thickets along the shoreline of streams and ponds. Also found here are highbush blueberry, swamp azalea, sweet pepperbush, and arrowwood. Can you solve the riddle of the dry wetland: why is there a band of freshwater wetland shrubs growing in this area of dry, sandy soil?

Sweet pepperbush (*Clethra alnifolia*) is easily identified in mid to late summer by its small white flowers grouped in elongated clusters. At other times, it can be distinguished by its spherical seed clusters which resemble peppercorns: hence the latter part of its common name. The "sweet" is readily apparent to anyone within range of its strongly scented flowers. Highbush blueberry (*Vaccinium corymbosum*) has a very distinctive bark which is pale and shaggy on the older stems and reddish on the new growth at the tips of its twigs. Its small pinkish-white, bell-shaped flowers appear in June; by mid-July the familiar fruit is ripe for picking.

These wetland plants are here because their roots are actually immersed in wet, marshy soil. As the northwest winds carried sand from the large dune to the left, the previous marsh has filled in. Today, the sand has completely covered the aquatic sedges, rushes, cattails, and ferns of the marsh, and all that is left are the taller shrubs. The buttonbush at (B), another wetland shrub, is already more than half buried by the flank of the dune. Unless the dune is stabilized, even these shrubs will be buried under the moving pile of sand. Since a picture is worth a thousand words, begin climbing the edge of the dune to (C) and you will see what this wetland area looked like before the dune sands encroached.

You are now standing on the tongue of the parabolic dune, its leading edge. As you can see, the dune is moving into a marsh inhabited with many species of herbaceous plants in addition to the wetland shrubs seen earlier, and will eventually fill at least a portion of it. Just up the slope from the marsh, the trail passes by a clump of small shrubs (6). This ia actually the top of a grey birch tree that is over 20 feet tall but is rapidly being buried by the moving dune. Only the protruding top can photosynthesize and keep the

184

tree alive. In 1990, the top two feet of a tupelo was visible; it is now completely buried.

There is no plant better adapted to the rapidly shifting sands and dry, nutrient-poor soil conditions found here than the American beachgrass (*Ammophila breviligulata*). Botanists have named it appropriately, for "ammophila" literally means "sand-loving." This plant actually requires some degree of sand burial to thrive and will turn brown and die once the source of blowing sand is cut-off. Another common name for beachgrass is compass grass, derived from the circle pattern in the sand that is drawn by bent leaf blades whose pointed tips are touching the surface of the sand. A slight breeze moving them etches a circular line, much like a compass used in geometry.

Beachgrass has evolved some truly amazing adaptations for growth in this harsh environment:

• Reproduction occurs both by seeds and underground horizontal stems called rhizomes. Beachgrass plants are often found growing in straight rows; are all connected by a rhizome, a reproductive strategy which enables beachgrass to quickly colonize a large area of bare sand. It also prevents the plant from becoming completely buried. As the dune sands build up around beachgrass stems, new rhizomes, from which new leaves can sprout, grow out and up on a diagonal toward the surface. In this way, beachgrass can "ride" the growing and shifting dune. With its lateral roots so near the surface however, beachgrass is highly vulnerable to surface traffic. Off-road vehicles and human feet will kill the plant. Please walk only in open sandy areas.

• The tough, coarse feel of the plant is due to the presence of silicon in its leaves. This adaptation enables the leaves to withstand the damaging effects of windblown sand, which can create small cuts in a leaf's outer surface and cause it to lose moisture, dry out, and eventually die.

• The vertical ridges extending the inside length of each leaf blade are another important adaptation for a plant trying to conserve water in these dry soils. Between these ribs are microscopic openings (stomata) where carbon dioxide is taken in, and oxygen and water vapor, by-products of photosynthesis, are released. To prevent too much water vapor escaping from the leaf on a hot dry day the leaf can fold lengthwise, bringing these ridges together like an accordion and sealing off the tiny openings.

Where the trail crosses over the crest of the dune (7), you can see the ridgetop extending to your left and right in such a way as to form a large U. This shape, to use another term from geometry class, is called a parabola— hence the scientific term for this type of dune, a "parabolic dune." Descending from this vantage point, look for upright wood timbers at the base of the dune's north side (D). These are the remnants of the pine-oak forest that grew on this site before the dune engulfed and killed everything in its path. Beyond this phantom forest you can see the tall, straight stalks of the common reedgrass (*Phragmites communis*), and further still it appears the pine-oak forest is attempting to reclaim its former territory. Remember that the dune once stood over portions of the area before you, destroying all the vegetation beneath it. However, unharmed plants nearby provided a ready source of seed so that the barren sand in the dune's wake was quickly revegetated.

Descend the dune into its bowl-like north side and follow the trail markers to the cranberry bog (8). It is not unusual for the northwest winds to blow so hard that they scour out a depression on the windward side of the dune. This depression sometimes gets deep enough to expose the water table, or at least the water-saturated soil just above it. Here, the perfect environment for cranberries was created: freshwater-saturated, nutrient-poor, acidic sandy soils and lots of sunshine.

This vine-like cranberry (*Vaccinium macrocarpon*) is the same species as the commercial cranberry. A low ground-hugging evergreen, its large fruit seems all out of proportion when compared to its tiny oval leaves and delicate white flowers. Its common name is a shortened version of "crane-berry," given by early colonists because its flower resembled a crane's head. As the cranberry plants multiply, spread, and thicken, they provide shade for sphagnum moss (*Sphagnum palustre*) to grow. Sphagnum tends to hold water in its tissues, causing the bog to become more consistently moist, rather than fluctuating from wet to dry with rainfall. Constant moisture slows bacterial decomposition in the soil and causes peat to build up on the surface of the sand. Peat, in turn, holds more water than pure sand and the bog becomes squishy underfoot.

Other plants found in this bog include two rare orchids, rose pogonia (*Pogonia ophioglossoides*) and calopogon (*Calopogon pulchellus*), best viewed in June when their pink flowers have blossomed (please don't pick). There is also a group of tiny insectivorous plants. Everyone has heard of the Venus flytrap, which captures and digests insects. Few know that there are several such insectivorous plants native to Long Island, two of which grow in this bog.

Both thread-leaved and spatulate-leaved sundews (*Drosera filiformis and D. intermedia*) are so small that you may have to stoop down to find them. Their mechanism for capture is a sticky, dew-like secretion on their leaf hairs. Once an insect is stuck, the leaf gradually folds over the insect, secretes digestive enzymes and absorbs nutrients from the carcass. Since the leaves are so tiny, the insects it can capture are also very small. See if you can find the carcasses of insects on any of the leaves. All three are green plants and therefore grow via photosynthesis, converting sunlight energy into chemical energy. The captured insects merely supply them with important nutrients such as nitrogen, phosphorous, and potassium, which most plants obtain from the soil. These plants have adapted to the sterile soils here by capturing insects as a source of fertilizer that is absorbed through their leaves rather than their roots. A truly unique evolutionary strategy.

Leaving the bog, the trail crosses a small dune ridge and eventually leads to the shore of Napeague Harbor (10). This is presently one of the least developed coastal bays on Long Island and, as a result of land purchases by the state of New York and the efforts of local conservation groups and town officials, it is likely to remain so.

As you return to the parking area, note the rusty color of the sand along the shoreline. This is the result of ferrous iron oxidizing and precipitating out as a solid, coating the sand and rocks. The large woodland east of here lies above a tremendous freshwater aquifer whose water is high in soluble ferrous iron. This freshwater, flowing underground toward the coastline in all directions, eventually seeps out of the sand and is exposed to oxygen, changing the water-soluble ferrous iron to ferric hydroxide, a solid which precipitates out and gives the shoreline its rusty tinge. Being a fairly enclosed harbor, with little tidal flushing at this end, the deposits of ferric hydroxide accumulate on the shore. In some areas, such as the Peconic River, this form of iron accumulated in quantities sufficient for mining and was used to produce ship anchors.

The walking dunes trail is a great place to visit at any time of the year. As you become more familiar with the area in different seasons, you may find yourself returning to the parking lot with more questions than answers. If so, you have been very observant!

Directions: Take Montauk Highway (Rte. 27) to Napeague Harbor Road (traveling east from Amagansett, continue across the Napeague stretch and look for the Hither Hills Racquet and Tennis Club on the left; Napeague Harbor Road is a left turn at the club directly across the highway from the Sea Crest Condos). Continue down Napeague Harbor Road, over the railroad tracks, and park where it dead-ends at the harbor. The trail begins on the right at the end of the road.

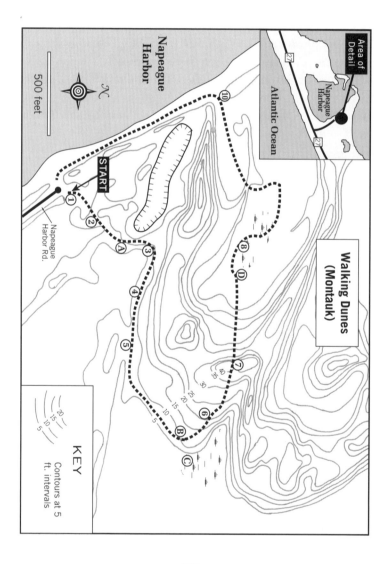

Paumanok Path:

Hither Woods Section

This section of the Paumanok Path traverses the largest forest preserve on the South Fork: an assemblage of state, county, and town properties totaling 3,000 acres. Visitors will be treated to an outstanding variety of plant communities, spectacular scenic vistas overlooking Block Island Sound and Fort Pond Bay, a remote area of the famous walking dunes complex, a beautiful secluded pond, several historic sites, and perhaps a glimpse of a wild turkey, a species that was recently reintroduced to the park. Of the 40-plus miles of trails in the Hither Woods area, the Paumanok Path is currently the only one marked; as such it provides a great opportunity to become familiar with the most extensive trail system on the South Fork.

The Paumanok Path crosses Napeague Harbor Road directly across from a private road (heading north on Napeague Harbor Road, look for the private road on your left and a white rectangular blaze on a telephone pole on your right). From this point to the Old North Road, a distance of approximately four miles, the Paumanok Path follows the Stephen Talkhouse Path, named for a Montaukett Indian whose hiking feats were legendary.

A dozen steps from the pavement takes you alongside a patch of our one and only native cactus. Although low-growing and easily overlooked, prickly pear cactus sports a striking yellow flower in the spring and reddish, edible fruit in the fall.

After winding through an oak forest, stunted due to its close proximity to salt-laden northwesterly winds blowing off Napeague Harbor, the trail climbs steeply up into a pitch pine forest. You have just ascended from the low-lying Napeague (Montaukett for "waterland") isthmus onto the Nominicks ("land seen from afar"). There is a major geomorphological distinction between the two: the Nominicks being composed of glacial debris deposited 10,000 years ago, while Napeague is largely composed of wind- and wave-deposited sands scoured from nearby bluffs over the past several thousand years.

These two distinct areas actually overlap somewhat over the first half mile of trail where the southernmost walking dune has migrated, driven by northwest winds, up onto the moraine. As a result, part of the steep climb involves ascending the western flank of one of the three parabolic (walking) dunes found in the area. Once on the ridge-like flank (1), a spur trail leads off to the right to the Nominicks overlook (2) with a great view westward across Napeague to the highlands of Amagansett.

Back on the Paumanok Path, the trail leaves the pitch pines and enters an oak–hickory forest. The main body of the oldest of the three walking dunes is off to the right (south), having come to a stop and towering over the LIRR tracks. The other two parabolic dunes are off to the left (north). The middle dune has also stabilized, while the northern and youngest dune is still active, marching southeastward and slowly engulfing a freshwater marsh (the latter dune is part of the nature trail described the Walking Dunes section).

As the southernmost dune migrated through this area, its sands smothered the trees and shrubs in its path, leaving a barren landscape in its wake. Note the presence of glacial erratics along the route here, evidence that the substrate is of glacial origin and not wind-blown dune sands. Over time, the area revegetated and today it is difficult to discern the impact of the disturbance caused by the wind-driven dune. However, much of the crescent-shaped ridge of dune sands is, not surprisingly, covered with pitch pines rather than the oaks found dominating the glacial soils on adjacent areas.

The trail exits the walking dunes area at a low point in the eastern flank of the dune where part of the steep face of the middle dune looms off to the left (3). As illustrated nicely on a topographic map of the area, the eastern flanks of all three dunes are connected into a dramatic dune ridge which extends for a mile between the LIRR and Napeague Bay and is easily negotiated by foot.

Once east of the dune system, the trail enters a more mature forest, following several old paths that circumvent swamps and marshes and eventually leads to the east shore of Fresh Pond. These well-worn paths may have been established by the Montauketts prior to the 1600s; they pass through an area that is thought to be the site of one of their forts. At Fresh Pond the trail passes near to the boat launch (4), which affords a good view of this pretty waterbody, and negotiates a maze of paths made by vehicles, fisherman, and picnickers before making its way to Fresh Pond Road, an important water access for baymen tending traps along this stretch of Napeague Bay.

A short distance further, at the next road crossing, leave the trail by turning left and following the road to the Waterfence Overlook (5) with views across Napeague Bay and Block Island Sound towards Gardiner's Island, the North Fork, and Connecticut. Waterfence refers to a fenceline spanning the 1.5 miles of land between the bay and the ocean. Constructed nearly three centuries ago, it was designed to keep livestock on Montauk, which for many years was a publicly owned commons used as a summer pasturing grounds by town residents.

East of Waterfence, the Paumanok Path parallels the shoreline of Hither Woods for four miles and offers several more interesting and scenic bay overlooks. In many places, such as the section west of Flaggy Hole, the adjacent oak forest shows signs of wind pruning. Salt-laden winds blowing off the bay have sculpted these old oaks into grotesque, contorted shapes with as much growth occurring laterally as vertically in some specimens. Just before reaching Flaggy Hole, a freshwater marsh with cattails and phragmites, a spur trail leads off a short distance to an old cellar hole (6). This is the site of a dwelling occupied by Montauketts including, at one time, Stephen Talkhouse.

Flaggy Hole is a low point in the 50-foot-tall bay bluffs scoured out by a glacial stream that is long gone. The relic streambed is discernible by closely examining a topographic map. In order to skirt the marsh, the trail swings seaward out of the forest and onto soft beach sands vegetated by beachgrass, beach plum, seaside rose, and goldenrod, then climbs back up onto the bluff and into the forest. East of Flaggy Hole to the intersection of the Old North Road (7), the trail is a narrow footpath established in the mid-1990s. In places, northerly winds have carried sand from the face of the bluff back into the stunted oak forest, creating deposits several feet thick. The orange or rusty hue to this sand reflects the high concentration of iron in Hither Woods' groundwater; as groundwater seeps out at the foot of the bluffs and comes in contact with oxygen, the iron precipitates out and stains the sand.

The Old North Road is a wide, well-established woods road once used to ferry smuggled liquor, unloaded from boats at several of Hither Woods' secluded landings (such as Quincetree) to their various destinations. A large grove of ironwood (*Ostrya virginiana*) grows along this section of trail; I know of no other place on the South Fork where it is found. In the autumn, the leaves resemble that of American beech, but the bark is much different, peeling away from the trunk in small, narrow curls. Ironwood is an understory tree, rarely growing more than 35 feet high and well-adapted to life in the shade of the forest canopy. The name derives from the characteristics of its wood, extremely hard and tough, accounting for its past use as wedges and sled runners.

After 0.75 mile on Old North Road, the trail takes a left fork (8) and continues through the Ironwood stand as a narrow foot trail, another recently created trail which accesses the Keyhole, an interesting cut in the bluff face and scenic view out over Block Island Sound. Beyond the Keyhole, the trail eventually joins an old coastal road (9) along a section of Hither Woods which juts out into the bay, exposed both to the northwesterlies and the powerful nor'easters. This stretch of trail weaves in and out of meadows, shrub thickets, and woods severely impacted by coastal storms, wind, and salt spray, with expansive views unobstructed to the west, north and east. Remnants of several old fishing outposts can be found here, and the area labelled "the tar works" is a large clearing where fishermen mended and tarred their fish nets, laying them out in the clearing to dry.

At Rocky Point the trail leaves the coast, crosses the LIRR tracks (caution: this is an unprotected crossing with no warning of oncoming trains) and enters a section of Hither Woods that was burned in the 1980s. Note the many multi-trunked oaks, the result of coppice shoots sprouting from root collars after the fire destroyed the above-ground portion of the trees.

Part of the firefighting effort involved creating fire breaks and new roads in the forest so that firefighting equipment could access the blaze. Both were done with brush hogs and bulldozers that not only cleared a path free of trees and shrubs, but also scraped away the leaf litter and exposed the underlying mineral soils. The latter is a perfect micro-environment for the germination of mountain laurel seeds; hence the proliferation of laurel along these roadbeds.

After crossing the tracks, the trail turns left onto one of the fire roads (10) and climbs over a ridge, descends to cross Rod's Valley Road, ascends another ridge (Riah's Ridge) for a beautiful quarter-mile traverse of several laurel thickets, and finally descends to and turns left on Flaggy Hole Road. Rod and Riah inhabited and tended livestock in this area in the 1870s.

The east-west trending ridges and valleys in this part of the Preserve are examples of the many push moraine features found there. A push moraine is a narrow, steep-sided ridge of glacial material created by a sudden, relatively short-lived forward thrust of the leading edge of the glacial ice that pushes soil into a pile before receding and leaving a low ridge behind.

Rick Whalen, who laid out most of the Paumanok Path route through Hither Woods, designed a short detour off Flaggy Hole Road to take hikers through a nice stand of American beech to a tremendous glacial erratic nicknamed Lost Boulder (11), then back to Flaggy Hole Road via another picturesque, laurel-lined roadbed.

The trail swings south toward the Montauk Landfill, which is now capped. Watch for a sharp left turn (12) onto a footpath cut recently to avoid the disturbed landfill area; it leads onto Old North Road, which in turn intersects Upland Road. Both woods roads are historic travel routes that date back several hundred years. Continue straight across this intersection onto a footpath that leads onto a 95-acre preserve acquired in 2000. The new acquisition provides an eastern extension to the Hither Woods preserve and provides a greenbelt connection, and possibly future trail link, to The Nature Conservancy's Montauk Mountain Preserve which fronts Second House Road.

The trail climbs up through a thicket of mountain laurel and along ridge. Near the high point of this long ridge (13) you can just make out the waters of Fort Pond Bay, even in the summer. Notice the number of oaks here with broken trunks and limbs; one broken limb, a massive piece of white oak, forms an arch over the trail. My guess is that this damage is a result of the ridge's exposure to strong northerly winds blowing across the long fetch of Block Island Sound and funneling in through nearby Fort Pond Bay.

Sharing the trail with me there on a June day was a female box turtle (*Terrapene carolina*), possibly searching for a suitable place to lay its eggs. Females can be distinguished from males by their brown, as opposed to red, eyes and the shape of the rear portion of their plastron (bottom side of their shell). The latter is concave in males and flat or slightly bulging outward in females, perhaps to accommodate developing eggs. This one's shell was a beautiful mix of yellow and chestnut colors and her annual growth rings numbered over twenty, a point beyond which they are difficult to count accurately. Although egg predation is very heavy, once box turtles reach several years of age their hinged shell provides adequate protection from most predators and, in a protected forest like this with no automobile traffic, they may live for over 100 years.

Dropping off the ridge, the trail next enters a steep sided gully which leads into the main ravine (14). This ravine (or as some would prefer, canyon) shelters some large oaks in addition to the large numbers of mountain laurel from which it derives its name: Laurel Canyon. Although some of us might feel the term canyon is a bit of a reach for this 75-foot deep gully with no vertical walls, others might argue that it is as appropriate as the nearby place name Montauk Mountain, only a thousand feet to the west.

Enjoy the walk along the leaf covered canyon floor, and note the unusual assortment of erratics dotting either side of the trail. Among the ones I could recognize were pure chunks of feldspar and quartz and what I think geologists refer to as a conglomerate, a large piece of sandstone embedded with other rocks. It would be interesting to visit the canyon with a knowledgeable geologist. My guess is the abundance of large rock material is related to the formation of the canyon: a stream of glacial meltwater that carried away the smaller sand and gravel and exposed these unmovable rocks.

Exiting the canyon at its southern end, the trail intersects Upland Road (15). Turn right and follow the woods road for a short distance to a footpath on the left that leads to an overlook on the east side of the Montauk Landfill (16). Fort Pond Bay, Culloden Point, and Rocky Point can be identified this side of Block Island Sound, while the shoreline of Connecticut and Rhode Island can be seen 15 miles away on a clear day. Before the landfill was capped in 2000, Gardiner's Island was visible over the green canopy of Hither Woods.

The next section of the Paumanok Path, between landfill overlook and the Parkway Trail, was nicely laid out and designed by Rick Whalen, particularly the traverse of a narrow ridge just south of the landfill. The ridge, at just under 200 feet above mean sea level, is the highest point of land between bay and ocean east of the landfill. This fact, and the implied exposure to winds off both bodies of water, may explain the unusual appearance of the oaks here: low, sprawling, multi-trunked specimens.

The trail descends the ridge into a jungle of catbrier and other vines. Turn right at the intersection of the Parkway Trail (17), leaving the Paumanok Path to hike out to the trailhead at the entrance road to the landfill (18).

Directions to Start of Trail: Eastbound on Rte. 27, pass through Amagansett, cross Napeague and turn left (north) onto Napeague Harbor Road. Follow Napeague Harbor Road across the LIRR tracks to the first road on the left. Park nearby on the road shoulder and look for a white paint blaze on a utility pole on the right (east) side of the Napeague Harbor Road that marks the trail entrance.

Directions to End of Trail: See directions to the start of Paumanok Path: Montauk Village Section.

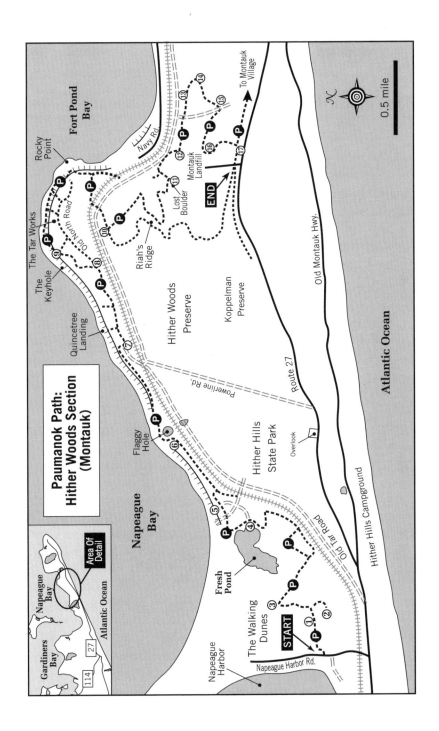

Paumanok Path:
Hither Woods Section
(Montauk)

Area Of Detail

Gardiners Bay

Napeague Bay

Atlantic Ocean

114

27

Napeague Bay

Fort Pond Bay

Rocky Point

The Tar Works

The Keyhole

Quincetree Landing

Napeague Bay

Flaggy Hole

Napeague Harbor

The Walking Dunes

Fresh Pond

START

Napeague Harbor Rd.

Hither Hills State Park

Overlook

Hither Hills Campground

Hither Woods Preserve

Riah's Ridge

Koppelman Preserve

Navy Rd.

Old North Road

Montauk Landfill

Lost Boulder

END

To Montauk Village

Powerline Rd.

Route 27

Old Tar Road

Old Montauk Hwy.

Atlantic Ocean

0.5 mile

195

Hither Hills Preserve:

Fresh Pond Loop

The Hither Hills and Hither Woods Preserve, an assemblage of state, county, town, and Nature Conservancy properties totalling over 3,000 acres, forms the largest block of protected open space on the South Fork. Its forests, wetlands and ponds, grasslands and dunes are bordered on the south by the ocean and Rte. 27, the north by Block Island Sound and Fort Pond Bay, Napeague Harbor on the west, and to the east a narrow finger of preserved land extends nearly to Second House Road. The preserve also boasts the largest network of protected trails east of the canal: some 40 linear miles.

The 3.5-mile-long Fresh Pond loop is my favorite route in the Hither Hills area, excluding the incredible Walking Dunes of course. It includes many of the area's most interesting historic and ecological features, as well as two outstanding scenic overlooks. Despite encompassing sections of at least ten different trails and having thirteen different trail intersections, the loop is easy to navigate using the attached map as a guide. Landmarks such as the LIRR tracks, the Old Tar Road, Fresh Pond, Gardiner's Bay, and Rte. 27 make pinpointing your location quite simple, even if you are map and direction challenged.

The first of the overlooks can be enjoyed right from your car at the parking lot on Rte. 27, with a better than 180-degree view encompassing Napeague Bay, Gardiner's Island, Napeague Harbor, the Atlantic, the Napeague isthmus, and the highlands of Springs–Amagansett in the distance. There are three informative displays worth examining before setting out on your hike. The Place Names and Formation of Napeague displays were researched and designed by Judy Cooper and myself in 1990 while employed for the summer as park naturalists. The excellent map of the entire Hither Hills State Park and Hither Woods Preserve, with trails, topography, and points of interest, was created by the Whalen brothers, siblings whose collective knowledge of the trails and history of this area is unmatched.

With your back to the ocean and highway, walk over to the left (northwest) corner of the parking area where trail signs point toward Elisha's Valley and Fresh Pond, and to the start of the Petticoat Hill Trail. The unmarked sandy footpath forks and branches several times. Take any of these paths, as they all head downhill through the open, sunlit secondary growth on the west side of Petticoat Hill. The abundance of shade-intolerant pioneer plants here indicates the area was subject to some type of disturbance not long ago. Various grasses, reindeer lichen, heather, bearberry, black cherry, and pines, all species genetically programmed to colonize areas devoid of any vegetation, are well-established and have stabilized most of the sandy soils.

A close examination of the pine's needles reveals that they are growing in pairs, each pair being wrapped at the twig end in a sheath, forming a fascicle. This key feature distinguishes this species of pine, the Japanese black pine, from our native pitch pine, which has three-needled fascicles. Both pines are well-adapted to the growing conditions found along Long Island's coastline: dry, nutrient-poor sandy soils and a fairly constant wind which often carries salt spray from ocean and bay waters.

Japanese black pine was chosen for landscaping purposes over our native pitch pine because of its faster and more luxuriant growth, and its longer, more attractive needles. The Long Island State Parks Commission planted black pines all along our State Parkways and in many of our State Parks, including Hither Hills, back in the mid-1960s. It did quite well for two decades (and still seems to fare well in its early years), but as it got older a native nematode developed a strong appetite for the exotic pine and began decimating it throughout Long Island. Today, the State Department of Environmental Conservation nursery grows pitch pine, among other native and non-native tree species, for replanting and landscaping projects.

Scattered among the pioneer plants are oak seedlings and saplings, mostly species in the black oak group. Since these species are very shade-tolerant, their seeds (acorns) can germinate in the shade created by the cherries and smaller shrubs. With time, the oaks will overtop the pioneer plants and cast shade over them, eventually killing them off and transforming this open sunlit habitat into an oak forest. This gradual process of change is called ecological succession. Various stages of this process are evident as you proceed down Petticoat Hill towards the junction with Old North Road: early successional grasses and low-growing shrubs dominate the upper slopes; a mix of taller shrubs and small trees (winged sumac, black cherry, and oaks) inhabit the mid slope; and further down the trail is a mature forest with large oaks and pines (1). These mature pines are our native pitch pines.

The Petticoat Hill Trail ends at Old North Road. Turn right, walk a short distance and take the next left onto the unmarked trail through Elisha's Valley. Named for a Montaukett Indian that once resided and tended livestock here, the valley is the upper reaches of an east-west trending swale that gradually slopes down to the swamp and marsh bordering Fresh Pond. Local naturalist and South Fork Natural History Society Director Jim Ash has had some luck finding short-eared owls and rough-legged hawks here in the winter months.

In striking contrast to the forested portion of the valley across the LIRR tracks, this area is quite open with pockets of grasslands interspersed with low woody shrubs: black cherry, sumac, bayberry, scotch broom, and poison ivy. Another example of ecological succession, Elisha's Valley is gradually changing from a maritime grassland-dominated community to one dominated by woody shrubs. The next step in the successional series is for the shrubs to give way to trees, such as oaks. Both Jim Ash and I are surprised that this change is happening so slowly here, since there have been no attempts to maintain the grassland. Perhaps the many years of grazing by livestock has had the effect of retarding the inevitable process of ecological succession.

At the west side of Elisha's Valley, turn right onto the Old Tar Road, whose pavement is barely discernible today, and hike a short distance to the first left, over the railroad tracks (caution: trains do run along these tracks) and into the forest. At the next intersection (2), turn right and follow the white rectangular blazes marking the Paumanok Path. This is a regional trail which spans the entire length of the Town of East Hampton and, when complete, will connect Montauk Point State Park with Rocky Point State Forest Preserve in Brookhaven, a hiking distance of 120 miles.

This particular section of the Paumanok Path, between Napeague Harbor Road to the west and Quincetree Landing to the east, is called the Stephen Talkhouse Path in honor of the legendary hiker and Montaukett Indian also known as Stephen Pharaoh. He apparently walked to Brooklyn on at least one occasion, and toured with P. T. Barnum's circus acts as the greatest walker of all times.

The trail passes through a hickory forest, indicative of richer soils than those supporting an oak dominated woodland. Note the understory/forest floor vegetation here, dominated by grasses, forbs, and Virginia creeper as opposed to the more common huckleberry–lowbush blueberry shrub layer. Perhaps this is also a reflection of slightly richer and moister soils, although our native grasses and Virginia creeper generally do not require good soils.

The Talkhouse Path soon reaches Fresh Pond's access and boat launch area (3). Enjoy the views westward over this pretty body of water here and at a few places further along the trail before moving on. The pond's western portion bends to the south around a point and is hidden from the trailside views. The best way to see the entire half mile long pond is to bring in a canoe or kayak.

The pond's fishery is managed by the New York State Department of Environmental Conservation, which periodically stocks it with gamefish and inventories species and sizes. Over a 40-year span beginning in the early 1950s, the state fisheries biologists documented three fish species in Fresh Pond: largemouth bass, yellow perch and freshwater killifish. The 1994 fish survey found brown bullhead, smallmouth bass, bluegill, pumpkinseed, and black crappie. The latter three introduced species made up a significant portion of the pond's fish community and, according to NYS DEC biologist Charles Guthrie, had a detrimental impact on the yellow perch and largemouth bass populations. Guthrie cites this as an example of a well-meaning angler introducing new species to a favorite pond and not only wreaking ecological havoc in the pond but destroying the quality of its fishing.

Paul Connor, another NYS DEC biologist and author of *The Mammals of Long Island*, set up mist nets here at Fresh Pond as part of his mammal survey in the early 1960s. He was collecting bats, and identified Keen's myotis (*Myotis keeni septentrionalis*) and red bats (*Lasiurus borealis boreali*) hunting for insects at this site. The former were caught in the nets throughout the summer and early fall, while red bats were only caught in late October. No specimens of Long Island's most common bat, the little brown myotis, were caught. Both the Keen's and little brown myotis overwinter in caves and mines, habitats not found on Long Island; the presence of Keen's myotis at Fresh Pond surprised Connor as, unlike the little brown, this bat's summer range is rarely far from its winter subterranean retreats.

The red bat was once Long Island's most abundant aerial mammal. It doesn't hibernate in caves, but migrates south and roosts in trees throughout the year. Connor found this species hunting large concentrations of moths along the shoreline of Fresh Pond on a mild October night. Included in his observations was the pursuit of a red bat by a merlin, a type of falcon only seen in this area during the fall or spring migration.

As the only living mammals capable of flight, and with nearly 1,000 different species worldwide, bats make for an interesting study in evolution, adaptation, and niche. An extremely successful order (Chiroptera) with an amazing variety of behavioral and structural characteristics, they account for almost one quarter of all mammalian species.

Bats have a serious public relations problem. What little information most people have about bats is either not true or grossly exaggerated. This undeserved reputation is slowly changing, and there are now commercially available "bat boxes" for attracting these amazing and beneficial creatures. Voracious insectivores, it has been estimated that the little brown myotis can consume 600 mosquitoes in a single hour!

Leaving the pond, stay on the white-blazed Paumanok Path until you reach Fresh Pond Landing Road. Turn left on this wide, sandy road and follow it to the Napeague Bay beachfront. This is one of several landings along the north shore of Hither Hills and Hither Woods where cordwood was loaded onto ships by day and, at least during the Prohibition era, liquor unloaded by night. The short but steep climb up onto the top of the bluff, called the Waterfence Overlook (4), affords beautiful views over Napeague Bay towards Amagansett, Springs, and Gardiner's Island, and along the bay's shoreline and bluffs to the east.

The name Waterfence refers to a split rail fence once spanning the 1.5 miles between the waters of the bay and the ocean. Constructed 300 years ago when Montauk was a summer pasturing commons for livestock owned by town residents, its purpose was to keep the animals from making their way home across Napeague. To keep an eye on things, a hired hand resided at First House, whose foundation can still be found in the thickets on the north side of Old Montauk Highway, just west of the Hither Hills campground entrance.

Another type of waterfence, fish traps, are generally visible here throughout the summer months. A long net stretched across a series of wooden poles is set perpendicular to the shore. Its purpose is not to catch fish, but to obstruct their movement along the shoreline. When confronted with an obstacle, fish will move around it by heading towards deeper water. The long net leads them seaward into the wide end of a V-shaped funnel, also made of netting, which gradually tapers to a smaller opening in the side of a circular corral, called the pound. Once in the pound, most fish swim in circles unable to find the small opening from which they came. The pound has netting on its bottom as well as its sides, so baymen can pull alongside in their dories, lift the pound net, sort through the catch and keep or release specimens as the fishing regulations and market dictate.

This overlook is the halfway point of the 3.5-mile loop. Before continuing on, note the appearance and shape of the oak and cherry trees found growing near the top of the bluff to the east. The most seaward trees are quite stunted and look as if they've been pruned with shears, creating an angled canopy. This sculpted look is the effect of wind, often laden with salt spray, blowing across the long fetch of Napeague Bay and damaging leaves and buds on the unprotected seaward side of the trees.

Heading south on the overlook road, look for the intersection with the Paumanok Path and turn left, following the path as it winds through an interesting stunted coastal oak forest whose limbs are festooned with arboreal lichens. At the next intersection leave the Paumanok Path (which turns left) by turning right and heading back to Fresh Pond Landing Road.

On Fresh Pond Landing Road, cross the LIRR tracks and the Old Tar Road (Fresh Pond Landing Road makes a quick right and left at the latter). The LIRR tracks were laid through this area in 1895, after which fire, along with grazing and woodcutting, shaped the park's landscape. This next section of trail shows evidence of the 1986 fire: nearly all the oaks have multiple trunks. This occurs when fire (or cutting) kills the above ground portion of the tree and the root system has enough stored energy to support the growth of previously dormant adventitious buds in the root collar. I noticed that this burned area is devoid of hickories, but I'm not certain of why. Hickory's ability to resprout from their rootstock following a damaging fire or woodcutting is well-known.

At the next intersection, Old North Road, turn left and walk 200 yards to the unmarked footpath on the right (5). Unlike most of the Park's trails, this one is fairly new, having been cut as a firebreak in the 1986 conflagration. Called the Ocean View Trail, it winds over fairly irregular topography, climbing to a knoll (6) that, for many years following the 1986 fire, afforded a view south to the Atlantic Ocean. Today, the multi-trunked oaks seem to have grown high enough to block this view.

At (7) the trail drops down into and traverses a long, narrow hollow or swale that was left unscathed by the 1986 fire, as evidenced by the many tall, single-trunked trees here, including some very large hickories.

Turn right at the next two intersections in order to make your way back to the overlook parking area on Rte. 27.

Directions: Travelling east on Rte. 27, pass through Amagansett and across the flats of Napeague. Stay on the main highway, passing the right fork (Old Montauk Highway) which leads to the Hither Hills Campground. The Hither Hills overlook is on the left, one mile east of the intersection of Old Montauk Highway and Rte. 27.

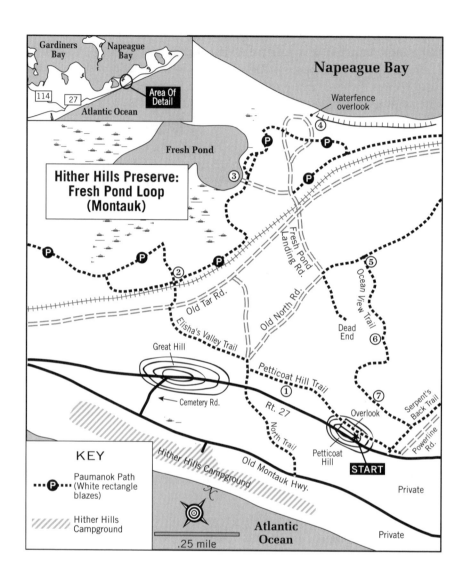

Hither Hills Preserve: Fresh Pond Loop (Montauk)

Napeague Bay

Gardiners Bay

Napeague Bay

114   27

Atlantic Ocean

Area Of Detail

Waterfence overlook

④

Fresh Pond

③

Fresh Pond Landing Rd.

Old North Rd.

Ocean View Trail

⑤

Old Tar Rd.

②

Elisha's Valley Trail

Dead End

⑥

Great Hill

Petticoat Hill Trail

①

⑦

Serpent's Back Trail

Cemetery Rd.

Rt. 27

Overlook

North Trail

Petticoat Hill

Powerline Rd.

START

Hither Hills Campground

Old Montauk Hwy.

Private

Private

KEY

● **P** Paumanok Path (White rectangle blazes)

Hither Hills Campground

.25 mile

Atlantic Ocean

N

HITHER WOODS PRESERVE:

RAM LEVEL LOOP

This four-mile loop includes a portion of the historic Old Montauk Road, as well as several unique features such as the grasslands at Ram Level, Split Rock, the Devil's Cradle, and Indian Jumps kettleholes.

From the trailhead parking area near the entrance to the Montauk Recycling Center (1), there are two trails leading into the woods on the west side (parking area side) of the road. Take the trail closest to the highway. This is one of several fairly new trails that were created in the 1980s by firefighters, either as fire breaks or as a result of driving a machine through the woods towards the fire area to suppress it. I believe this route, now called the Parkway Trail, was created as a fire break.

The Parkway Trail closely parallels Montauk Highway between here and the Powerline Road, approximately two miles to the west. Over that distance there are at least a half-dozen trails not shown on the map that lead a short distance out to the highway.

The vegetation along both sides of the trail near the start is that of a very young forest. Note the number of vines (Virginia creeper, bittersweet, and catbriar) and early successional tree species such as sassafras and black cherry. These are all species that quickly colonizes clearings but are not generally common in well-established mature forests. Some of the sassafras trees are quite large. They are easily identified at any time of the year by their distinctive bark: cinnamon-colored with a very regular-spaced, diamond-shaped pattern.

As you walk west, the forest composition quickly changes to predominately oaks. In a 1982 report entitled "A Brief Description of Hither Woods," Larry Penny of the town's Natural Resources Department surmised that approximately 75% of the oaks in Hither Woods were white oaks (*Quercus alba*). There are several interesting aspects to the vegetation along the Parkway Trail, characteristics and changes that can be recognized by observant hikers with no botanical training.

One is the change in growth form of the oaks, from the usual tall, single-trunked specimens to that of smaller, shrubby, multi-trunked plants. The latter forms nearly impenetrable thickets in places along the trail, and reflects the impact of fire. There were two large forest fires in Hither Woods over the last twenty years: one in 1982 and another in 1986. If severe, fire can completely destroy the above-ground portion of an oak. But the root system usually survives and, in an area of the plant called the root collar, dormant buds draw on energy reserves stored in roots to send out new shoots.

As many as 50 shoots will sprout around the root collar, creating a growth form called coppice growth. Each competes to become the new tree trunk and, over time, most of the shoots die back. Now, 15–20 years later, I could find a few with as many as a dozen surviving shoots, but most have less than six. A close inspection of these coppice oaks often reveals the lower portion of the old trunk, now a dead snag, still standing in the midst of the new growth. Evidence of the fire, in the form of blackened charcoal, can sometimes be seen on those trunks.

As with many forest fires, there are many variables at work that influence its spread and impact. In some areas, the canopy trees escaped unharmed. Most vulnerable are the ridgetops and knolls which tend to have drier soils and are more exposed to the wind. Least vulnerable are the bottoms of kettleholes and swales, whose soils tend to be richer and moister. This fact is evident where the trail intersects three kettleholes known as the Indian Jumps (at 2, 3 and 4 on the map).

As legend would have it, these kettleholes were not created by glacial processes but by a mortally wounded Indian brave. Arranged to marry an Indian maiden, he was shot with an arrow by a jealous rival and made quite a lasting impression with his three final death leaps. A fourth, more dramatic, and much elongated depression is found off Old Montauk Road between (6) and (7). Known as the Devil's Cradle, it is a good example of the northeast–southwest trending ridges and valleys common to Hither Woods. These are somewhat unusual landforms, called push or thrust moraines, created by abrupt changes in movement of the glacial ice sheet.

Note that there is little, if any, evidence of fire damage in the Indian Jumps. Large hickory trees and red maples comprise much of the forest composition there. Much of the forest floor is covered with a short, clumpy grass called Pennsylvania sedge. Near the westernmost Indian Jump (4) is a stand of American beech, a very fire-sensitive species.

The right turn onto Old Montauk Road is not marked, but hard to miss (5). The only other right turn is 150 yards east of Old Montauk Road, but you will soon realize your mistake as it quickly dead-ends. Rick Whalen and I reopened this trail, which had been completely overgrown, about ten years ago. Several sections had nearly impenetrable thickets of black cherry saplings; it seemed the slight opening in the forest canopy provided by the old roadbed created ideal conditions for its seeds to germinate.

Despite being very overgrown, it was fairly easy to trace the exact location of the roadbed. This section of Old Montauk Road was part of the original roadway west to Montauk, predating Old Montauk Highway along the ocean bluffs and the new Montauk Highway (Rte. 27) just to the south. Rick and I were both impressed by the road's straight and consistently level aspect; clearly the early route finders succeeded in finding an easy, flat traverse through an relatively hilly section of Hither Woods.

Note the large patch of ferns, which I am told is hayscented fern, and the ten-foot-high glacial erratic on the right (6). The latter, called Split Rock, has a small shadbush growing on it. A short distance further is a concrete monument used to mark property lines, in the middle of the trail. I'm uncertain as to its origin, and am not aware that there was ever a property line in this area.

As with the Parkway Trail, there are areas along Old Montauk Road that were obviously burned in one or both of the fires in the 1980s. An easy-to-miss footpath cuts off to the right (7) and descends into the Devil's Cradle. Unfortunately, this interesting depression is not very obvious from the trail.

At Ram Level (8), the trail emerges from the forest and intersects another trail in a brushy grassland. Take the left turn, leaving Old Montauk Highway, and follow an unnamed trail through the remnants of a maritime grassland. This area was once used as a pasture ground for male sheep, hence the name. It is slowly reverting back to an oak forest, and there has been some talk of doing a prescribed burn here to maintain the grassland community.

I couldn't find any mention of this grassland in Norman Taylor's botanical work "The Vegetation of Montauk: A Study of Grassland and Forest" (published in 1923 through the Brooklyn Botanical Garden), nor do I know when the area was last used for pasturing sheep.

Climb a steep, badly eroded knoll (9) with a large patch of bearberry on top before making your way back onto Ram Level Road and exiting the grassland through a section of shrubby oaks (10). Turn right at the next intersection onto Flaggy Hole Road for a short distance, passing through a nice stand of mountain laurel (11) before making another right onto Midland Road. Much of the Midland Road area shows evidence of being burned (12). Midland eventually joins Old Montauk Road a half-mile east of Ram Level. Turn left onto Old Montauk Road to return to the start.

Directions: Heading east on Montauk Highway (Rte. 27), turn into the entrance to the Montauk Recycling Center (left turn two miles east of the Hither Hills Overlook). A trailhead parking area is found on the left side of the Recycling Center access road, one100 feet from the highway.

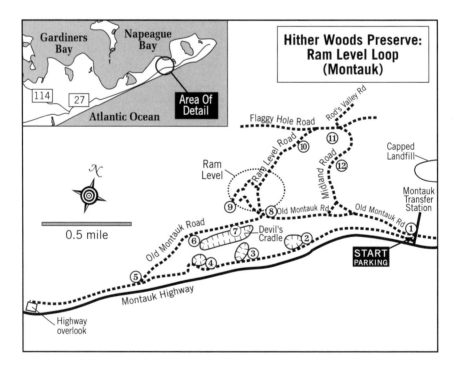

Montauk Mountain Preserve

A mountain in Montauk? Well, that's what this Nature Conservancy preserve has been named and, like the "canyon" just west of it, it is a bit of a stretch of the imagination. However, it does offer spectacular views from the summit and an opportunity to hike through an interesting and rare plant community.

The half-mile-long trail begins at a well-marked entrance just off Second House Road west of Fort Pond. Following the trail markers from the preserve's parking area, proceed through the opening in the split rail fence (1) and begin ascending the first of two knolls that comprise the mountain. The trail here is quite steep, and has been terraced with wood to stem erosion. The trailside vegetation is a variant of the typical oak-hickory forest found on much of the South Fork, with a thick understory of huckleberry and lowbush blueberry. Note the growth form of the oaks: short in height with canopies as wide as they are tall, and many of their lateral branches are as thick as the main trunk. Unlike the low shrubby multiple-trunk growth form found in burned or logged areas, these oaks generally have only one trunk. This growth form is indicative of exposure to wind and, here on the South Fork, salt particles in the wind also play a role in sculpting the characteristic low, spreading shape. This is not unlike the "krummholz" growth form of trees in the windy alpine zone of our New England mountain tops.

There are two other things of note here. One is the lack of any of our native hickories, usually found mixed in with the oaks and common in Hither Woods just a stone's throw to the west. The other is the unusually large leaves found on many of the oaks. I can't explain either and would appreciate hearing from any readers who can.

At (2) the trail swings to the right onto the top of the smaller of the two knolls, where a small patch of maritime grassland plants and break in the forest cover provides a nice view to the east. In addition to the common grasses found in this community (wavy hairgrass, little bluestem, panic grass, and Pennsylvania sedge), look for bearberry, a ground hugging woody evergreen with bright red berries, and reindeer lichen (*Claudonia* spp), both comprising a significant portion of the ground cover.

Contouring around the north side of the knoll, the trail intercepts a brick-size piece of concrete containing a round brass plate inscribed with the words "U.S. Coast and Geodetic Survey Reference Mark, CL Rear, R.M.

ONE" and an arrow pointing in the direction of true north (3). Just beyond this point is a section of woods thick with catbriar (*Smilax* spp.). Vines grow very quickly; instead of expending energy in the development of woody tissue for support, they utilize other plants or objects. Catbriar climbs by means of modified curling stems called tendrils. Despite the presence of numerous and formidable thorns along their stems, this plant is heavily browsed by deer. Its blue-black berries are an important winter food for many birds, raccoons, and fox.

Shadbush, or Juneberry, is also more noticeable in the surrounding woods here and easily identified by its bark and growth form. Both younger and older specimens have smooth bark and multi-stemmed (as many as 20) trunks. The bark color of the young trees is a uniform gray, while older ones have a distinctive vertical light-and-dark-gray streaked pattern. This appears to be the more common shad (*Amelanchier canadensis*) as opposed to the rare Nantucket shad found on the higher knoll ahead. Both the presence of shadbush and catbriar are used by some who have studied this area to delineate the Hither Woods forest on the west from the old Hither Plain, a maritime grassland that extended east from hither Woods to Fort Pond.

After swinging close to the edge of a deep gully on the left, the trail descends slightly towards an old man-made pit (4) before beginning the ascent of the second, and higher, knoll. Just before reaching the boundary or lopped tree at (5), note the large shadbush specimen on the left side of the trail. It currently has 18 live trunks. Over time, the older trunks will weaken and topple, to be replaced by new shoots sprouting from the root collar. Traditional methods of determining the age of these trees are biased towards the tree parts that are above ground and do not necessarily reflect the age of the root system, the latter comprising the bulk of the tree's mass.

The boundary tree at (5) is a white oak (*Quercus alba*) and appears to delineate the eastern edge of the Midland Road right-of-way, unopened in this area. Many of the oaks between this point and the top of the knoll (7) are white oaks, whose scaly, light-colored bark provides more insulation against the damaging effects of fire than the bark of the scarlet and black oaks which dominate the lower slopes.

A large patch of the low-growing woody evergreen, bearberry (*Arctostaphylos uva-ursi*) is found at (6), just before the forest gives way to the maritime grassland community that dominates the top of the knoll. This interesting plant is well adapted to nutrient-poor dry soils and windy conditions; it forms a major component of the back dune community along our coastal areas and is a common plant in the pine barrens. Being shade-intolerant, it will eventually disappear as the oaks and black cherries encroach on the knoll. Its shallow root system does not provide it with good protection from fire, and its prevalence here is an indication that the knoll has not been subject to fire in recent years.

Continue to the top of the knoll, where a sign directs you to turn right (7). On a clear day, there is an excellent view north and east over Montauk and Block Island Sound. The Atlantic Ocean is visible in line with the Fisher Office Building, a tall brick building built in 1927 to house the Montauk Beach Development Corporation and converted to condominiums in the 1980s. Scanning from there to the left (north), is the radar tower at Camp Hero, the wooden poles marking the GATR site at Prospect Hill (Theodore Roosevelt County Park), the Montauk Manor (sitting on top of Signal Hill), and, beyond Fort Pond Bay and Culloden Point, the coastline and hills of Rhode Island and Connecticut.

Given the proximity of this hilltop ridge to Fort Pond, many believe this was the site of Dayton's Ruse. At one point in the Revolutionary War, the British anchored their ships in Fort Pond Bay and appeared to be preparing to raid Montauk. Clearly outnumbered, Captain John Dayton had the local militia march single file on the hilltops overlooking the bay, loop back out of sight of the British, and continue the march again, giving the enemy the impression of an army of much greater size. Apparently the ruse worked; the British never came ashore.

According to The Nature Conservancy, this small area atop the knoll contains one of the best maritime grasslands and heathlands in New York State and is home to three rare plants: the New England blazing star (*Liatris borealis*), bushy rockrose (*Helianthemum dumosum*), and Nantucket shadbush (*Amelanchier nantucketensis*). The latter is much smaller than *A. canadensis*, barely reaching above the huckleberry in which it is often found, but I'm not able to distinguish a mature Nantucket from a young common shadbush.

The Nature Conservancy has recently removed most of the Japanese black pines from the knoll, and the rare plants are being carefully monitored. Today, the dominant plant community appears to be the maritime heathland, as evidenced by the amount of area covered by bearberry, lowbush blueberry, and huckleberry. Rounding out the mosaic of bearberry mats are scattered clumps of small oaks, shadbush, and black cherry. The common maritime grasses (little bluestem, hairgrass, poverty grass) are dotted among the bearberry patches and their total coverage at this site is quite small. TNC staff are developing a management plan for the site to address the loss of grassland species to ecological succession.

Heading east away from the high point of the preserve, pass an eight-foot-tall gray birch (*Betula populifolia*) on the left (8) and, just before reentering the woods, a ribbon of trailing arbutus (*Epigaea repens*) hugging the sides of the trail. Further down the side of the knoll, not far from the edge of the heathland, are four clumps of mature gray birches, approximately 25 feet in height. Considered an early successional or pioneer species, gray birches are well adapted for quickly colonizing disturbed sites, their small seeds preferring to germinate on litter-free substrate or soils free of leaves and other organic material. A short-lived species which requires direst sunlight, these birches will soon be overtopped and shaded out by the adjacent oaks, another example of ecological succession.

Continuing downhill, the trail winds through the oak forest and traverses a low ridge of black cherries, another early successional or pioneer tree species (10). Dropping steeply off the ridge through a thicket of young shadbush (11), cross a gully (the one which leads up to the saddle between the two knolls crossed earlier) and climb back up to an old roadbed (12). Once a paved access to several vacant residential lots, The Nature Conservancy had the asphalt removed and the roadbed is now vegetated with a variety of grasses, sumac shrubs, and locust trees. Follow this roadbed back to the parking area and trailhead.

Directions: Take Montauk Highway (Route 27) east towards Montauk and turn left onto Second House Road (just before Montauk's business district). Travel 0.7 mile on Second House Road, to a sign on the left marking the entrance The Nature Conservancy's Montauk Mountain Preserve (it is the first left after Dewey Place). Drive about one hundred yards up the preserve's access road and park in the designated trailhead parking area. The trail entrance is marked by another sign and an opening in a split rail fence.

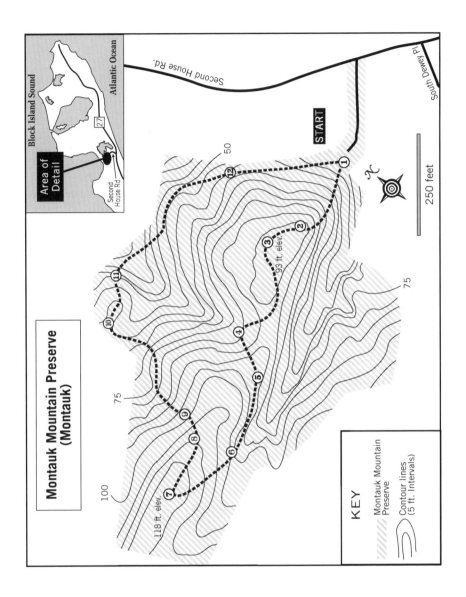

Montauk Mountain Preserve
(Montauk)

KEY

Montauk Mountain Preserve

Contour lines
(5 ft. Intervals)

START

250 feet

Second House Rd.

South Dewey Pl

Block Island Sound

Atlantic Ocean

Area of Detail

Second House Rd

27

93 ft. elev.

118 ft. elev.

50

75

75

100

Paumanok Path:
Montauk Village Section

This five-mile section of the Paumanok Path essentially follows the unopened portion of the Montauk Point State Boulevard right-of-way between the Hither Woods Preserve and Theodore Roosevelt County Park. This was the last, and most difficult, section to open of East Hampton's 45-mile long Paumanok Path. Through cat briar, shadbush, and arrowwood thickets, skirting marshes and bridging dreens, even the most optimistic of the original Paumanok Path planning crew wondered if we'd really be able to open this part of the trail. Several of us had made short forays into this ribbon of jungle, and we realized we needed some fresh blood: new recruits who had no idea what they were getting themselves into. In 1997, with one year left before the Paumanok Path's grand opening ceremony, they materialized, fondly referred to as the "Over the Hill Gang."

While we all saw the utilitarian value of this trail, linking the Hither Woods Preserve, Second House and Kirk Park, Fort Pond and Lion's Field, the Montauk Library, the town beach at the south end of Lake Montauk, and Third House/Theodore Roosevelt County Park, we were pleasantly surprised to see it evolve, as bits and pieces were opened and connected, into a scenic and attractive trail of its own. Despite its close proximity to the highway and powerlines, it meanders through thickets, over irregular topography and along the edges of ponds, marshes, and pasture land and provides a great trail experience.

The trail begins on the east side of the entrance road to the Montauk Recycling Center, within 200 feet of Montauk Highway. This is the eastern section of the Parkway Trail, which parallels Route 27 as far west as the Hither Hills overlook. After a short traverse of a dense tangle of shrubs and vines including catbrier (*Smilax rotundifolia*), wild grape (*Vitis sp.*), bittersweet (*Celastrus scandens*), honeysuckles (*Lonicera spp.*) and arrowwood (*Viburnum dentatum*), all fast-growing and well-adapted to take advantage of openings in woods, the trail enters the shade of the oak forest. Here, out of the direct sunlight, the tangle of vines and shrubs diminishes somewhat, but none of the sun-loving plants is eliminated. Scattered along either side of the trail are openings in the forest canopy where conditions are again optimal for the formation of a seemingly impenetrable tangle of vines and shrubs. When flagging this section of the Parkway Trail back in 1998, I had two main considerations for determining the route: staying within the narrow public right-of-way (Montauk State Parkway) and avoiding the worst of the catbrier and thickets.

Within 0.2 mile of the start, the Parkway Trail intersects the Paumanok Path: a left turn heads westbound into the Hither Woods Preserve; straight leads east towards the Montauk business district.

Cross a paved drive (the access road to a Suffolk County Water Authority well field) and, at 0.5 mile from the start, a wide concrete road called Upland Road. Just east of Upland Road the trail barely skirts a low area that acts as a storm drainage sump. Over the course of the next 0.4 mile to South Delphi Street, the trail follows a boundary scrape: the northern border of the highway right-of-way that was delineated many years ago by bulldozing an eight-foot-wide swath through the shrubs. Over the years, the cleared area revegetated with some of our more aggressive and invasive shrubs and vines: black cherry, sumac, and honeysuckle comprising the former and Virginia creeper, wild grape, cat briar, and bittersweet representing the latter (vines).

Crossing South Delphi Street, the trail climbs onto an 80-foot-high knoll before veering northeasterly (following the right-of-way) and crossing South Dewitt, Dearborn, and Second House Roads as it heads for the narrowest part of Fort Pond. I was surprised to learn that the unopened right-of-way here is as much as 750 feet north of Rte. 27. Apparently there was a plan at one time to construct a highway to bypass downtown Montauk by way of a bridge over Fort Pond, continuing across what is now the Fort Pond boat launch and Lion's Field, passing north of the library and rejoining Rte. 27 at South Fox Street.

On the east (pond) side of Second House Road the trail turns right (south) through town parkland along the shore of Fort Pond, and passes close by the Second House Museum. Fort Pond is a large freshwater pond regularly stocked with fish by the New York State Department of Environmental Conservation. Its name is derived from the fact that the original inhabitants of the area, the Montauketts, had a stockade fort nearby.

Second House is one of three dwellings constructed on the Montauk peninsula in the 1700s for housing the overseer and his family of Montauk's common pasturage. Spaced approximately four to five miles apart, First House (near Hither Hills campground), Second House, and Third House (near Deep Hollow Ranch) were encountered successively in the 1800s while travelling eastward on Old Montauk Highway from Amagansett. At the time, most of Montauk was grassland either owned as common land by the residents of East Hampton, who used it as summer pasture for their livestock, or was held by the remaining Montaukett, who also tended livestock.

On the south shore of Fort Pond the Paumanok Path joins the main trail through Kirk Park. Owned and managed by the Montauk Village Association, the park has benches and a pavilion on the water, a nice place to stop for a snack. Beyond the park, the trail follows the sidewalk along Montauk Highway to Emery Street, where a left turn commences four blocks of road walking: left onto Emery, right onto South Euclid, left on Embassy (unpaved) and right onto South Erie (also unpaved). The last two blocks run alongside state land which the trail may be rerouted through in the future, with the potential of eliminating three of the four stretches of road walking.

Taking care while crossing busy Edgemere Street, the main thoroughfare to the docks, the trail threads its way across the Lion's Field recreation area to the foot of a steep hill, which it climbs to Essex Street.

East of Essex Street, the trail follows the LIPA powerline right of way to a knoll just north of the Montauk Public Library. The 80-foot high knoll offers an interesting view westward overlooking the village and Fort Pond. The variety of native grasses here are also worth noting: switch grass, little blue stem, and wavy hair grass all add a distinct golden hue to the autumn landscape. From the knoll, a foot trail leads south to the library and the Paumanok Path takes leave of the powerline, entering a classic Montauk thicket of arrowwood, black cherry, shadbush, and highbush blueberry. A fairly large hawthorn is worth looking for, just below the knoll. Over the remainder of the distance to the next road intersection, South Fox Street, and eastward to West Lake drive, the trail is a pleasant traverse of thicket-covered, undulating terrain which, typical of Montauk, encounters several small bridged dreens, a shrub swamp dominated by sweet pepperbush, and an interesting marsh full of grasses, sedges, and rushes.

East of West Lake Drive, the trail once again enters a thicket, but only for a short distance before emerging onto the powerline right of way just south of a horse stable operation. For the next 0.5 mile, the trail follows the powerline, also used as a bridle path, with broad vistas north over badly overgrazed horse pastures and degraded freshwater wetlands.

East of the pasture, the trail meanders back and forth between the powerline and adjacent thicket to avoid wetlands, until reaching Old West Lake Drive, just south of the Crow's Nest Restaurant.

Between Old West Lake and East Lake Drives, a distance of 0.4 mile, the trail negotiates some very low-lying and wet areas near the south end of Lake Montauk. A culverted dreen under the highway, carrying groundwater and storm water runoff from as far away as Ditch Plains, enters a five-acre marsh extending from the lake to the highway, forcing the trail up against the Route 27 guard rail for a short distance. Turning back into the shadbush–cherry–arrowwood thicket, the trail comes quite close to the eastern edge of the same marsh, with good wildlife viewing opportunities to be had. Two foot bridges, a red gravel private drive, and the short dead-end South Lake Drive need to be crossed before reaching East Lake Drive. Be sure to make the short side trip down to the beach at the end of South Lake Drive, for a great view of Lake Montauk, before continuing east.

Crossing East Lake Drive, the trail makes use of the powerline for 0.3 mile to the LIPA substation, then heads north into the woods. The top of a knoll roughly marks the boundary for Theodore Roosevelt County Park. A short distance from the knoll is a large, obviously man-made clearing leading up a hill (to the right) to a pic-nic area. The trail stays left on what is now a ten-foot-wide grass path, crossing a wooden bridge and leading up a slope to a well-worn dirt road.

From the road, the large building to the north is Third House, now county park headquarters and a museum. The trail swings off to the west (left) and follows the edge of the field up to a high hill behind the park buildings with an awesome view over Lake Montauk. Theodore Roosevelt County Park, extending from Route 27 to Block Island Sound and Lake Montauk to Oyster Pond, has much to offer the naturalist, hiker, horseback rider, and historian: wetlands of all types, dunes, majestic beech and tupelo forests, maritime grasslands being managed by burning, a varied trail system with three incredible overlooks, and an interesting history as rich, colorful, and varied as its flora and fauna.

Directions to Start of Trail: Take Montauk Highway (Route 27) to the Montauk Recycling Center, two miles east of the Hither Hills overlook and one mile west of Montauk Village. Park on the left side of the recycling center entrance road. The trail begins on the right side of this road, directly across from the parking area. This trail is not part of the Paumanok Path, therefore it is not marked with the white rectangular blaze. However, it is very easy to follow and, within 0.2 mile, intersects with the marked Paumanok Path.

Directions to End of Trail: See directions to the start of Paumanok Path: Montauk Point Section.

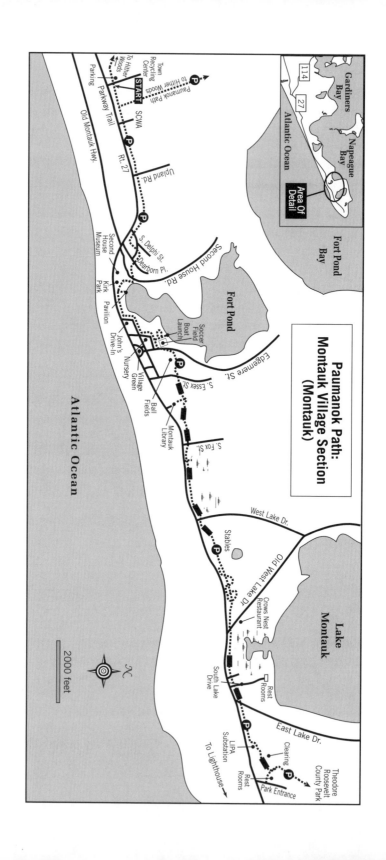

Paumanok Path:
Montauk Village Section
(Montauk)

2000 feet

Atlantic Ocean

Gardiners Bay

Napeague Bay

Atlantic Ocean

Fort Pond Bay

Area Of Detail

Fort Pond

Lake Montauk

To Hither Woods

Town Recycling Center

Paumanok Path

START

to Hither Woods

Parking

Parkway Trail

SCWA

Rt. 27

Upland Rd.

S. Delphi St.

Dearborn Pl.

Second House Museum

Kirk Park

Pavilion

John's Drive-In

Nursery

Village Green

Ball Fields

Soccer Field

Boat Launch

Second House Rd.

Fort Pond

Edgemere St.

S. Essex St.

Montauk Library

S. Fox St.

West Lake Dr.

Stables

Old West Lake Dr.

Crows Nest Restaurant

Rest Rooms

South Lake Drive

East Lake Dr.

LIPA Substation

Rest Rooms

Park Entrance

Clearing

Theodore Roosevelt County Park

To Lighthouse

Old Montauk Hwy.

Atlantic Ocean

SHADMOOR PRESERVE

A quick look at the accompanying map reveals a maze of unmarked trails criss-crossing over the 100 acres that comprises the newly established Shadmoor State Preserve. For those unfamiliar with the area and planning their first hike there, that can be intimidating. Don't be. Two World War II concrete bunkers provide landmarks easily identifiable from much of the preserve over its generally short moorland vegetation. As well, the Atlantic Ocean, which delineates the entire southern border of the preserve, is visible from nearly half of the trails.

The entrance to the preserve is east of Montauk Village on the south side of Montauk Highway (1), and well-marked. Hike along the unpaved roadbed leading from the parking area. This was very close to becoming the private access road to four oceanfront homesites for which the owners had received final subdivision approval.

Various proposals to develop the property, as well as efforts to preserve it, date back to 1981. The diverse attributes of the site—a federally endangered plant, breathtaking trails, historic structures, extensive freshwater wetlands, and unusual fluted bluffs called hoodoos—rallied an equally diverse group of residents, public officials, and organizations to keep pushing for its acquisition even when all hope seemed lost. Despite the interest expressed by the federal government, and a large pot of federal monies available through the Land and Water Conservation Fund, no federal funding came through in the end (Long Island has been unsuccessful in securing these monies for acquisition over the past two decades). Fortunately, the state, county, town, and Nature Conservancy all pitched in to meet the huge price tag: $17.6 million dollars. The deal was finalized on October 18, 2000.

Take the first right off the wide road (2), onto a narrower footpath which makes for a more pleasant hike. This trail heads due south to the ocean bluffs, climbing a knoll en route to where some remnant maritime grassland species are evident. Although the ecological interest in Shadmoor stems from the presence of sandplain gerardia and the maritime grassland community it is associated with, much of the preserve has succeeded to woody shrubs and small trees: black cherry, sumac, honeysuckle, arrowwood, shadbush, bayberry, red maple, and a few Japanese black pines.

After descending the knoll, and before dropping further down into a wet swale, look for a trail to the left which leads uphill to the World War II bunker (3) and two smaller ancillary concrete structures. For the agile and adventurous, a rope ladder on the north side of the bunker provides access to the flat roof, and a breathtaking 360-degree panorama of the Atlantic Ocean, much of the Montauk peninsula, Lake Montauk, Block Island Sound, and the hills of Connecticut.

The bunker is one of two such structures on the Shadmoor Preserve that were part of an elaborate communications and defense network, known as the Eastern Defense Shield, established by the United States Army during the Second World War. Both bunkers were positioned such that they could provide, by visual triangulation, exact coordinates of targets at sea for the sixteen-inch guns located at Camp Hero (3.5 miles to the east) to aim at.

The fate of these historic structures, which apparently qualify for placement on the State and National Registers of Historic Places, is uncertain. A preserve management plan is needed to address these issues, as well as trails, restoration of the roadbeds and bluff top, and protection of rare and endangered flora on the site. The latter is related to the general issue of restoring the maritime grassland plant community, and reversing the ecological succession of grassland to woody shrubs and trees, a management issue which may require the use of prescribed burns.

Take the trail leading downhill from the west side of the bunker, which intersects the north-south trail hiked earlier. Turn left and make your way south to the east-west bluff top trail. Here is a great view of the usual landform called hoodoos, the fluted spires and ridges of the bluff face. I first encountered hoodoos while doing graduate research in Banff National Park, Alberta, where hoodoo formations were found along the bluffs of the Bow River.

Most explanations and examples of hoodoo formations are based on those in the southwest, particularly Bryce Canyon National Park. In those situations, the hoodoos are pinnacles or pillars of sedimentary rock created by the presence of a hard cap rock (boulder or cobble) or material more resistant to erosion, which protects the underlying sediments. After the material surrounding the hoodoo is washed away by direct rainfall and surface erosion, the hoodoo stands as a small tower. The caps often resemble heads and the pillars a robbed figure—hence the term hoodoo, of African derivation and translating as ghost or spirit.

In his book *The Natural History of Long Island*, author Rob Villani explains that the formation of Montauk's hoodoos are the result of "differential erosion of soft sands and resistant clays within the bluffs. The action of wind and water washes away the sand, leaving bizarre fluted pinnacles of hard clay."

Head east along the bluff-top trail, which extends the entire length of the Shadmoor Preserve, and enjoy the magnificent ocean scenery. The persistent ocean breeze, combined with a touch of ocean salt, keeps the bluff-top vegetation from growing to a height that might obscure the 360-degree view. However, much of the bluff top here is completely barren of any vegetation at all, and somewhat unsightly—the result of years of vehicular traffic compacting the soil. Hopefully the preserve management plan will include some sort of re-vegetation strategy.

The trail climbs to the highest point of the bluff at (4), 70 feet above mean sea level, where a sliver of Lake Montauk is barely discernible to the north. Descending the eastern side of this bluff-top knoll, the trail is quite eroded, forming a deep gully and leading to a crude stone stairway which provides access to the ocean beach (9). Continue along the bluff top and into the twelve acre Rheinstein Town Park which, in turn, lies adjacent to the town's Ditch Plains beach parking lot and rest rooms.

Another smaller knoll is climbed to an elevation 37 feet above the sea (5). Note the pieces of concrete, brick, and flagstone on the knoll, and a long vertical pipe protruding from the bluff. These are the remnants of the Rheinstein house foundation, patios and what appears to be the old well pipe. Scattered at the foot of the bluff are more pieces of the foundation and an old boiler. According to Russell Drumm, a writer for the East Hampton Star and very knowledgeable local historian who at one time resided in the house, it was once quite an elaborate affair, including a windmill, dating back to the 1920s. The windmill was later moved, by helicopter, to Peter Beard's property on the ocean bluffs near Camp Hero. The remaining structures were dismantled and removed in the mid-1970s, leaving the foundation, septic system, boiler, and some stonework to the mercy of the relentless ocean surf.

The trail joins the Rheinstein's old concrete driveway as it descends this final knoll into the lowlands and sandy soils of Ditch Plains. Off to seaward, the ocean bluff gives way to a coastal sand dune which is bisected in two places to provide pedestrian access to a popular swimming and surfing beach. The main trail continues eastward to Ditch Plains Road and the parking area (town residents only) for the beach. From the top of the Rheinstein knoll, take your second right turn (6) toward the beach access point (7) to incorporate a beach walk into part of your return trip.

Check the tide before proceeding west. A high tide may force you right up against the bluffs, in which case you may have a difficult, ankle-wrenching traverse across the cobble beach. At the foot of the Rheinstein knoll, look for the cluster of bank swallow burrows in the upper face of the bluff (8). The burrows, approximately three inches in diameter and up to four feet deep, are excavated by both the male and female, and a nest of grass and feathers is constructed at the far end. Bank swallows nest in close proximity to one another, forming colonies of varying sizes. The main advantages of this nesting strategy are thought to be twofold: group mobbing reduces predation of eggs and young, and information can be shared as to the whereabouts of food resources. As with many species of swallows, the diet of bank swallows is almost entirely insects, which are generally caught on the wing.

Another 200 yards west along the beach, climb the stone stairway (9) to return to the top of the bluff and continue westward to the trail intersection at the bluff's highest point (4). Take the well-defined right fork, leading away from the bluff and onto the main access road for the preserve. This will take you past the second of the bunkers; from there it is less than a half mile back to the start.

Directions: The entrance to Shadmoor State Preserve is on the south side of Montauk Highway, approximately 0.7 mile east of the Montauk Village green. A large sign marks the preserve entrance and parking area. East Hampton Town residents may prefer to park at the Ditch Plains bathing beach and enter Shadmoor via the Rheinstein Park trail.

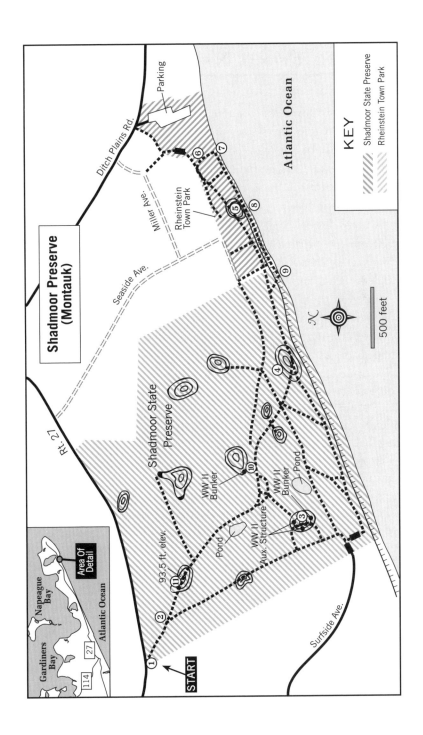

Shadmoor Preserve
(Montauk)

KEY

Shadmoor State Preserve
Rheinstein Town Park

Atlantic Ocean

Shadmoor State
Preserve

WW II Bunker

WW II Bunker

WW II Aux. Structure

Pond

Pond

93.5 ft. elev.

START

Rt. 27

Seaside Ave.

Miller Ave.

Ditch Plains Rd.

Parking

Rheinstein Town Park

Surfside Ave.

500 feet

Gardiners Bay

Napeague Bay

Atlantic Ocean

Area Of Detail

114

27

BIG REED POND NATURE TRAILS

Located in the northwestern corner of Theodore Roosevelt County Park, the Big Reed Pond nature trail system provides access to several unique ecological communities not normally associated with the 1,100 acre park, largely composed of pastureland and grasslands in various states of ecological succession. Here on the south and east shores of Big Reed Pond, a series of three interconnected trail loops varying in length from one to three miles showcases a wide variety of ecological sites: salt marsh, cattail marsh, freshwater pond, red maple–tupelo swamp, and a magnificent hardwood forest inhabited by several species unusual for the South Fork. One of the most botanically rich areas on Long Island, over 500 species of vascular plants have been documented in the park. In addition, the trail crosses many small picturesque brooks and accesses one of the most significant archeological sites on the South Fork: the remnants of a Montaukett village dating back several hundred years and inhabited as recently as 1885.

The Blue Trail, a one-mile loop which begins and ends at the parking area off East Lake Drive, provides access to the other two trail loops in the Big Reed Pond nature trail system. The middle loop, or the Green Trail, adds a half-mile to the Blue Trail for a total loop of 1.5 miles (to and from the parking lot). Highlights of the Green Trail are the Montaukett archeological site, a large stand of blue beech, or musclewood, and a long boardwalk section through a red maple swamp. The final loop, the Brown Trail, is 1.5 miles in length. Since it is accessed from the far end of the Green Trail, it provides a total distance to and from the parking lot of 3.0 miles. Along the Brown Trail are several viewpoints over Big Reed Pond, including two from duck blinds which provide excellent opportunities to view aquatic wildlife. This section of the book corresponds to trail markers found along the Blue and Green Trails, a 1.5-mile loop which can be hiked, without stopping, in one hour. Allow more time to read through the guide and observe the variety of flora and fauna found along the route.

Interpretive Stations

1) Pioneer forest community

This section of the trail traverses a young forest dominated by black cherry (*Prunus serotina*). Able to thrive in a wide variety of soil and moisture conditions, black cherry can reach heights of 60 to 80 feet with trunk diameters of two to three feet. These specimens, rarely seen on the South Fork, are valuable for their lumber; in fact its reddish-brown, close-grained hardwood is considered one of the best among furniture makers and woodworkers in general. On less than ideal sites, such as this one with its exposure to salt-laden strong winds, growth can be quite stunted. On dry sandy soils, black cherry often resembles a shrub rather than a tree.

If unsure of identification based on its dark scaly bark, drooping clusters of white flowers, or pea-sized fruit, there are several other key features which are easy to recognize. Its twigs, when broken, have a distinctive smell described as bitter almonds. Also, visible from a distance and found on nearly every black cherry in this area is a black warty mass, called black knot, on the twigs and branches. This is caused by a fungus which kills plant cells and distorts the growth of the branch, but doesn't seem to destroy the entire tree. Finally, as with other members of the *Prunus* genus, black cherries are favorite host plants for the Fall Webworm (*Hyphantria cunea*) and Eastern Tent Caterpillar (*Malacosoma americanum*), whose silken web "tents" are easily spotted. The former is active in late summer and fall, spinning its tent around the tips of twigs, while the latter is active in spring and early summer, building tents in the forks of twigs and branches.

Black cherry is an important successional tree in old fields on the South Fork. Its presence here indicates that this area was once cleared, perhaps as part of the once extensive pasture land found in Montauk or possibly an extension of the clearing associated with the sand and gravel pit at what is now the parking area. There are two key features which enable black cherry to quickly colonize a clearing: its fleshy fruits are eaten by a wide variety of birds which help disperse its seeds, and its seeds remain viable in the soil for many years.

Found among the black cherries is another plant, poison ivy (*Toxicodendron radicans*), which also tolerates a wide variety of growing conditions, both wet and dry soils in addition to shade and full sunlight, and whose small grayish-white berries are also eaten and dispersed by many species of birds. Learn to identify this hardy and adaptable plant in all seasons, including the winter months when its telltale three shiny green leaflets are not visible. All parts of this plant (leaves, stems, berries, and roots) contain the poisonous oil which gives it its name and reputation. The oil's toxicity is legendary: botanists have contracted the itchy rash after handling dried herbarium specimens that were 100 years old! A strong soap will remove the oil from skin and clothes, but its best to avoid contact by staying on the trail. The specimen here is growing as a vine, with its characteristic hair-like aerial roots. It is also commonly found growing as a shrub, in which case it often lacks the aerial roots.

2) TIDAL WETLAND COMMUNITY

The next stop is at the end of a short spur trail off to the left. A tidal waterbody connected to Lake Montauk, Little Reed Pond has changed dramatically in appearance and size since 1926. Prior to that year a sandy beach, infrequently breached by storms and man, separated Lake Montauk from Block Island Sound. In 1926, Carl Fisher dredged a permanent channel between lake and sound, altering the salinity and ecosystem of most of the lake and its tributaries, including Little Reed, which had been a freshwater ecosystem. Deposition of spoils during the construction of East Lake Drive further altered the pond: today it is a fraction of its original size and resembles a marsh more than a pond. Salt hay, groundsel bush, and phragmites now dominate the marsh. Alewives (a type of herring) and eels navigate the narrow ditches connecting the tidal waters of Little Reed with Big Reed Pond, a large freshwater body. Look for one of the wide assortment of piscivores that hunt here, including terns, herons, and egrets. If you are lucky, you might glimpse the elusive least bittern hunkered down in the marsh grasses, or the rare northern harrier hovering above.

3) ECOLOGICAL SUCCESSION: SHRUB AND VINE COMMUNITIES

This area is a mosaic of vines, shrubs, and small trees typically found where a grassland is succeeding towards forest. One of the more common shrubs here is sumac, both winged (*Rhus copallina*) and smooth (*Rhus glabra*). Both are short-lived, fast-growing plants with a tight cluster of small red berries located near the tips of their shoots. Their striking berries are not particularly favored by wildlife and are often evident throughout the winter, a useful characteristic for identification. Sumac has several adaptations for quickly colonizing abandoned fields, including the ability to sprout from underground runners and hollow-pithed shoots which require less energy per unit of growth.

Many of the plants found here are vines, a growth form commonly found in abandoned fields as well as other areas with abundant sunlight such as forest gaps and edges. Vines illustrate another energy conservation strategy or adaptation which compromises development of a strong support system (woody tissue) in favor of rapid growth and reliance on other plants or objects to support their growth. Using very little energy for woody tissue, vines can grow very quickly outward and upward and maintain their position in full sunlight by clinging to other plants via hair-like aerial roots (poison ivy), aerial roots with adhesive pads (Virginia creeper), tendrils (tiny curling stems which are actually modified leaves as found on cat brier), entwining around the host plant (bittersweet), or simply draping themselves over the host (wild grape).

Vines often slow down reforestation. Wild grape (*Vitis* spp.), bittersweet (*Celastrus scandens*), and cat-brier (*Smilax glauca*), in addition to poison ivy, combine to shade out tree seedlings and, in some cases, actually strangle them by entwining tightly around their narrow trunks and eventually damaging their xylem and phloem. Some vines, such as poison ivy, also inhibit seedlings by secreting a toxin into the soil.

4) Swamp Community

Look closely at the large red maple trees here and you will note several demonstrating an amazing resilience to being toppled. Despite the loss of much of their root systems, they have readjusted and begun to sprout a set of new shoots from their now horizontal main trunks. Some are also rooting where the old trunk has come in contact with the ground. Also commonly known as swamp maple, this tree is actually quite tolerant of a wide range of soil moisture conditions and can grow well on dry, upland sites. However, in these waterlogged, oxygen-poor soils it can out-compete most other trees and form pure stands of *Acer rubrum*.

Depending on the season and amount of rainfall, the floor of the swamp may be moist or completely submerged. The latter is often the case in spring, when a host of amphibians seek these temporary or vernal pools of water to breed in. Their temporary nature ensures that fish, potential predators of the amphibians and their eggs, are absent. Spring peepers, wood frogs, and spotted salamanders make their way to these breeding pools in late winter and early spring, sometimes before the ice has completely melted, and their eggs and larva develop very quickly, within several months. These are all adaptations to ensure that the young will have metamorphosed and be ready to leave the pools before they completely dry up in summer.

5) THE YELLOW-BELLIED SAPSUCKER

A close look at the trunk of this large hickory reveals a series of small uniform drill holes in the bark: the sap wells of the yellow-bellied sapsucker. This unusual member of the woodpecker family takes advantage of a tree's energy-rich sap, which flows between roots and leaves in vessels located just under its bark. The bird's long, sharp, pointed tongue is well-designed for licking the nourishing sap out of these wells, but it should be noted that the sapsucker is also a versatile insect predator. While some insects are attracted to the sap wells, only a small portion of the sapsucker's prey is caught there.

Sapsuckers drill holes in a wide variety of trees, but concentrate their efforts on individual trees and locations on such trees related to tree physiology and sap flow. Studies have shown that drill holes are most often concentrated on injured trees, and specifically just above the injured site. The correlates to the fact that a tree will increase nutrient (sap) flow to these areas in order to repair the injury.

Many commensal relationships have been documented between sapsuckers and other wildlife. Paper wasps, ruby-throated hummingbirds, chipmunks, and black-throated blue warblers feed at the sap wells, while chickadees, bluebirds, tree swallows, and squirrels nest in abandoned sapsucker nest cavities.

6) UPLAND HICKORY FOREST

Depending on the elevation of the surrounding area, which in turn determines its height above the water table and moisture content of the soil, the trail meanders among large hickories (drier sites) or large tupelos (wet areas). Although all trees provide leaf litter which to some degree enriches the forest soil, some play a more important role in building soil fertility than others. Of our common South Fork forest species (oaks, pitch pines, hickories, beech, red maple, black cherry), hickories add the most nutrients (calcium, magnesium, potassium, phosphorus, and nitrogen) to the soil via decomposing leaves.

Hickories play another important ecological role in our South Fork forests: they are an important mast tree, along with the oaks and American beech. All of these produce seeds in the form of nuts, also referred to as mast. These high energy food packages are available to wildlife in the autumn, when animals are preparing for the rigors of winter or a long southward migration. Some of our local wildlife that rely on this important food source are deer, turkey, ruffed grouse, wood ducks, gray squirrels, chipmunks, and mice.

Hickory is also considered an important resource among Homo sapiens: hickory wood is prized for its combination of hardness and stiffness, and ability to withstand sudden shock and impact, making it the wood of choice for automobile wheel spokes (in the past) and ax handles even today.

7) EMERGENT WETLAND COMMUNITY

The U.S. Fish and Wildlife Service defines wetlands as "lands where saturation with water is the dominant factor determining the nature of soil development and the types of plant and animal communities living in the soil and on its surface." Wetlands can be flooded permanently, as illustrated by the large cattail marsh seen here, or seasonally, as seen in the swamp at stop 4. One method of classifying freshwater wetlands is based on this spectrum of wetness, with wooded swamps on the drier end and floating or emergent vegetation such as the smartweed (*Polygonum* spp.) and cattail (*Typha* spp.), found here, on the other. Uphill from the wooded swamp, on drier ground still, is the oak–hickory–beech or other types of upland forest; downhill from the smartweed and cattail is the open water of the pond. This boundary between the wetland and pond is roughly delineated by a permanent water depth of two meters: the maximum depth in which emergent plants can grow.

In addition to providing a classification method, this spectrum of wetland types describes another example of ecological succession. Over time, the deposition of material (sand and silt eroding from upland areas and organic matter from dead wetland vegetation) elevates the site above the water table, enabling drier plants to compete and become established. The direction of wetland succession here is as follows: open water with submerged plants; floating-leaved plants (e.g. water lilies); emergents; wet meadow community dominated by grasses and sedges; shrub swamp; tupelo–red maple swamp; oak–hickory–beech forest.

8) BIG REED POND

The observation deck is a good vantage point to scan the pond for waterfowl. No matter the season, you are likely to see something interesting: spring and fall migrants; an unusual overwinterer; or perhaps one of the wide variety of summer residents. In addition to waterfowl, Big Reed is home to muskrat and mink; snapping, spotted, and painted turtles; largemouth bass, yellow perch, and white perch; and spring peepers, green frogs, and gray tree frogs. Bluegill sunfish dig saucer-shaped depressions in the sandy bottom, some of which are visible in the shallow water near the deck. Into these nests the eggs are deposited, which the males vigorously defend.

Two migratory fish also inhabit the pond for part of their life cycle. Alewives, an example of an anadromous species or one which migrates from salt to fresh water to spawn, swim in every spring via the narrow ditch which connects to the tidal waters of Little Reed, Lake Montauk, and Block Island Sound. Eels, on the other hand, are catadromous, moving into the pond as young elvers and residing in freshwater until ready to spawn (between five and 20 years of age), at which time they begin the long journey south to the Sargasso Sea (southeast of Bermuda) to lay their eggs amid the floating rafts of Sargasso weed.

9) GLACIAL ERRATICS

The large boulders just off the side of the trail here are referred to as glacial erratics. This geologic term refers to the fact that the boulders are not originally from this area (hence the term erratic), and that their method of transport was glacial ice. During the last ice age, tens of thousands of years ago, these pieces of granite were plucked off some mountain in New England or Canada by glacial ice and slowly carried here by that same ice sheet. Approximately 12,000 years ago, the huge ice sheet began to melt and gradually retreat northward, dropping its cargo of soil, gravel, and boulders in the process.

How much material did the glacial ice unload? To give you an idea, nearly all the material (largely sand, gravel, clay, and boulders) between the surface of the land and bedrock on Long Island is glacial deposits; here in Montauk they are over 1,000 feet thick.

Take a close look at the surface of the granite and note its variety of colors. The pink coloring is due to the mineral composition of the granite, while the gray, green, and black stains are actually a type of plant growing directly on the rock's surface. These are crustose lichens: remarkable plants that can grow where no soil exists and which are often the first plants to colonize bare rock surfaces. The crustose forms of lichen hug the rock face so tightly that they appear to be paint stains. All lichens are actually a symbiotic relationship between two very different types of plants, an alga and a fungus, which grow in such an intimate arrangement that they appear to be a single organism. The alga captures sunlight, photosynthesizes, and creates food for the organism, while the fungus provides structure and grips the rock surface.

10) INTERFACE OF WET MEADOW, WETLAND SHRUB, SWAMP COMMUNITIES

On the pond side of the boardwalk (trail left) is an example of a wet meadow community dominated by sedges and grasses well-adapted to water-logged soil and full sunlight. Most field situations are not uniform, clearcut textbooks examples of specific community types; rather they are a mosaic of intergradations among community types. Representatives of the emergent wetland community (cattails), shrub swamp (swamp azalea), and wooded swamp (red maple) can be seen interspersed among the grasses and sedges.

This is a great spot to hunker down with a good field guide and botanize, as there is quite a variety of interesting and unusual plants found in this small area. In addition to the usual wetland herbs (sensitive fern, cinnamon fern, skunk cabbage, jack-in-the-pulpit, sphagnum moss), there is marsh horsetail (*Equisetum palustre*) and rattlesnake fern, the largest, most common and earliest to appear of the grape ferns in our area. In the spring, look for two diminutive plants in flower here: marsh marigold, with a five-petalled, yellow, buttercup-like flower; and the ubiquitous marsh blue violet.

The horsetails, also known as scouring rushes due to their rough outer surfaces containing gritty silex particles, are considered the most primitive genus of the ferns and their allies group. Three hundred million years ago, giant horsetail and clubmoss (*Lycopodium*) trees over 100 feet in height formed vast jungles whose carbon-rich remains are the origin of much of the coal deposits we mine today. The present day ancestors are less than three feet tall; their cylindrical, bamboo-like stems and symmetrical, whorled branching pattern are quite distinctive.

To the right of the boardwalk, woody shrubs and trees have shaded out much of the marsh grasses and herbs. One such shrub or small tree, smooth alder (*Alnus serrulata*), can be seen growing along the edges of the small brook. Smooth alder requires moving water that is rich in nutrients and oxygen; in such situations it can seemingly defy the concept of succession and endure indefinitely. Alder is easily distinguished by its multiple clumped trunks, and cone-like fruit which persists through the winter.

A word of caution: there is a poison sumac shrub (*Rhus vernix*) growing near the left side of the boardwalk (northwest corner of the marsh), so take care to identify everything before you touch it! Its oil is apparently even more virulent than that of its close relative, poison ivy.

11) MUSCLEWOOD: A FOREST UNDERSTORY TREE

Alongside the trail, from this bridged brook to the next, are quite a few specimens of *Carpinus caroliniana*, known by the common names hornbeam, blue beech, ironwood, and musclewood. I'm not sure of the derivation of hornbeam, but the other common names are related to the tree's appearance and characteristics of its wood. The leaves are somewhat beech-like, with prominent veins that are very straight and evenly spaced, and the smooth bark is a slate, blue-gray color; hence the name blue beech. One of its most striking features is its fluted trunk and larger branches, aptly described by George Symonds in his excellent *Shrub Identification Book* as "muscular-looking," hence the name "musclewood." And finally, the nickname "iron-wood" refers to its extremely hard and heavy wood which, due to the tree's small size, found limited use as handles, wedges, and sled runners.

The number of common names for one species is one good reason or having (and using) scientific names; another is the fact that *Ostrya virginiana*, an unrelated tree species found in nearby Hither Woods, also goes by the name ironwood. Both species are understory trees, well-adapted to growing in the shade of taller, forest canopy trees. Their typical growth form, low and spreading, is designed to maximize capture of the limited light penetrating the canopy layer. Contradicting this generalization, several specimens have taken advantage of the narrow canopy openings over the brooks here, and growing out from the edge of the bank have reached heights of 30 to 50 feet.

12) SPRING

This natural spring is unusual in that the groundwater is seeping out at a point that is elevated in relation to the surrounding land (most of the springs or "seeps" on the South Fork are found in low-lying swales and kettles). This situation is most likely created by groundwater, traveling through the soil, hitting a water-impermeable barrier which prevents it from moving downward or horizontally. As the water builds up behind this underground dam, pressure forces it upward and out of the ground. Further north, in New England, the dam is usually some type of rock in the form of a large underground ledge; here it is likely a layer of confining clay, a common feature of Montauk's soil and one which is notorious for wreaking havoc on construction sites involving installation of conventional septic systems.

13) SWEAT LODGE

Note the arrangement of the large rocks forming an eight-foot-diameter circle on the left side of the trail. Their size, shape, and location near the brook make it a possible Montaukett sweat lodge site, with the stones forming the outline of the sweat lodge's wigwam-style structure. Flexible saplings (hickories would work well) were bent over and lashed together to form the frame upon which layers of hides, which served as insulation, were laid. A pit in the center of the structure received the hot rocks which would have spent several hours in a small bonfire. At periodic intervals, water was poured over the rocks, creating steam and an incredible amount of heat. The combination of glowing rocks, darkness, chanting, and confined, intensely hot space can be a powerful experience, and played an important role in Native American culture.

14) WOLF TREE

The large oak tree off the left side of the trail stands out not only because of its size but also its wide-spreading growth form. The latter is due to its unusually thick and long branches. What is the ecological advantage of a tree growing squat and wide versus tall and narrow? The answer lies in the environmental conditions present during most of a particular tree's life. In a typical forest setting, canopy trees (such as most of the oak genus) put most of their energy into the growth of their main trunk; growing tall as quickly as possible enables them to reach the forest canopy and maximize their exposure and capture of direct sunlight. When growing in a more open setting, such as a field or meadow, these same trees can capture more sunlight by putting most of their energy and growth into their lateral branches and developing the characteristic wide-spreading growth form found here. A second advantage of a short-trunked, spreading growth form is usurping canopy space and shading out future competitors. Because these trees once stood alone in clearings, they are referred to by foresters as wolf trees.

15) MONTAUKETT VILLAGE SITE

Stone-lined depressions of varying sizes and a stone-walled enclosure delineate the Pharaoh Site, an area inhabited by a group of Native American known as the Montauketts until 1885. Between 1975 and 1977, an archeological study of the area led by Edward Johannemann of SUNY-Stony Brook determined that the former were houses, barns, and food storage pits, while the latter was a pen for livestock. The entire complex sits on the south side of a knoll, maximizing warmth from the sun and protection from the cold north wind. These permanent structures reflect a dramatic shift in the Montauketts normally nomadic lifestyle, a change brought about largely by the loss of their ancestral land to the new inhabitants of East Hampton and various town policies imposed upon them.

This and the surrounding area, known as Indian Field, were designated by the settlers of East Hampton as a reservation for the Montaukett. Between 1703 and 1885, as many as 200 members of the tribe resided here. Most of the Montauk peninsula was a common pastureland, managed by the Town Trustees for the settlers' sheep, cattle, and horses.

The changing economics of the cattle industry and a growing interest in this area among sportsmen and tourists prompted the sale of the entire Montauk peninsula to resort developer Arthur Benson in 1879. Benson's legacy includes the eviction of all the remaining Montaukett from Indian Field in 1885.

16) SPICEBUSH AND WITCH HAZEL: FOREST UNDERSTORY SHRUBS

Two forest understory shrubs or small trees associated with stream banks and moist woods are common along this section of trail: witch hazel (*Hamamelis virginiana*) and spicebush (*Lindera benzoin*). Spicebush, so named due to its strongly aromatic leaves, twigs, and berries (when crushed), is one of the earliest shrubs to flower in the spring, gracing the forest with clusters of small yellow petals in April before most trees and shrubs have begun to leaf out. In contrast, witch hazel flowers at the other extreme end of the growing season, producing small, stringy yellow petals in late autumn when most trees and shrubs have already dropped their leaves. These flowers persist into early winter, and most nature photographers have at least one picture of snow-covered or ice-encrusted witch hazel flowers in their portfolio.

17) MICROENVIRONMENTS AND DIVERSITY OF A RED MAPLE SWAMP

This is an excellent place to study the herbaceous flora of the maple swamp: a wide assortment of wildflowers, sedges, ferns, and mosses. Here, one can view firsthand the subtle microenvironments and their resulting plant diversity within the swamp itself. The more water-tolerant species such as sensitive fern, skunk cabbage, marsh violet, and Pennsylvania bittercress can be found in the lowest, wettest areas, while woody species such as sweet pepperbush, highbush blueberry, and spicebush cling to small elevated and slightly drier mounds or hummocks scattered throughout the swamp.

Skunk cabbage (*Symplocarpus foetidus*) is named for the odor emanating from all parts of the plant, a strong and garlic-like smell not nearly as disagreeable as an aroused skunk. This interesting perennial has something visible at all times of the year. From late spring through summer its plate-sized leaves are hard to miss; possibly the most massive leaf of any of the native flora in the park. Despite the size and succulence of their leaves, few wildlife seek them out as food. An anti-browsing agent in the form of calcium oxalate keeps all but the resident slugs at bay, including the ubiquitous white-tailed deer.

By September, the leaves have died back but next year's flower and leaf buds are visible: the former a mottled purple-yellow and the latter a light green. Both are pointed and up to six inches tall. These remain visible through the winter and, in late winter, the flower bud begins to enlarge. Beneath its spongy covering (spathe) is the knob of male and female flowers (spadix); heat generated through the process of respiration is trapped by the insulating spathe and enables the spadix to maintain a temperature of 70 degrees while ambient temperature may be as low as freezing. This unusual phenomenon can result in the flower buds actually melting the surrounding snow.

When in bloom, one side of the spathe opens and the tiny flowers are visible. This occurs in early spring before the leaves emerge. There are not many insects available to pollinate the flowers at this time of year, but the warmth of the flower and odor of the plant help attract honeybees and small flies. The pollinated flowers develop into dark, marble-sized seeds in late summer, a source of food for wood ducks, pheasant, and grouse.

18) ECOLOGICAL SUCCESSION: GRASSLANDS TO FOREST

The composition of the trailside vegetation alters dramatically here, as the diverse mix of hickory, oak, beech, red maple, and tupelo comprising the mature forest gives way to a shrubbier mix of sumac, black cherry, bayberry, honeysuckle, and hawthorn. Scattered among the woody plants are pockets of a grassland community: predominantly switch grass (*Panicum virgatum*) and little bluestem (*Andropogon scoparius*). This area may have been part of the extensive complex of pasture land covering much of Montauk, used for several hundred years to graze livestock. Now that grazing has been eliminated from this area, certain woody species have been able to invade and become established. These opportunistic pioneer species shade out the grasses, converting the open grassland to a thicket of woody shrubs and small trees. These pioneers tend to be short-lived and their seeds don't germinate well in the shade of the parent plants. As a result, this shrub community is generally a relatively brief stage between grassland and forest: an ongoing and intriguing process called ecological succession.

In order to halt this successional process and maintain some of the grassland species here, County Park managers are periodically mowing the vegetation. Unlike woody plants, which have the growing part of their stems (called meristematic tissues) located at the tip of the plant, grasses have their meristematic tissues at the base of the plant. Therefore, grasses grow back quickly after being mowed (or grazed); woody plants, on the other hand, will eventually perish after several years of regular mowing. Prescribed burns are another management tool to maintain the grassland community, and are being done elsewhere in the park.

19) ECOLOGICAL SUCCESSION OF A SAND PIT

The parking area and trailhead is situated on the edge of an old sand pit, an area first stripped of its vegetation, organic humus layer, topsoil, and subsoils sometime after 1947. The remaining bare sandy soil is a harsh environment for most plants to colonize, particularly in this windy location, but there are several species well adapted to these conditions. Beach heather (*Hudsonia tomentosa*), a low-growing evergreen shrub with tiny scale-like needles designed to minimize water loss through transpiration, thrives here. A close look reveals a thick coat of whitish hairs enmeshed in its leaves, another adaptation towards water conservation. Its tiny yellow flowers add a splash of color to the area in May and June.

Two grasses (switch grass and little bluestem), both found in the nearby grassland community, also do well here. Their thick, fibrous root systems, which can comprise up to 90% of the plant's total weight and have the ability to go dormant through Long Island's typical mid-summer drought, enable them to survive in dry sandy soils. Northern bayberry's (*Myrica pennsylvanica*) waxy leaves help conserve water loss. Although not a legume, it is a nitrogen-fixer, a big advantage over other plants in this nutrient-poor sandy soil. The process of nitrogen fixation—taking gaseous nitrogen from the atmosphere and converting it into a solid form which, essentially fertilizer, can be taken up by the plant's roots—is actually done by a bacteria (*Rhizobium* spp.). These bacteria invade the plant's tiny root hairs, causing them to develop tumor-like growths, called nodules, in which the nitrogen fixing takes place. Since this arrangement benefits both the bacteria and host plant, it is a form of symbiosis called mutualism.

Not surprisingly, a variety of lichens and mosses can be found growing on the bare sand. Also found in the arctic tundra, along alpine ridges and colonizing bare rock, these are extremely hardy plants able to cope with some of our harshest environments. Visitors may be surprised to find a cactus here. I found one specimen of our native cactus growing in the sand pit: a low, spreading plant with large yellow flowers (in June) called the prickly pear cactus (*Opuntia humifusa*). The extreme structural characteristics and specialization of cacti, while enabling the prickly pear to thrive in these poor soils, comes with a price: it is extremely slow growing.

The Brown Trail

Rounding a bend on the trail, my heart skipped a beat as what appeared to be a dark branch, lying in a grassy, sunlit opening on the path, sprang to life and disappeared into the nearby shrubs in an instant. I'm not sure who was more startled, the black racer or myself, but the snake certainly had quicker reflexes.

Named for its uniform glossy black appearance (although its undersides are a light gray color), and the speed with which it can disappear, the black racer (*Coluber constrictor*) is a relatively common snake on the South Fork and one which I have often seen along the trails in Theodore Roosevelt County Park, where the mix of overgrown fields, pastures, grasslands, dunes, and open woods provide the perfect habitat for this harmless creature. In this case, I happened to be on the easternmost and least-visited loop of the Big Reed Pond Nature Trail system: the Brown Trail. Although only 1.5 miles in length, hikers must traverse the Blue and Green trails in order to reach it from the East Lake Drive parking area, and again to return, adding another 1.5 miles for a total distance of 3 miles to complete this loop.

The Brown Trail intersects the Green Trail in two places, both in the vicinity of the Montaukett Indian Village site (15). I started at the northern of the two access points (A) where the Brown Trail crosses a brook via a long section of boardwalk. There, on the downstream side of the trail at the edge of the brook, a shrub with a paired branching pattern and compound leaves can be found. *Sambucus canadensis*, otherwise known as common American or black-berried elder, has clusters of small white flowers that develop into edible fruit in time to help fuel the fall bird migration.

Past the boardwalk, the trail diagonals up a hillside onto firmer, drier ground where patches of pink-flowered wild geranium (*Geranium maculatum*) and New York fern grace sunlit openings on the forest floor. At (B), take a break on the bench to listen for the sounds of spring in the nearby cattail marsh and pond: the high-pitched "chirp" of spring peepers; "plunk" of green frogs; and the "ookaleeee" of resident red-winged blackbirds. There is a service road which dead-ends at the bench, so be sure to look for the brown trail marker before continuing on.

After crossing a short bridge, the trail enters a section of beech forest before reaching a fork. Take the short detour to the left (C), which leads down to a duck blind on Big Reed Pond. This is a great vantage point to observe the waterfowl, herons, and egrets which frequent the pond. Peer over the left side of the structure: the large clump off ferns growing there are cinnamon ferns. Among the large and graceful sterile leaves, look for an unusual leaf with a dense growth of brown (cinnamon) fuzz on the end of its leafless stalk; this is the fertile leaflet on which the spores (as many as 50 million per plant) will develop.

On the right side of the blind is a large shrub, obviously well-suited to growing in wet soil, with tiny white bell-like flowers when in bloom. This is the highbush blueberry; come again in mid-summer to enjoy its delicious fruit. Growing underneath this shrub is the very unfern-like royal fern (*Osmunda regalis*) whose spores develop on the tops of its leaves.

Back on the trail, cross another small bridge before reaching a nice knoll overlooking the pond (D). Some type of ornamental fruit tree is growing here, doing quite well amidst the oaks and hickories. Between here and the next point (E), there are no views of the pond despite the trail's course quite close to the shoreline. Just before reaching the east duck blind, the composition of the trailside vegetation alters dramatically, with mature forest—a diverse mix of hickory, oak, beech, red maple, and tupelo—giving way to a more open canopy, a shrubbier mix of sumac, black cherry, bayberry, honeysuckle, and sassafras. This area may have been part of the huge complex of pasture land covering much of Montauk, used for several hundred years to graze livestock. Now that grazing has been eliminated from this area, certain woody species have been able to invade and become established. These opportunistic pioneer species have shaded out much of the original grasses, converting the open grassland to a thicket of woody shrubs and small trees. These pioneers tend to be short-lived and their seeds don't germinate well in the shade of the parent plants. As a result, this shrub community is generally a relatively brief stage between grassland and forest: an ongoing and intriguing process called ecological succession.

Again, a left fork leads a short distance to another duck blind, which provides an excellent view of a different section of the pond. A word of caution: there is a poison ivy plant growing in the blind. Visible along the path just behind the blind are patches of two herbaceous plants that are quite beautiful when in flower: wild geranium (pink) and bulbous buttercup (yellow).

The geranium's thick, woody rhizome has medicinal uses traced back to the Native Americans and was listed in the official United States Pharmacopoeia. A powder from the dried and ground rhizomes was applied to external cuts to stem bleeding; it was also mixed with liquid for use as a gargle for sore throats.

The geranium flowers are short-lived, lasting only several days. After being pollinated by an insect, the petals are shed and the ovary develops into a long thin fruit somewhat resembling a crane's bill. In late summer, tensioned stringy bands holding the ripened seeds let loose, flinging the seeds several feet away from the plant.

Just before climbing a short hill at (F), the trail swings close by a large hickory with its typical compound leaf and stout twigs, but whose bark is peeling off in large slabs, very atypical of our common South Fork hickories. This is the shagbark hickory, a species unknown to me anywhere else on the South Fork.

At this point, the trail has left the shrub community and reentered the forest. While hiking through there one winter, after a late March snowfall, I came upon the headless remains of a black racer. For some mysterious reason, the unknown predator had apparently abandoned what looked to be a substantial chunk of prime meat. I had seen this once before, while tracking a fox in the snow near Little Poxabogue Pond. The unusual drag mark alongside the typical fox print pattern turned out to be caused by the aft end of a black racer hanging out of the fox's mouth. In the middle of the pond, at that time frozen over, the fox dropped its uneaten meal and left.

Perhaps the predators involved in these two cases had discovered black racer denning sites, consumed their fill of snake meat at the site and decided to discard their awkward doggy bags. In autumn, racers will migrate up to several miles to reach their underground den sites and, although they will sometimes overwinter alone, these sites are usually communal and used year after year. In spring, they emerge and the mature adults linger nearby to mate before traveling to their respective summer territories. According to Tom Tyning, in his excellent book *Guide to Amphibians and Reptiles*, racers will normally try to escape when cornered but, during courtship and mating, may not only stand their ground but actually advance toward an intruder, even a two-legged one.

This large snake, commonly reaching four feet in length but documented to six feet, does not even remotely resemble its parents during its first three years. Up until that time, the black racer has a bold pattern of gray and brown or red markings. Racers prey on a wide variety of insects, birds, reptiles (including other snakes), amphibians, and small mammals. Chris Chapin, a local expert on our South Fork reptiles and amphibians, has found that any area populated by racers will not have garter snakes, a fact he attributes to predation by the former on the latter.

The next section of trail passes by some particularly large specimens of trees and shrubs: between (F) and the next boardwalk are sizable tupelos, red maples, witch-hazels, and shadbushes. Further along, just before reaching

(G) on the map, is a section of huge oak trees. In the wetland just behind the bench at (G) is a quite distinctive, somewhat fern-like emergent plant, called water parsnip (*Sium suave*). This is approximately the halfway point, 1.5 miles from the parking area. At this point the trail forks, so look for the brown trail markers which will direct you to take the first right. If time permits, you might consider a detour up to the pond overlook (noted on the map).

The long stretch between (G) and (H) is a continuation of the band of shrubs encountered earlier, with the addition of the spike-laden hawthorn and a large patch of thorny brambles.

Approaching (H), the shrubs give way to woodland of oaks and hickories. A grove of tupelos, some with poison ivy vines growing forty feet up their trunks and branches, marks the descent into the red maple swamp and a series of boardwalks. Here, one can view firsthand the subtle microenvironments and their resulting plant diversity within the swamp itself. The more water-tolerant species such as jewelweed, sensitive fern, skunk cabbage, marsh violet, and Pennsylvania bittercress can be found in the lowest, wettest areas, while woody species such as sweet pepperbush and spicebush cling to small elevated and slightly drier mounds or hummocks scattered throughout the swamp.

The final two boardwalk sections (I) in this series are situated in a patch of beech forest with an understory of predominantly beech saplings. An ecological community which has the same species in its canopy and understory is considered one which is stable and self-sustaining, or a climax community. Provided all else remains unchanged—no fires, hurricanes, devastating insect blights, clearing (by man), or major climate shifts—this area will remain a beech forest for a long time.

Crossing an unpaved service road, the final stretch of the Brown Trail drops down into a steep-sided swale to a boardwalk and brook (J) at the edge of the old Montaukett Village site. This brook, which flows steadily throughout the year, probably provided drinking water for the small Montaukett settlement (15). Look for the two ferns named for states: New York fern, with its lower leaflets tapering down to tiny stubs, and Massachusetts fern, whose two lower leaflets are reduced in size and point downward. Of the two quite similar looking species, the latter prefers slightly wetter sites. A third species which can be confused with these, the marsh fern, prefers even wetter sites still. It can also be distinguished, by those with sharp eyes or a hand lens, by the forked vein pattern of its leaflets.

Directions: Travel east on Montauk Highway through Montauk Village. Turn left onto East Lake Drive and continue for 1.8 miles to a sign marking the entrance to the nature trails, an unpaved road on the right. Follow the dirt road to a parking area; the trail begins near a large trail head sign at the far end of the parking area.

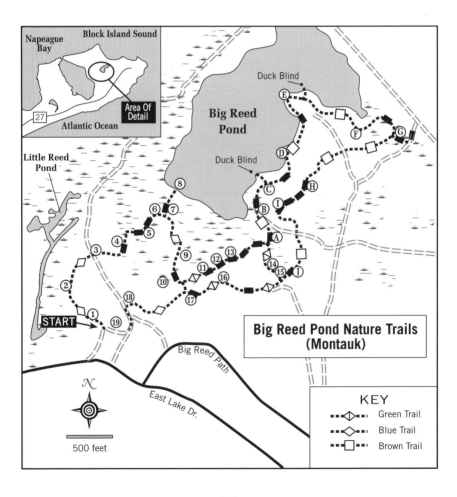

Paumanok Path:

Montauk Point Section

The final five miles of the Paumanok Path begins at historic Third House, set amid the rolling grasslands and pastures of Theodore Roosevelt County Park, and finishes at equally historic Montauk Point. The trail contours around a recently completed rock revetment just beneath the lighthouse and perched spectacularly above the ever changing Atlantic; the hiker will be treated to numerous vistas across parklands, secluded ponds, Block Island Sound and, of course, the Atlantic Ocean. Depending on the visibility, these lookouts offer views of Block Island, Connecticut, and Rhode Island on the horizon while, nearer at hand, there is the chance to glimpse one of the many unusual species of wildlife attracted to this area including several types of seals and a wide variety of seabirds. Sound enticing? Well, there's more. The route traverses a portion of the Point Woods, an enchanted forest of American holly, beech, black birch, white oak, swamp maple, and pepperidge interwoven with tiny, picturesque brooks.

Entering Theodore Roosevelt County Park from Montauk Highway, park near the large building at the end of the driveway. Known as Third House, this building is now park headquarters but has a long an interesting history dating back to the original structure (since replaced) built in 1747. At that time it was headquarters for the overseer of livestock which grazed the surrounding common pasturage; hence its claim to fame as the first cattle ranch in America. In 1898, at the end of the Spanish American War, it was the headquarters of Camp Wikoff: the destination of thirty thousand American troops, including Teddy Roosevelt and his Rough Riders, where they were quarantined until found free of yellow fever and typhoid.

From the parking area adjacent to Third House, walk up the drive heading uphill with the pastures of Deep Hollow Ranch on your right and Third House, several small cabins and the Pharaoh Museum on your left. Just beyond the cluster of buildings is a fence line and gate where you will pick up the Paumanok Path blazes: continue straight through the gate onto a large grassy knoll (1) with a stunning view of Lake Montauk in the distance.

Closer at hand, keep an eye out for kestrels, our smallest and most colorful falcon, which frequent the hilltop.

On the far side of the knoll the trail swings right and begins to descend, offering a fine view to the east, including the very top of the Montauk Light-house poking above the distant forest. As the trail levels off, take care to watch for the trail blazes: a maze of paths winds in and around woody thick-ets of sumac, bayberry, and black cherry, laced with vines of bittersweet. One third of a mile from the start is a fence with a narrow gate: squeeze through and follow a fence line, with outstanding views south over the pastures of Deep Hollow Ranch, for another third of a mile.

Leaving the fence, the trail enters a classic Montauk thicket and climbs onto a ridge, part of the Shagwanac Hills, which it follows northward. The thicket here is dominated by sumac, with its terminal clusters of dried red berries and black cherry easily identified by a fungal distortion of its twigs, a disease commonly referred to as black knot. These woody plants, along with bayberry, are the first wave of ecological succession, or change, from the mar-itime grassland plant community which occupied this area, and roughly three-quarters of the Montauk peninsula, for over 300 years. Many factors seem to have played a part in determining the composition of plants in the grassland community: wind, soils, moisture, fire, and grazing. The relatively recent elimination of fire and livestock grazing from the equation has resulted in a shift from grassland species to woody species, a concern of many botanists who see this trend as a threat to the survival of several rare plants associated with the grassland complex.

After dropping down off the ridge to cross a gully, the trail climbs steeply and begins a traverse just below the top of the ridge. Here, two small remnants of the grasslands are encountered in quick succession (2). The first offers a great view of Oyster Pond and, on a clear day, Block Island. A fox has been exploring the den possibilities here with little luck: the sandy soil is too unstable for successful excavating. The second remnant offers a view across Block Island Sound to Connecticut and Rhode Island.

The trail next climbs up onto Cornergate Ridge, one of the highlights of the county park which can not be adequately described in words. Suffice it to say that the 180-plus-degree view, at an elevation of 100 feet, is quite dra-matic. Much of the area to the north has been intentionally burned over the past four years as part of an effort to reclaim the grassland community, including several rare plants, from the encroaching sumac and cherry: in effect, reversing the normal course of ecological succession. It will take time, intensive monitoring, and perhaps repeated prescribed burns over many years to determine the success of this project.

At the top of the ridge, exactly one mile from the start, the trail turns right and, following the ridge's spine, begins a long, gradual descent to the intersection of the main bridle path, known as Cornergate. Note that the ridge walk has been refurbished with jute mesh, transplanted plant material, and wood terracing, all part of an effort by Group for the South Fork, the East Hampton Trails Society, the East Hampton High School Environmental Club, and County Parks personnel to stem the erosion there. This is one of many trail improvement projects completed in the park under the tenure of Park Superintendent, knowledgeable naturalist, and Friend of the Trails award recipient Peter Liss, who retired in 2002.

From Cornergate, the trail continues straight across first one and then a second bridle path before making a sharp right turn and essentially straddling the boundary between county and state parkland. This trail was also used as a bridle path and has been worn down in places to a narrow, four-foot-deep gully. One such place is the fairly steep descent down to an intermittent creek that drains into the southwestern arm of Oyster Pond. Although the pond is not visible from the trail, it lies just beyond the stand of phragmites growing to the left.

At the next trail intersection (4), the Paumanok Path turns left onto a narrow foot trail and into Montauk Point State Park (straight ahead leads to Montauk Highway and the Oyster Pond Overlook). A sign post at the intersection with West Oyster Pond Road (5) directs you straight across the unpaved road toward Ogden's Brook. From this point east to East Oyster Pond Road the Paumanok Path overlaps the Ogden Brook Trail, the latter blazed with dark blue trail markers.

If you have the time, consider a side trip down West Oyster Pond Road to enjoy a great view of the pond (roughly 0.75 mile round-trip) and explore its southern shoreline (A).

Heading eastward, descend to Ogden's Brook, crossing several small boardwalks en route and the substantial Ogden's Brook bridge itself (6). The latter is situated in a beautiful setting: the brook courses through the forest, over boulders and under the bridge where it empties noisily into the upper reach of Oyster pond, here a narrow waterway bounded by maples, pepperidge, large shadbush trees, and a small stand of phragmites. A few winterberry hollies, with their showy clusters of red fruit, and the evergreen American hollies provide a splash of color in the early winter season. This is one of a dozen places along this section of trail worth lingering at.

Nearby, a second, smaller bridge is crossed before the trail veers just out of view of the pond in an attempt to avoid more bridging through this low-lying and flood-prone area. Oyster Pond is separated from Block Island Sound by a narrow berm of sand which can be breached in the event of heavy rains or storm-driven waves, resulting in large fluctuations in the pond's water levels. At times the bridges may seem completely unnecessary; at others, they may seem completely inadequate. The first winter after it was constructed, flood waters carried the heavily timbered Ogden's Brook bridge, completely intact, off its footings and upstream approximately ten feet!

The Ogden Brook bridge roughly marks the western entrance to the Point Woods: a climax forest of white oak, American beech, red maple, and tupelo with an understory of shadbush, American holly, spicebush, mountain laurel, and witch-hazel. It may also mark the eastern limits of livestock grazing on the Montauk peninsula.

Before leaving the pond's environs altogether, the trail makes a final swing out of the maritime oak-holly forest and onto a sandy beach where one of the best vistas of the pond can be had (7). Binoculars are helpful for sorting out the various waterfowl plying the pond's waters. Home to an unusual assortment of reptiles, amphibians, and birds, Oyster Pond has provided me with several nature encounters that I will never forget: one being my first sighting of a bald eagle on Long Island and the other a comical run-in with a newly born fawn.

A short distance from the beach, the narrow trail intersects and turns right onto East Oyster Pond Road. Although now closed to motor vehicles, you may run into a bayman driving down with a truck load of fishing gear to access the pond. Follow the road out to Montauk Highway, a quarter-mile away and three miles from Third House, passing the start of the Seal Haulout Trail en route.

Cross the highway and walk a short distance west to pick up the trail on the south side of the road. This next section of the Paumanok Path, 1.2 miles between Montauk Highway (Rte. 27) and Old Montauk Highway, is called the Point Woods Trail and covered in more detail elsewhere in this book.

Within a short distance of the highway, two bridges span narrow creeks which eventually drain into Oyster Pond. Between the bridges is the junction of the trail leading in from Camp Hero Road (8). Worth noting here, in addition to the large beech and maples, are the black birches, a tree not commonly found on the South Fork. Further along, near the third bridge (9), is an old cyclone fence which marked the boundary between state parkland and the privately owned Sanctuary, a 340-acre mosaic of swamps and brooks recently acquired and preserved by New York State. This trail-less area made the news several years ago when a birder wandered in and spent the next 24 hours trying to figure a way back out, somehow managing to avoid several search parties and the nearby roads.

Crossing the bridge, the trail heads into a stand of immense mountain laurel, their trunks contorted such that it appears they are reluctant to climb any farther off the forest floor. One spring, Jim Ash and I watched a pair of fledgling great horned owls near here. Not often seen, I often heard their low, muffled hoot call in the early evenings when I was exploring the Point Woods to lay out this trail. With the exception of the barn owl, this is our earliest nester on the South Fork, laying eggs as early as February. They are quite vocal when they begin to occupy breeding territories in November. Keep an ear out for flocks of noisy crows: their habit of "mobbing" roosting great horned owls is a good way to locate them during the day.

At the Battery 112 Trail intersection (10), the trail swings within sight of a looming bunker, part of a coastal defense system built throughout the Montauk area during World War II. Between here and the next bridge (actually nothing more than a few well-placed stones in a narrow brook), look for linden (or basswood) and the telltale mottled bark of the sycamore, apparently planted in the area 50 years ago when the Camp Hero Air Force Base was built to mimic a quiet fishing village. One more wooden footbridge is negotiated before the trail intersects with Old Montauk Highway (11): here a wide, unpaved roadbed but at one time the main thoroughfare to the lighthouse.

Turn left (east); the Paumanok Path follows Old Montauk Highway for the next 1.1 miles. Consider making a short detour by taking the next right (200 yards away) onto a paved road that heads south (12); the road climbs to the top of a knoll where the pavement ends, and eventually leads to the ocean bluffs at Driftwood Cove (B). The round trip adds 0.4 mile to your hike and takes you to another great lingering spot: a grassed clearing perched atop an 80-foot-high bluff overlooking what I consider the best ocean view on Long Island.

Back on Old Montauk Highway heading east, the Paumanok Path should be a spectacular section of trail with several more bluff-top overlooks, ocean, and lighthouse views. Unfortunately, our state park's stewardship of this unique area has been nothing less than a travesty: "state-protected" wetlands have been cleared to make way for motor vehicles and two parking lots have been established, one atop a particularly high section of bluff with views of the lighthouse in the distance.

Stoney Brook has worn a cut in the ocean bluff (13) where it empties into the ocean, providing the only easy access to the ocean beach along the route until you reach Turtle Cove. The remains of the outfall pipe from the Camp Hero military facility are still visible in the surf here.

Back on Old Montauk Highway, the trail negotiates a bluff-top parking area, passes close by Bunker Hill (worth scaling for a view), and slowly descends through a head-high, wind- and salt-spray-pruned forest to Turtle Cove (14). At the split rail fence, provided the sea conditions are not too wild, turn right and clamber onto the rock walkway for an interesting quarter mile walk at the very eastern most edge of Long Island, just beneath the lighthouse. (If conditions look unsafe, a narrow path leads off to the left towards the Point parking lot.) This rock revetment was recently completed to prevent the 200-year-old lighthouse, commissioned by President Washington, from toppling into the sea. Since it was first constructed much of the eastern flank of Wamponamon (the Native American term for Turtle Hill on which the lighthouse sits) has been eroded and carried westward by shoreline currents, or littoral drift. The huge rocks are only one part of the defense system: wooden terraces underlain with special permeable fabric and planted with salt resistant beachgrass form the upper bulwark. It will be interesting to see how well this project works over time; for now it offers a pleasant observation platform from which to scan the seas for seals, eiders, scoters, oldsquaw, mergansers, grebes, loons, and some of our pelagic birds such as gannets, petrels, razorbills, and shearwaters. So, find a sunny spot out of the wind, dig out the binoculars and field guide, and enjoy "Montauk: the end" before heading home.

Directions to Start of Trail: This section of the Paumanok Path begins at Third House in Theodore Roosevelt (a.k.a. Montauk) County Park, located on Montauk Highway (Rte. 27) 5.5 miles east of Montauk Village. The park entrance is on the left (north) side of the highway, east of East Lake Drive, and well-marked.

Directions to End of Trail: This easternmost section of the Paumanok Path terminates at the Montauk Point Lighthouse. Take Rte. 27 east to Montauk Point State Park and leave a car, or arrange to be picked up, at the parking lot/concession area.

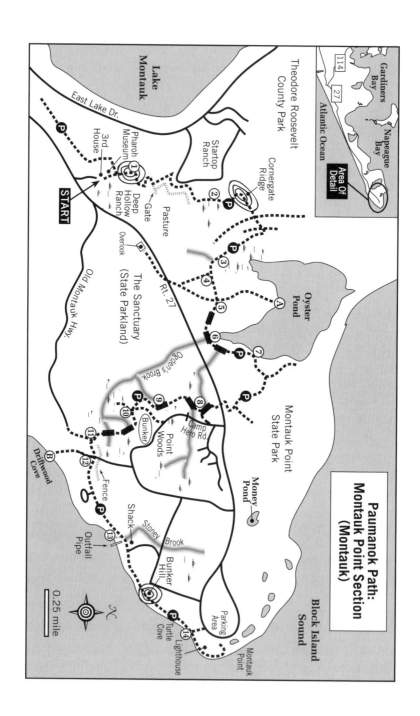

Paumanok Path:
Montauk Point Section
(Montauk)

246

SEAL HAULOUT TRAIL

The 0.75-mile-long (one way) Seal Haulout Trail winds its way through the northern section of the Point Woods to the low bluffs bordering Block Island Sound, where an unusually large cluster of flat-topped glacial erratics, called the Stepping Stones, are used as haul-out sites by seals overwintering in the area. If you are hoping to observe seals, plan your trip to coincide with low tide (check the tide tables for Montauk: North Side). Seals are most abundant in this area during the winter months (December through March).

Completed in the spring of 1999, this popular trail is a mirror image of the Point Woods Trail just south of the highway. Both traverse a spectacular maritime oak-holly forest with particularly large specimens of white oak, American beech, shadbush, and mountain laurel; both cross picturesque babbling brooks; and both skirt a wide variety of freshwater wetlands including vernal ponds, marshes, and extensive red maple-tupelo swamps. Such is the beauty and tranquility of this trail that, even if seals are not spotted, a delightful hike is guaranteed.

From Camp Hero Road, where road shoulder parking is permitted (1), cross to the north side of Montauk Highway and walk west a short distance to the first dirt road on the right. This is Oyster Pond Road, a trailhead link to Oyster Pond (red blazes), Ogdens Brook (blue blazes), and the Paumanok Path (white rectangular paint blazes) in addition to the Seal Haulout Trail (yellow blazes). Follow this road a few hundred feet to the trail sign directing you right onto the much narrower Seal Haulout Trail (2).

The trail follows a low ridge along the western edge of a large swamp, just visible off to the right, and threads through a thicket of mountain laurel before reaching a small, open beech grove (3) on the edge of a running brook. American beech is easily identified at any time of the year by its uniform smooth gray bark. These majestic trees are also distinctive in their shallow root systems that make for awkward footing. Note the small beech saplings growing from the roots; these clones of the larger trees are another method of reproducing and colonizing the upland areas.

The beech and brook setting is one of the most scenic spots on the entire trail. Not wanting to spoil it, we've created an awkward but functional footbridge by repositioning a few rocks in the brook. There will likely be a wooden bridge constructed here in the near future; until then, watch your footing here.

After crossing the brook (which eventually empties into Oyster Pond), you pass close by several quite large mountain laurel shrubs and sassafras trees (the latter considered an understory species, but reaching into the canopy here). The trail skirts along the edge of several more picturesque swamps and vernal pools, crossing a long, narrow arm of one of the swamps via a short section of wooden boardwalk (4). Look for skunk cabbage growing along the edge of the wetland near the boardwalk. These shallow, fishless wetlands are breeding areas for a variety of forest amphibians: wood frogs, gray tree frogs, spring peepers, and several rare salamanders (four-toed, spotted, and blue-spotted).

The trail soon ascends a 60-foot-high hill (5). A remnant of the grassland that once covered much of the North Road area between here and Oyster Pond is found on the eastern half of the hilltop which the trail traverses (6). Patches of little bluestem grasses remain, but the grassland has now largely succeeded to small black cherry trees, thorny cat briar vines, and bayberry shrubs, an intermediate stage before it reverts to an oak forest. The foam-like egg masses of the praying mantis can often be found on the low shrubs here. Also note the piles of bare sand that mark the entrances to old fox dens.

Descending the north side of the hill, note the remarkable oak specimens with huge, spreading crowns to the left. Trees with this type of growth form are called wolf trees and these only develop on open, sunny sites, providing further evidence that this area was once not forested. Many years ago when they were first developing, these then young oaks were lone wolves dotting a grassland landscape. Their wide, spreading shape may have also been influenced by the strong northwesterly winds that regularly roaring off nearby Block Island Sound.

Descending into a swale that drains westward towards Oyster Pond, the trail swings close to a large vernal pond visible off to the right (7) and another extraordinary wolf oak. Depending on rainfall, this pond can be dry enough to easily walk across or brimming over with freshwater, the latter situation creating a temporary brook through the bottom of the swale and necessitating a standing broad jump to continue along the trail.

Just beyond the swale, the trail emerges from the oak forest and enters another, much larger section of grassland (8). As with the hilltop grassland, this area is slowly changing from a grassland to a forest with woody plants, predominantly bayberry and black cherry here, beginning to shade out the sun-loving little bluestem and switch grasses. An interesting question is how the grassland originally became established here: this may have once been an eastern extension of the pasture lands managed for grazing at Third House. The cessation of grazing may have enabled woody plants to reestablish themselves, just as they have in many areas of Theodore Roosevelt County Park now closed to horses and cattle.

At the junction of an old unpaved road, turn left. This is North Road, which spans the northerly edge of Montauk Point State Park between Oyster Pond and the lighthouse concession. The road is usually passable for hikers heading east to the Point; at the western (Oyster Pond) end it is often flooded. Head west and take the first right off North Road, which is directly across from a magnificent old white oak whose lower branches have more girth than many main trunks on our South Fork trees (9).

It is a short walk from this point to the Block Island Sound bluffs and seal observation blind: approach the open bluff top cautiously and quietly so as not to needlessly disturb seals that may be hauled out on the nearby ledges. Biologists doing research on seals at this site are concerned that it is being impacted by human disturbance: noisy visitors, dogs, and vehicles. A proposal to move the observation area back from the edge of the bluff to the top of a nearby knoll is being considered by NYS Parks.

Seal watching is fun, and with binoculars a careful and patient observer can make valuable contribution to our understanding of these fascinating creatures. In the words of Valerie Rough, a seal researcher from Maine, "There are other benefits too, for a quiet session of observation, punctuated only by the cries of gulls and the muffled barking of seals across the water, can restore one's sense of time, patience and well-being."

MORE ON SEALS

Although you are most likely to see harbor seals (*Phoca vitulina*) here, there are five species currently found in Long Island waters. All five (harbor, grey, ringed, hooded, and harp) are members of the earless or true seal family and, although quite awkward on land, all are both extremely well-adapted to life in the cold northern waters and very effective predators with keen, well-developed senses. The combination of a dense fur coat and thick blubber layer insulates them well from the icy waters they inhabit. Powerful webbed rear flippers help propel their torpedo-shaped bodies through the water fast enough to catch fish, and their large whiskers are extremely sensitive to vibration and touch, useful features when closing in on a darting fish or foraging for bottom-dwelling shellfish in limited light.

Despite the lack of large external ears, their hearing is acute both in and out of the water; this is due to internal ear bones that, compared to terrestrial mammals, are massive. Their olfactory sense is also well-designed for both aquatic and terrestrial situations: when underwater, a structure surrounding the nostrils (which are closed) is able to detect stimuli from dissolved molecules, not unlike a dog's nose. Oddly enough, although the seal's large eyes enable it to see well in limited light conditions underwater, sight is apparently not essential to survival—there are numerous reports of blind but otherwise healthy seals in the wild.

So why do these animals, so perfectly designed for aquatic life, periodically climb out of the water onto large rocks, ledges, and sand spits? According to biologists, this behavior is primarily associated with thermoregulatory balance, a biological term for energy conservation. Although naturally well-insulated, seals still need to expend energy to maintain their specific body core temperature. Water is much more efficient at conducting heat away from an organism than air, hence the danger of getting hypothermic over time in water that is only room temperature. Because of this, our visiting seals can actually conserve calories (and maintain that "torpedo" figure) by hauling themselves out of our near-freezing sea water and basking in the subfreezing winter air.

Haulout may be associated with several other functions such as reducing skin parasites and, depending upon the species, establishing a social hierarchy among the group. And even the hardy seals have a bottom line: when the wind chill hits -15 degrees F, or rough seas make snoozing on the rocks difficult, they won't bother coming out.

Long Island seal population censuses completed between 1991 and 1993 revealed some interesting trends: total numbers increased fivefold, and the number of ringed, harp, and hooded seals (considered arctic species) increased dramatically, with harp seals outnumbering greys in 1993. Subsequent censuses indicated that the seal population in Long Island waters continues to grow, with both increases in numbers of seals and numbers of haulout sites noted. There are now several haul-out sites within the limits of New York City. There is even some evidence that seals have given birth to young this far south. The 1997 census found a twofold increase over the previous year, and the 1999 census estimate for Long Island waters was 6,000 seals with 2,000 found hauled out on Great Gull Island (just east of Plum Island) alone. This latter number makes Great Gull Island one of the largest haulout sites on the east coast.

Seals have been inhabiting Long Island's coastal waters for many winters, as noted in the writings of naturalists dating back to 1670. Why the sudden population explosion? According to Sam Sadove and Dr. Paul Forestell, researchers associated with Southampton College and the Coastal Research and Education Society of Long Island, reduced seal hunting has increased populations up north and caused the seals to re-inhabit former territories further south. Bounties on seals were instituted in Maine, Massachusetts, and eastern Canada many years ago, resulting in local exterminations. This practice ceased in the eastern U.S. in 1962, and in eastern Canada in 1976.

Directions: Take Rte. 27 east past Montauk Village, Theodore Roosevelt County Park, and Deep Hollow Ranch. At 1.4 miles beyond the ranch, turn right onto Camp Hero Road and park on the shoulder. The trail begins on a dirt road on the north side of the highway, 100 yards west of Camp Hero Road.

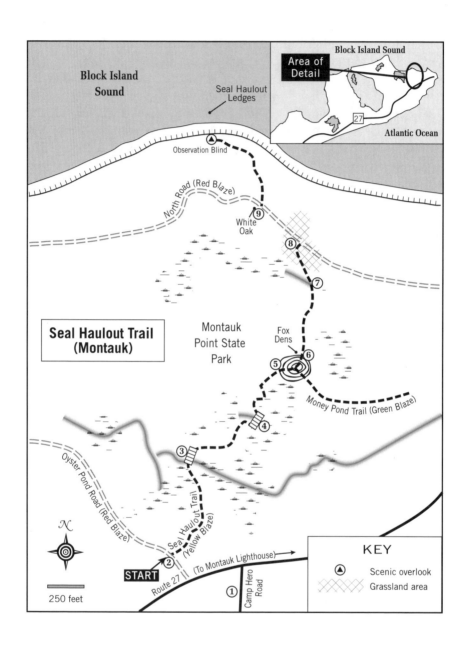

Block Island Sound

Seal Haulout Ledges

Block Island Sound

Area of Detail

Atlantic Ocean

27

Observation Blind

North Road (Red Blaze)

⑨

White Oak

⑧

⑦

Seal Haulout Trail (Montauk)

Montauk Point State Park

Fox Dens

⑥

⑤

Money Pond Trail (Green Blaze)

④

③

Oyster Pond Road (Red Blaze)

Seal Haulout Trail (Yellow Blaze)

𝒩

START

②

(To Montauk Lighthouse)

Route 27

250 feet

①

Camp Hero Road

KEY

Scenic overlook

Grassland area

Money Pond Trail

I designed this trail over the winters of 2000–2001 to provide an interesting alternative route from the Montauk Point parking area to the Seal Haulout Trail and, of course, access to the picturesque pond that bears its name. It was a challenge to find a route that avoided the extensive freshwater wetlands in this section of Montauk Point State Park, and to negotiate the unusual fluted sand ridges east of Money Pond. The trail route was approved by NYS Parks in 2002 and opened by the East Hampton Trails Preservation Society in the spring of that year.

Leaving the highway loop road, walk across a wide, flat-topped grassy knoll overlooking Block Island Sound. Little bluestem and Pennsylvania sedge grasses and clumps of reindeer lichen give the knoll an open, windswept feel, and windswept it is. The dominant woody plants here, black cherry trees, are wind-pruned to the height of a low shrub.

Near the north edge of the knoll, where it begins to drop steeply towards a series of small coastal ponds near the bay beach, is a witness post (1) or benchmark, used by the Federal Army Corps of Engineers for interpreting aerial photographs and measuring changes in the coastline. On the horizon, the hills of Rhode Island and Connecticut are visible to the north. Eastward a portion of Block Island sits low on the horizon and to the west the hills of Theodore Roosevelt County Park are prominent.

The trail heads west into a stand of shadbush and descends somewhat awkwardly into a steep-sided gully. At the lower elevation, the trees (shadbush and black cherry with a few American hollies and oaks) gain some protection from the wind and grow overhead but the woods still do not resemble a mature forest. This early successional forest covers the quarter-mile span between 1 and 4 on the map, including the northern flanks of the three small hills and the two steep-sided gullies between each.

Note the fine-grained nature of the soil and absence of any glacial erratics, or even pebble-sized rocks, as you hike this same section of the trail east of Money Pond. It appears that the surface soil here is wind-blown deposits of sand that originated from the bay beach and dune. The U.S. Soil Conservation Service's "Soils of Suffolk County" publication, a very useful reference, verifies this with the following passage: "Included with this soil in mapping… are sandy soils without stones that are underlain by till. These small included areas appear to be aeolian in nature." Aeolian is a somewhat obscure term that is defined as "of or caused by the wind; wind-blown." They also characterize the soil here as having many small, steep-sided ridges, mounds, knobs and hogbacks.

These latter features, which I first described as "fluted ridges" in my field notes, are striking. I designed a section of the trail to follow along the top of two of these small but dramatic steep-sided ridges or hogbacks that meet at a point to form a wedge somewhat resembling a parabolic dune (2).

The trail soon emerges from the woods and turns left, heading uphill, on a fairly wide sandy road (3). This road once connected to North Road which in turn connects the lighthouse area with Oyster Pond. Today the route to North Road (there are actually several old paths) are quite over-grown and difficult to follow, particularly when the seasonally high water table floods the lower area with several inches of water.

Look back over your shoulder as you climb for views of Block Island Sound and False Point. The trail soon turns right and re-enters an early successional forest, mostly black cherry and shadbush. There are also quite a few honeysuckle shrubs here. This vegetation, the interesting fluted-ridge topography, and the lack of stones and boulders on the surface continues to 4. Here the trail enters a mature oak-hickory forest and begins to descend to the eastern edge of Money Pond.

Money Pond is a small picturesque pond situated at ten feet above mean sea level. Although it intercepts the water table, it is also partially perched above it. Several small intermittent streams direct freshwater into it, but it is mostly groundwater fed. On its western side, a stand of tupelo separates the main body of the pond from a smaller section. In dry years it is possible to walk from south to north through the tupelo swamp; at other times the tupelos form an island.

Nearly the entire perimeter of the pond is bordered by thick vegetation, and although the trail passes close to its edge on the east side there isn't a good view here, even in winter. Continue on the trail around the pond's southeast corner (5), stepping over two of the pond's intermittent inlets. These two spots, and another at 7, will get small boardwalks sometime soon. The best view over the pond is found at 6.

Money Pond is apparently named for the treasure hidden nearby by the legendary Captain Kidd in the late 1600s. More recently, there has been speculation that the pond and its environs hold another type of treasure: the endangered tiger salamander. Local herpetologist and president of the South Fork Natural History Society Andy Sabin uncovered some old natural history records that refer to sightings of this large and unmistakable mole sala-mander in a pond in the Montauk Point area. Inventories of the pond by Sabin, an awkward endeavor made on cold, dark nights in late winter, have not been able to verify this.

From the pond, the trail climbs onto a low ridge, crosses another inter-mittent stream (7) and continues westward through some arrowwood thick-ets on firm ground just north of a large red maple swamp. The swamp occupies the drainage divide between Money Pond and Oyster Pond; further west it widens into a complex series of beautiful swamps and running brooks that can be seen on the Seal Haulout Trail.

Two hundred yards before reaching the Seal Haulout Trail (9) the vege-tation changes dramatically to a mature forest (8). Oaks, tupelos, and red maples form the dominant canopy species, and there are quite a few large American holly specimens here as well.

At (9), hikers have a choice. One option is to turn left, follow the Seal Haulout Trail to the Paumanok Path and turn left again on it to return to the parking area via the Point Woods and ocean bluffs. Another is to go right on the Seal Haulout Trail and return via the North Road. The latter route is shorter: two miles round trip as opposed to approximately 3.5.

If returning via North Road, look for the concrete and brick remnants of the coal bins tucked in the side of a large dune (10). This was where sup-plies, including fuel to light the lighthouse lamp, were unloaded from ships anchored in Clark's Cove and driven to the point by horse-drawn wagon in the nineteenth century.

The activity associated with the unloading provides a clue as to the source of the aeolian deposits found inland between here and the concession. Over the years, this activity destroyed much of the vegetation anchoring the bayfront bluff and dune. This, in turn, enabled our strong northwesterlies to widen the breach and carry the finer sands and sediments southeast and up against the hill situated there, covering its unsorted morainal till of rocks and boulders in interesting patterns of ridges and swales.

Directions: From the Montauk Point State Park parking area, cross the loop road near the concession area and turn left, walking 100 yards westward along the shoulder of the road to the top of the hill. The trail begins on the right just before reaching a Speed Limit 15 MPH sign.

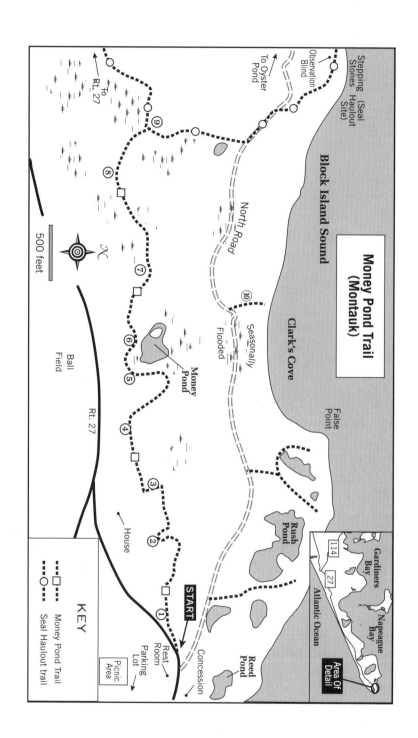

Money Pond Trail (Montauk)

Block Island Sound

Clark's Cove

False Point

Stepping (Seal Haulout Stones Site)

Observation Blind

To Oyster Pond

To Rt. 27

North Road

Seasonally Flooded

Money Pond

Ball Field

Rt. 27

House

Rush Pond

Reed Pond

START

Rest Room

Parking Lot

Concession

Picnic Area

KEY

- - - □ - - - Money Pond Trail
- - - ○ - - - Seal Haulout trail

500 feet

N

Area Of Detail

Gardiners Bay

Napeague Bay

Atlantic Ocean

114

27

POINT WOODS TRAIL

Designed by Group for the South Fork and opened by the East Hampton Trails Preservation Society in 1996, the Point Woods Trail provides public access to the western portion of Camp Hero State Park. From the trailhead on Camp Hero Road to the bluff overlooking the ocean, the route is a two-mile hike (one way).

Camp Hero, a military base military base established in World War II, was deeded over to New York State Parks by the federal government in 1984. With many attractive nuisances in the form of buildings, bunkers, and underground tunnels scattered over the 420-acre site, public access was prohibited to the park, with the exception of the Point Woods Trail, until 2002. Two years after the trail opened, State Parks officials announced their interest in developing an 18-hole golf course at Camp Hero, portraying the area as a severely disturbed one. However, the Point Woods Trail had already become one of the most popular hiking routes on the South Fork. Hikers, birders, and nature enthusiasts who had used the trail helped galvanize opposition to the proposal, which was eventually withdrawn.

Point Woods is a somewhat historical name referring to the large forested area east and south of Oyster Pond. A botanist, Norman Taylor, described the Point Woods in his classic work "The Vegetation of Montauk," published in 1923. Most of the Montauk peninsula was depicted as a treeless area occupied by grazing sheep and cattle and vegetated by low growing shrubs and maritime grasses. These areas were, in addition to being grazed, periodically burned. At that time, the Point Woods area stood as a relic forest: an island of woodlands amid a sea of moor land and pasture. Today, despite some loss of forest associated with construction of the Camp Hero military base, the Point Woods remain largely intact. Some ecologists believe that areas of the Point Woods have never been cut or burned, noting the girth and height of not only the canopy trees such as beech, tupelo, American holly, black birch, and oaks, but the understory vegetation as well. Some of the largest specimens of mountain laurel, spicebush, witch hazel, and shadbush on the South Fork can be found here. Considering the close proximity of the ocean and bay and the constant, at times formidable, winds at Montauk, two abiotic factors which normally lead to the creation of a shrubby moorland or low-stunted forest at best, the physical stature of the Point Woods is truly remarkable.

The trail, identified with white plastic trail markers, begins on the west shoulder of Camp Hero Road. Shortly after winding its way through a dense stand of mountain laurel, black birch, and American holly, it intersects the Paumanok Path (marked with rectangular white blazes) at a very picturesque beech, red maple, and black birch forest at the confluence of two small brooks. To the right is the Paumanok Path (westbound) which leads to a footbridge, Rte. 27, and the Oyster Pond trail. The Point Woods Trail continues to the left, joining the Paumanok Path (eastbound), crossing and paralleling a small brook (1). This wooded wetland—with its slow-moving brook, stagnant pools of freshwater, and forest floor thickly carpeted with leaf litter and furnished with logs in various states of decay—is perfect habitat for the blue-spotted salamander. Rarely encountered by the casual hiker, this beautiful and fragile-looking animal is an important member of the forest community, moving through the leaf litter and subterranean tunnels in search of a wide variety of insects. Studies of a related woodland salamander in upstate New York found that it accounted for the greatest amount of biomass of any vertebrate in the forest ecosystem: an astounding finding that underscores its potentially valuable role in controlling insect numbers.

Continuing to the top of a small ridge, enter a very dense mountain laurel grove which leads to a small vernal pond (2). Unlike most small vernal wetlands elsewhere on Long Island, this classic Montauk wetland is perched on the top of a hill, indicating the presence of clay soils. These vernal ponds may completely dry up in the summer, but provide important breeding areas for many species of amphibians (frogs, toads, and salamanders) whose egg-laying and development stages are either synchronized with our wet springs or fast-tracked to take advantage of a mid-summer deluge. Descending to the edge of a skunk cabbage marsh, note the large beech tree (3) before ascending another ridge with many large shadbush and black birch. Reaching the edge of a red maple swamp, you may notice an old chain link fence on the right. This marks the boundary between two sections of state parkland: the Camp Hero property (annexed from the federal government in 1984) and the Sanctuary, 340 acres sandwiched between Old Montauk Highway and Rte. 27 (acquired in 1997).

After crossing the brook at the outlet to the swamp (4), enter a stand of mountain laurel containing some of the largest specimens I have ever seen. Further along, at a sharp left turn, note one of the largest black birch specimens in the area. Black birch twigs have a strong wintergreen taste and smell, a reliable feature for identifying them should you be able to reach a branch. At (5) the trail crosses an old woods road, not very easy to discern, associated with the 1940s military installation and soon after passes close by a brook with a small, one-foot-tall waterfall on the right (6). This is approximately the halfway point to Old Montauk Highway.

Paralleling the brook, the trail crosses a low-lying wet area via a stone pathway, passes through an opening in an old cyclone fence, and enters a beech forest. Climbing very slightly as it contours around a knob (hill), there are nice views through the beech forest down towards the brook and adjacent swamp. At (7) is an unusual concentration of large boulders (glacial erractics) strewn about.

One hundred yards further, the trail enters a thicket of shrubs, including the very early flowering spicebush, before crossing a very obvious old road and the intersection with the Battery 112 Trail, noted by the red trail markers (8). From the road, enter a thicket of arrowwood and shadbush. Between here and the next brook crossing is an area hosting a mixture of native and non-native plants, a result of disturbance during the construction of the nearby bunker. There are some very large basswoods and sycamores (distinctive mottled bark) worth looking for along the trail. On the other side of the brook, ascend a small ridge of mostly shrubs (witch hazel, arrowwood, shadbush) and then a stand of holly. To the right is another small vernal pond, this time tucked in a notch between two hills. On higher ground, the trail roughly follows a ridge forested with many large oaks and hollies. Cross a very narrow brook (9), the fourth and last brook crossing since leaving Camp Hero Road. All of these brooks drain westward onto the Sanctuary property, taking a long convoluted route before swinging north under Rte. 27 and into Oyster Pond.

Not far beyond the brook, the trail follows an old roadbed until its intersection with Old Montauk Highway (10). It is interesting to note that although only 200 yards from the ocean, this last section of trail still traverses through a forest of sizeable trees. This is largely due to the protection afforded by the ocean bluffs, which are at their tallest just to the south of the trail.

At this point it is worth continuing up onto the bluffs. Turn left (east) onto Old Montauk Highway, which was once the only way to reach the lighthouse by automobile until the new highway was completed in 1932. In places pieces of the old pavement are still visible, but today the "highway" is mostly used by hikers, mountain bikers, and horseback riders, and provides access to the beach for fishermen and surfers. Take the first right, a narrow paved road ascending a steep hill (11), and bear left at the top where the road pavement ends (12). This leads to one of (if not the) most dramatic ocean views on all of Long Island. Note the bizarre fluted ridges, called hoodoos, on the bluff face. Depending on visibility, Block Island can be seen on the eastern horizon. Take the time to fully enjoy this spectacular overlook before making the return trip.

Directions: Take Montauk Highway (Rte. 27) east through Montauk Village, past Theodore Roosevelt County Park and Deep Hollow Ranch. At 1.4 miles beyond the ranch, turn right onto Camp Hero Road. Look for the Point Woods trail sign on the right approximately 0.1 mile from the intersection with Route 27. Park on the road shoulder.

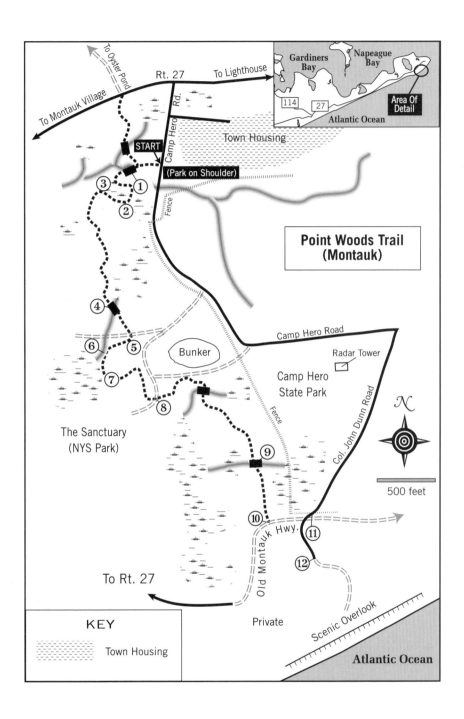

Point Woods Trail
(Montauk)

KEY

Town Housing

CAMP HERO STATE PARK

The loud BOOM! shook the walls and rattled the windows of every home in Montauk, some over five miles distant from the source: one of the four big guns positioned at Camp Hero. Each gun, or battery, had a barrel diameter of sixteen inches, fired 2,240-pound bullets, and was capable of launching it far out over the Atlantic at enemy ships. Fortunately, the firing was part of a training exercise. In fact, between 1943–44 when they were constructed and 1949 when they were removed, none of the gun emplacements at Camp Hero were ever fired at an enemy target.

Camp Hero is a part of Montauk's long and interesting military history, a history that stretches back to pre-colonial times when the Montauketts fended off attacks from the Pequots of Connecticut. Some of Montauk's place names, such as Fort Pond and Massacre Valley, date back to that period. The area played a role in the Revolutionary War and the War of 1812, and served as a quarantine station for soldiers returning from Cuba and Puerto Rico, including Teddy Roosevelt and his Rough Riders, in the Spanish American War of 1898.

Camp Hero was established in 1942 as part of our Coastal Defense System to protect approaches to New York City and Long Island Sound. Named in honor of Major General Andrew Hero, who was Chief of Coast Artillery during the 1920s, Camp Hero's facilities included three self-sufficient batteries (#112, #113, and #216 on the map), housing, a medical clinic, water supply and sewage systems, a repair shop, and a recreation center. Over six hundred soldiers were stationed there.

From 1947 until 1982, the Camp was used for a variety of military purposes, including anti-aircraft artillery training and air traffic surveillance. The latter was aided by the construction of a large radar tower in late 1960, today a prominent feature of the Montauk skyline, but made obsolete with advances in satellite technology and closed in 1982. Between 1974 and 1984 various portions of the 400-acre site were deeded over to the Town of East Hampton (Camp Hero Housing and Turtle Cove Preserve) and New York State Parks.

Most of the state holdings were off-limits to visitors until 2002, pending a cleanup of asbestos and live ordnance on the site. In addition to the cleanup work, State Parks added a new hiking trail, picnic area, and other visitor facilities, including some interpretive information about the site's military history. The new trail is a pleasant half-mile-long route called the Battery 113 Trail. Despite its name, the trail heads off into the lovely maritime oak-holly forest that comprises a portion of the Point Woods, well out of view of the Battery and other military features of the park.

From the edge of the parking area (1), the trail crosses through a narrow band of second growth woods and quickly reemerges to turn right and follow along a fence line. The metal fence is part of a network spanning over two miles in length that was constructed years ago to prevent people from gaining access to Camp Hero's attractive nuisances: bunkers, batteries, the radar tower, and various buildings associated with its military past.

In erecting the fence, an area 100 feet in width was cleared (and possibly periodically mowed later), enabling some of the grassland species that covered most of Montauk a hundred years ago to survive here. A photo in Albert Holden's *A Pictorial History of Montauk,* taken of Battery 113 sometime in the late 1940s, depicts a grass-covered landscape completely devoid of trees and shrubs. How much of the 400-acre Camp Hero was once a maritime grassland or cleared of trees, and how much was a mature forest that was left intact, is difficult to say.

One clue is found in botanist Norman Taylor's 1923 publication "The Vegetation of Montauk." He describes the Point Woods, located east and south of Oyster Pond, as one of two significant forested areas on the Montauk peninsula at that time (the other being Hither Woods). The area he describes correlates to what is known today as the Sanctuary, Camp Hero, and the western part of Montauk Point State Park. Here we can find a climax forest of American beech, scarlet, black and white oaks, American holly, black birch, red maple, and tupelo, with specimens of each attaining tremendous size in height and girth despite their location in close proximity to the ocean and bay. Visiting ecologists have also noted the size of the understory vegetation. Some of the largest specimens of mountain laurel, spicebush, and witch hazel on the South Fork can be found here.

Passing through the fence the trail reenters the forest and crosses over a knoll covered with shadbush trees (2), whose distinctive gray bark along with its crooked, multi-trunked growth form makes its easy to pick out any time of the year. Dropping down off the knoll, the terrain flattens; look for a slight circular depression off to the left (3) that likely collects water and attracts breeding amphibians in the spring.

The first of five wooden footbridges is encountered at (4). It spans a low-lying swale hosting a few interesting wetland plants. Among others look for jewelweed, iris, highbush blueberry, and a sedge (probably *Carex stricta*) whose dense root system and clumpy growth form creates an unusual knob or "tussock" elevated well above the wet soil. Just beyond the bridge I encountered one of my favorite animals also using the trail: the eastern box turtle. This one was a large female whose mottled yellow-brown coloring was well-matched with the leaves covering the forest floor here. With a life-span that often reaches 50 to 75 years (some have been aged at over 100), she may have been around to hear the big guns roar in the 1940s.

Approaching the next footbridge (5), note the witch hazel shrub growing atop the glacial erratic on the left. This unusual plant flowers in November when there is little competition (no other plants in bloom) for insect pollinators. The down side of this strategy is that there are few insect pollinators active at that time of year.

Take a look at the larger oaks along the trail as you hike. Most oaks growing in a forest are fairly straight-trunked, with upper branches that put leaves high up into the canopy where sunlight is more abundant and intense. Oaks that grow in a field or other type of clearing don't need to grow straight and tall; they can capture more sunlight by sprawling out horizontally with large lower limbs. A tree displaying this latter growth form is referred to as a wolf tree in reference to its being a "loner" apart from the forest. Many of the larger (and older?) oaks in this area of the park (and in the vicinity of 10 on the map) resemble wolf trees, seeming to indicate that much of this area was once cleared.

Within sight of a maintenance building, the trail skirts a small swale wet enough to support a stand of tupelo and red maple trees (6) and a colony of ferns (7).

After following a pretty ridge of mountain laurel (8), the trail drops down to another footbridge. The last two bridges cross small streams that were channeled with creosote timbers, probably back in the 1950s. There is also evidence that they were once partially excavated; note the unnatural looking piles of earth nearby. I'm not sure why this work was done, but it may have been part of an effort to reduce mosquito populations via providing better drainage of the wetlands, a practice that is frowned upon by many biologists today.

The last stretch of trail partially follows an old unpaved roadbed that is noted on an old map of the area dating back to the early 1940s. I believe this area (10) was cleared based on the presence of the road, a few structures still evident, and the number of wolf trees.

The trail ends at Rough Riders Road. There are several options for creating a loop to return to the trailhead parking area. The shortest way back (0.5 mile) is by road, turning left at all intersections. Another option is to take all rights: right on Rough Riders Road, Old Montauk Highway (follow the white rectangular Paumanok Path blazes), and Col. John Dunn Road. Be sure to take advantage of a low point in the ocean bluffs to access the beach, and make the side trip to the bluff overlook (see map) for a mile-long return trip.

A third option is to continue past Col. John Dunn Road on the Paumanok Path and turn right onto the Point Woods Trail (also part of the Paumanok Path). Keep an eye out for the Battery 112 Trail intersection for a 1.5-mile return trip.

Directions: The Battery 113 Trail is located in Camp Hero State Park, which is adjacent to Montauk Point State Park at the eastern terminus of Rte. 27. After reaching Montauk Point State Park on Rte. 27, make a right turn a quarter-mile past where the highway divides and forms a one-way loop around the Point parking area. Drive through the parking toll booth and take your first right (Coast Artillery Road). Continue past a maintenance building to a "T" intersection and turn left onto Camp Hero Road. The second left (Col. John Dunn Road) leads to the parking area and trailhead.

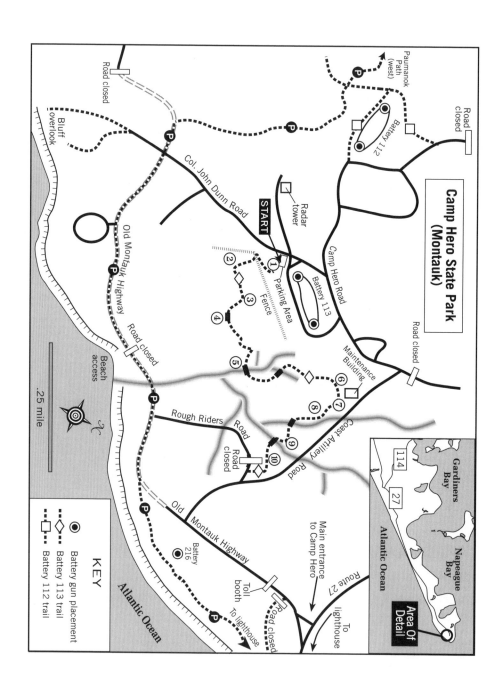

Camp Hero State Park
(Montauk)

KEY

Battery gun placement ⊙
Battery 113 trail ◇
Battery 112 trail ▢

Area Of Detail

Gardiners Bay

Napeague Bay

Atlantic Ocean

Route 27

114
27

To lighthouse

Main entrance
to Camp Hero

Coast Artillery Road

Maintenance
Building

Road closed

Battery 113

START

Parking Area
Fence

Radar
tower

Col. John Dunn Road

Camp Hero Road

Road closed

Battery 112

Paumanok
Path
(west)

Road
closed

Bluff
overlook

Old Montauk Highway

Road closed

Beach
access

.25 mile

Rough Riders Road

Road
closed

Battery
216

Old Montauk Highway

Toll
booth

Road closed

To lighthouse

Atlantic Ocean

1
2
3
4
5
6
7
8
9
10

MAIN KEY

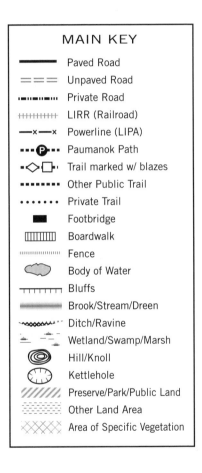

━━━━	Paved Road
═══	Unpaved Road
▪━▪▪━▪▪	Private Road
++++++++++++	LIRR (Railroad)
━×━×	Powerline (LIPA)
▪▪▪🅿▪▪▪	Paumanok Path
▪◇▪□▪	Trail marked w/ blazes
▪▪▪▪▪▪▪	Other Public Trail
▪ ▪ ▪ ▪ ▪ ▪	Private Trail
▬	Footbridge
⊞⊞⊞⊞	Boardwalk
'''''''''''''''''''''	Fence
⬭	Body of Water
┬┬┬┬┬┬	Bluffs
▬▬▬	Brook/Stream/Dreen
～◇◇◇◇～	Ditch/Ravine
⹀ ⹀	Wetland/Swamp/Marsh
◎	Hill/Knoll
⊛	Kettlehole
/////	Preserve/Park/Public Land
⋯⋯⋯	Other Land Area
✕✕✕	Area of Specific Vegetation

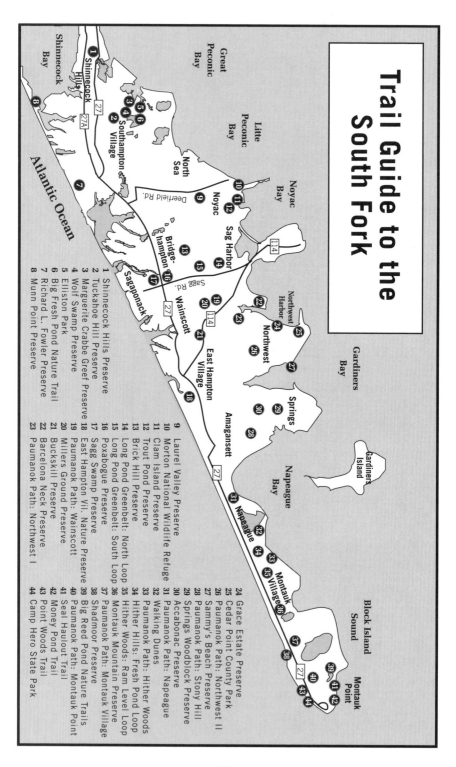

Trail Guide to the South Fork

1 Shinnecock Hills Preserve
2 Tuckahoe Hill Preserve
3 Marguerite Crabbe Greef Preserve
4 Wolf Swamp Preserve
5 Elliston Park
6 Big Fresh Pond Nature Trail
7 Richard L. Fowler Preserve
8 Munn Point Preserve
9 Laurel Valley Preserve
10 Morton National Wildlife Refuge
11 Clam Island Preserve
12 Trout Pond Preserve
13 Brick Kiln Preserve
14 Long Pond Greenbelt: North Loop
15 Long Pond Greenbelt: South Loop
16 Poxabogue Preserve
17 Sagg Swamp Preserve
18 East Hampton Vil. Nature Preserve
19 Paumanok Path: Wainscott
20 Millers Ground Preserve
21 Buckskill Preserve
22 Barcelona Neck Preserve
23 Paumanok Path: Northwest I
24 Grace Estate Preserve
25 Cedar Point County Park
26 Paumanok Path: Northwest II
27 Sammy's Beach Preserve
28 Paumanok Path: Stony Hill
29 Springs Woodblock Preserve
30 Accabonac Preserve
31 Paumanok Path: Napeague
32 Walking Dunes
33 Paumanok Path: Hither Woods
34 Hither Hills: Fresh Pond Loop
35 Hither Woods: Ram Level Loop
36 Montauk Mountain Preserve
37 Paumanok Path: Montauk Village
38 Shadmoor Preserve
39 Big Reed Pond Nature Trails
40 Paumanok Path: Montauk Point
41 Seal Haulout Trail
42 Money Pond Trail
43 Point Woods Trail
44 Camp Hero State Park

Notes

Notes

Notes

NOTES